# MONTY PYTHON SPEAKS!

## THE COMPLETE ORAL HISTORY

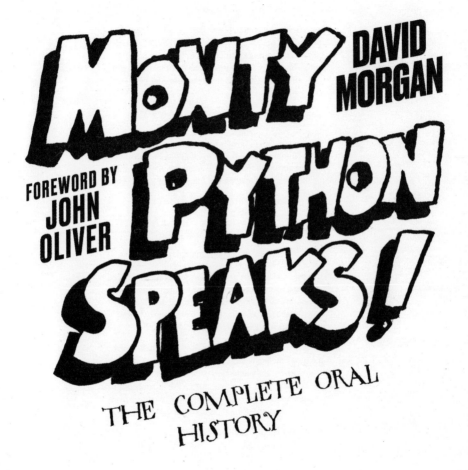

# MONTY DAVID MORGAN PYTHON SPEAKS!

FOREWORD BY JOHN OLIVER

### THE COMPLETE ORAL HISTORY

4th ESTATE • London

4th Estate
An imprint of HarperCollins*Publishers*
1 London Bridge Street
London SE1 9GF

www.4thEstate.co.uk

This edition first published in Great Britain by 4th Estate in 2019
This edition first published in the United States of America by
Dey Street, an imprint of William Morrow, in 2019
First published in Great Britain by 4th Estate in 1999
First Dey Street paperback published in 1999
Reissued in Harper paperback in 2005

1

David Morgan asserts the moral right to be identified
as the author of this work in accordance with the
Copyright, Designs and Patents Act 1988

Designed by Paula Russell Szafranski

A catalogue record for this book is
available from the British Library

ISBN 978-0-00-833680-6

Printed and bound in Great Britain by
CPI Group (UK) Ltd, Croydon, CR0 4YY

*To Gwen Dibley,*
*who was (almost) there at the start*

# CONTENTS

CONTENTS

# FOREWORD

## BY JOHN OLIVER

Writing about the importance of Monty Python is basically pointless. At this point, citing them as an influence is almost redundant. It's assumed. In fact, from now on it's probably more efficient to say that comedy writers should have to explicitly state that they *don't* owe a significant debt to Monty Python. And if someone does that, they'll be emphatically wrong.

This strange group of wildly talented, appropriately disrespectful, hugely imaginative, and massively inspirational idiots changed what comedy could be for their generation and for those that followed.

I first discovered Monty Python when I was probably ten years old, and back then it felt like something I shouldn't be watching. That was already a pretty big appeal. Then I saw *Life of Brian* in middle school, when a substitute teacher put it on to keep us quiet on a rainy day. I'm not sure he knew exactly what he was showing us, but I've always been hugely grateful for the reckless professional mistake he made that day, because I've never forgotten how it made me feel.

I think what I've always loved about all of Monty Python's work is that they've never been afraid to get into trouble, and *Life of Brian* is the perfect distillation of that. There was a famous episode of a BBC talk show back in 1979, when John Cleese and Michael Palin were being interviewed alongside the Bishop of Southwark and a writer called Malcom Muggeridge, both of whom were furious about the film. Incidentally, the very name 'Malcolm Muggeridge' is so stereotypically English, it's almost racist. It's the name of someone who should be looking after the owls at Hogwarts. Anyway, for twenty minutes, Muggeridge told them off like a pair of naughty schoolboys, calling what they'd done a 'miserable little film,' 'a squalid number' and 'tenth rate,' and said it contained laughs that were 'rather easily procured.'

And while everything he said was titanic nonsense, it was that last part that drove me crazy. Because nothing about what Monty Python did was easy – not their TV show, not their albums, and certainly not *Life of Brian*. It's fucking hard to write such incredibly smart, incredibly stupid comedy.

I got to interview all the Pythons after a screening in New York a few years ago. It was total, beautiful chaos. The audience seemed to turn up in reverence of them, but you're not going to find a group of people less interested in hearing how important they are. So, they took it in turns to try and create mayhem – turning their chairs the wrong way around, walking off stage when they got bored, and sitting with the microphones in their mouths. They treated the evening, each other, and their own legacy terribly, and it felt like a far more meaningful tribute.

That's why one of the greatest acts of love I've seen was the funeral for Graham Chapman. It was a *de facto* roast. They saw him off in the spirit he would have wanted, with no respect whatsoever. Here's what John Cleese said about one of his best friends:

'I guess we're all thinking how sad it is that a man of such talent, such capability and kindness, of such intelligence should now be so suddenly spirited away at the age of only forty-eight, before he'd achieved many of the things of which he was capable, and before he'd had enough fun.

Well, I feel that I should say, "Nonsense. Good riddance to him, the free-loading bastard! I hope he fries. And the reason I think I should say this is, he would never forgive me if I didn't, if I threw away this opportunity to shock you all on his behalf.'"

With that in mind, I'll say this to you: Monty Python are a bunch of decaying old men, and they'll all be dead soon. Their shrivelled testicles will become dust in the wind of history. But people will be laughing hysterically at their work long, long after they're gone.

I really hope you enjoy this book. After you're finished, find a ten-year-old who probably shouldn't have access to it and give it to them. It might change their life.

**John Oliver** is a stand-up comedian and the host and writer of the Peabody and multi-Emmy Award-winning HBO series *Last Week Tonight*.

# ACKNOWLEDGEMENTS

Having covered the work of one Python or another over the years, it was a pleasure to finally have the opportunity to write on their work as a team. For that I wish to thank Tom Dupree, who believed in the value of taking a (somewhat) serious approach to examining a (somewhat) silly group.

My heartfelt thanks for the generosity of the Pythons: to John Cleese for his thoughtfulness; Terry Gilliam for his enthusiasm; Terry Jones and family for their hospitality; Michael Palin for his charm; and Eric Idle for the battery drain on his laptop.

My great appreciation extends to Douglas Adams, Howard Atherton, Hank Azaria, Terry Bedford, Carol Cleveland, Julian Doyle, Mark Forstater, John Goldstone, Ian MacNaughton, David Sherlock, and Barry Took, and a big thank-you to Nancy Lewis and Simon Jones for their generosity.

I am thankful for the help of Sophie Astin; Peter Becker and Sean Wright Anderson at the Criterion Collection; Lisa Brody; Cathy McDonnell at

HBO; Bobbie Mitchell of the BBC Photo Archives; Amanda Montgomerie; Roanne Moore; Roger Saunders; Jessica Tipping; and Kirsten Whiting, each of whom smoothed the process considerably.

Thank you to Matthew Daddona at HarperCollins for agreeing that fifty-year anniversaries are worth celebrating, and for supporting this revisit to one of my most enjoyable projects; and to Holly Gilliam for her aid and zeal. Also, I am grateful for guidance and wisdom over the long haul from Deborah Cabaniss, Martha Kaplan, Lucille Rhodes, and Richard Spitaleri.

Finally, loving thanks to my wife, Tessa Wardlaw, who understands.

# INTERVIEWEES

## THE PYTHONS

### JOHN CLEESE

Cleese escaped a projected career in law when he accepted a job writing jokes for the BBC. Beside Python, his talent made him a valued presence on radio (*I'm Sorry, I'll Read That Again*), TV (*The Frost Report, At Last the 1948 Show,* and *Fawlty Towers*), in films (*Silverado, A Fish Called Wanda, The World Is Not Enough,* and the *Shrek* series), and in a frighteningly long list of commercials. He also penned the autobiography *So, Anyway . . .*

### TERRY GILLIAM

Born and raised in Minnesota and Los Angeles, Gilliam's early career as a magazine illustrator and advertising agency copywriter somehow pointed him towards creating animations for British television. As a director his films away from Python include *Time Bandits, Brazil, The Adventures of Baron Munchausen, The Fisher King, Twelve Monkeys, Fear*

*and Loathing in Las Vegas*, *The Imaginarium of Doctor Parnassus*, and, finally, *The Man Who Killed Don Quixote*. He also directed the operas *The Damnation of Faust* and *Benvenuto Cellini*.

## ERIC IDLE

A razor-sharp wit with a poison pen, Idle professes to shun acting for writing and yet has acted in a plethora of non-Python projects (*Nuns on the Run*, *Casper*, *An Alan Smithee Film: Burn Hollywood Burn*, *Quest for Camelot*, and *South Park: Bigger, Longer & Uncut*). He authored the novel *The Road to Mars*; a Grammy-nominated children's story; and the Tony Award–winning musical 'lovingly ripped off' from *Monty Python and the Holy Grail*, *Monty Python's Spamalot*.

## TERRY JONES

Most likely of the Pythons to appear in drag, Jones is a noted history buff who has written on Chaucer and hosted the documentaries *Ancient Inventions*, *The Crusades*, and *Barbarians*. He also directed *Personal Services*, *Erik the Viking*, *The Wind in the Willows*, and *Absolutely Anything*; wrote several fanciful children's books; and has contributed political op-ed columns.

## MICHAEL PALIN

The most innocent-looking of the group (and consequently able to play some of the most subversive parts), Palin starred in *The Missionary* and *A Private Function*. He has since become a trusty guide for armchair travellers with his globetrotting series, including *Around the World in 80 Days*, *Pole to Pole*, *Full Circle*, *Himalaya*, and *Sahara*. He also wrote the novels *Hemingway's Chair* and *The Truth*.

# CO-CONSPIRATORS

## BARRY TOOK

A veteran television producer and writer, Took's credits on radio and television include *Round the Horne, The Frost Report,* and *The Marty Show* (with Marty Feldman). It was Took who proposed the teaming of the six members that made up Python to the BBC. He did duty in Los Angeles as a producer of *Rowan and Martin's Laugh-In* but soon returned to the UK to work as a programming executive, columnist, and comedy writer. (Took died in 2002.)

## IAN MACNAUGHTON

A veteran of the BBC's drama department before being abducted by Light Entertainment and Spike Milligan, MacNaughton was the producer of all of Python's TV output and director of all but a handful of their shows, as well as the feature *And Now for Something Completely Different.* He later worked as a television, stage, and opera director out of his home base in Germany. (MacNaughton died in 2002.)

## DAVID SHERLOCK

A drama teacher and writer, Sherlock was Graham Chapman's companion of twenty-three years and witnessed the birth of Python. He also collaborated with Chapman on several projects, including *Yellowbeard.*

## CAROL CLEVELAND

Born in the UK, Cleveland was raised in the United States but pursued acting (both comedic and dramatic) in England. Aside from her Python roles, she has appeared in numerous television series (including *The Avengers, The Persuaders,* and *Are You Being Served?*), films (*The Return of the Pink Panther*), and stage shows (*The Glass Menagerie, Dial M for Murder*), as well as her own one-woman show, *Carol Cleveland Reveals All.*

## JOHN GOLDSTONE

The executive producer of *Monty Python and the Holy Grail*, Goldstone was the producer of *Life of Brian* and *The Meaning of Life*. He also co-produced quasi-Python projects such as Terry Jones' *The Wind in the Willows*.

## MARK FORSTATER

A flatmate of Terry Gilliam's in New York City in the 1960s, Forstater served as producer of *Monty Python and the Holy Grail*. His other film and TV credits include *The Odd Job*, *The Fantasist*, and *Grushko*.

## JULIAN DOYLE

Doyle's duties as production manager on *Holy Grail* included staging the Black Knight sequence in East London, locating a Polish engineer in the wilds of Scotland to fashion a cog for a broken camera, and transporting a dead sheep in his van at five o'clock in the morning. He took the more sedate job of editor for *Life of Brian* and *The Meaning of Life*. He has also edited *Brazil* and *The Wind in the Willows*.

## TERRY BEDFORD

Director of photography for *Monty Python and the Holy Grail*, Bedford also served as DP for Terry Gilliam's *Jabberwocky*. He has since become a director for television and commercials, and helmed the feature *Slayground*.

## HOWARD ATHERTON

A fellow alumnus of the London International Film School with Bedford, Doyle, and Forstater, Atherton was camera operator on *Holy Grail*. He has served as director of photography for such directors as Adrian Lyne (*Fatal Attraction*, *Lolita*) and Michael Bay (*Bad Boys*).

## NANCY LEWIS

Python's New York-based publicist and, later, personal manager during the Seventies and Eighties.

## DOUGLAS ADAMS

Not a Python, but an incredible simulation. Before creating *The Hitch-hiker's Guide to the Galaxy*, Adams collaborated with Graham Chapman in the mid-Seventies, and even contributed a few morsels to Python. He later collaborated with Terry Jones and John Cleese on the video game *Starship Titanic*. (Adams died in 2001.)

## HANK AZARIA

A six-time Emmy Award winner, Azaria has appeared in the Mike Nichols film *The Birdcage, Cradle Will Rock, Mystery Men*, and *Tuesdays with Morrie*, and the series *Mad About You, Huff, Ray Donovan*, and *Brockmire*. But he is probably best known as the voices of Moe, Chief Wiggum, Apu, Comic Book Guy, and several dozen other characters on *The Simpsons*. Azaria was a Tony Award nominee for the original Broadway production of *Monty Python's Spamalot*.

# INTRODUCTION

This revolution *was* televised.

When the six members of Monty Python embarked on their unique collaboration fifty years ago, they were reacting against what they saw as the staid, predictable formats of other comedy programmes. What they brought to their audience was writing that was both highly intelligent and silly. The shows contained visual humour with a quirky style, and boisterous performances that seemed to celebrate the group's creative freedom. But what made Monty Python extraordinary from the very beginning was their total lack of predictability, revelling in a stream-of-consciousness display of nonsense, satire, sex, and violence. Throughout their careers they were uncompromising in their work, and consequently made a mark on popular culture – and the pop culture industry – which is still being felt today.

Two of the more revolutionary concepts of *Monty Python's Flying Circus* (the BBC Television series which premiered in Britain in 1969 and in the United States five years later) were the lack of a 'star' personality (around whom a show might have been constructed), and the absence of a specific formula. Typically, the most popular or influential comic artists in film or television were those who had shaped a powerful persona, either of themselves or of an archetypal character. Charlie Chaplin, Buster Keaton, Harold Lloyd, the Marx Brothers, W. C. Fields, Bob Hope, Woody Allen, and Richard Pryor all worked within a formula in which the comedy would be built around a recognizable character. And while a few experimented with the conventions of motion pictures (such as Allen's character Alvy Singer breaking the fourth wall while standing in a cinema line in *Annie Hall*), it was still in support of a comic personality.

Television (and radio) also perpetuated the situation comedy, in which narrative possibilities were limited by being subordinate to the conventions of already-accepted characters, with no deviation allowed. Even *Rowan and Martin's Laugh-In,* which was heralded in its time for its fast, freewheeling format, nonetheless *had* a format, in addition to recurring characters and situations.

Python would have none of that. Apart from a few repeated characterizations such as the Gumbys (irrepressible idiots, which were themselves pretty vaguely drawn), the series' forty-five episodes marked a constant reinvention. Each production had its own shape, with only rare reminders of what other Python shows were about. There might be a theme to a particular episode's contents, but even that was a pretty loose excuse for linking sketches together. It was that fluidity of style that made the Pythons seem like a rugby team which kept changing the ground rules and moving the goalposts, and still played a smashing good game – one could barely keep up with them. And even as audiences became more familiar with each Python's on-screen personality, the six writer/performers were so adaptable and chameleonic that no one ever stood out as the star of the group – the cast was as fluid as the material.

This very flow of action and ideas was the most potent source of humour for Python. The comedy had an inner logic (or illogic) that was not contingent upon generally accepted notions of drama: there was no narrative drive, no three-act structure, and no character development (and in fact, there was often *anti*-character development, as when the camera turns away from a couple deemed 'the sort of people to whom nothing extraordinary ever happened').

As the series progressed, the troupe experimented with doing longer and longer sketches, or (as in 'Dennis Moore') creating characters or situations which would reappear at different points throughout the show. By the end, a couple of episodes ('The Cycling Tour', 'Mr Neutron') were in effect half-hour skits, though their lack of dramatic arc pointed to the fact that separate, disparate sketches were in effect draped over a specific character serving as a linking device.

*Monty Python's Flying Circus* never had the tight adherence to form or place that John Cleese's *Fawlty Towers* had, and never really told a story, as the Michael Palin and Terry Jones series *Ripping Yarns* did. What it did have were odd and surreal juxtapositions, a penchant for twisted violence, and a belief that the human condition is, on the whole, pretty absurd.

The films that followed – *Monty Python and the Holy Grail, Life of Brian,* and *The Meaning of Life* – demonstrated quite vividly that this stream-of-consciousness approach could be transferred to feature-length films, but the Pythons also showed that they could (when they wanted to) have the discipline to tell an actual story. *Brian* is a fast-moving, fully formed tale whose comic asides never distract from the central figure's arc. More importantly, the filmmakers offer some serious social commentary mixed in with the humour, without ever seeming pedantic or boring – a very rare talent.

Python was not about jokes; it was really about a state of mind. It was a way of looking at the world as a place where walking like a contortionist is not only considered normal but is rewarded with government funding; where people speak in anagrams; where highwaymen redistribute wealth in floral currencies; and where BBC newsreaders use arcane hand signals when announcing the day's events. And as long as the world itself is accepted as being an absurd place, Python will seem right at home. That is why the shows and films remain funny to audiences fifty years after their premiere, even after the routines have been memorized.

*Monty Python Speaks!* explores the world of the Pythons, who describe in their own words their coming together, their collaboration, their struggles to maintain artistic control over their work, and their efforts to expand themselves creatively in other media. It also documents the stamp they have made on humour; the passion of their fans; and the lasting appeal of their television and film work, books, recordings, and stage shows, in Britain and around the world. It also reveals what is perhaps the definitive meaning of 'Splunge!'

And now, 'It's . . .'

❀    ❀    ❀

# PRE-PYTHON

## IN THE OLD DAYS WE
## USED TO MAKE OUR OWN FUN

If there is a progenitor to credit (or blame!) for Monty Python, the innovative and surreal comedy group that turned the BBC and cinema screens on their ends, one need look no further than a tall, undisciplined, manic-depressive Irishman, born and raised in India, who spent his young adulthood playing the trumpet for British troops in North Africa, before wrestling his fervent notions of humour onto paper in the back of a London pub.

Spike Milligan, author of such pithy memoirs as *Adolf Hitler – My Part in His Downfall*, created the revolutionary BBC Radio series *The Goon Show*, which was to radio comedy what Picasso was to postcards. Aired between 1951 and 1960, and featuring Milligan, Peter Sellers, Harry Secombe, and (briefly) Michael Bentine, *The Goon Show* was a marvellously anarchic mixture of nonsensical characters, banterish wordplay, and weird sound effects all pitched at high speed. The surreal plots (such as they were) might concern climbing to the summit of Mt Everest from the inside, drinking the contents of Loch Lomond to recover a sunken treasure, or flying the Albert Memorial to the moon.

Milligan's deft use of language and sound effects to create surreal mindscapes showed how the medium of radio could be used to tell stories that did not rely on straightforward plots or punchlines; it was the *illogic* of the character's actions bordering on the fantastic (e.g., the hero being turned into a liquid and drunk) which moved the show along. It was a modern, dramatized version of Lewis Carroll and Edward Lear – fast-paced and hip, its language a bit blue around the edges.

The artistic and popular success of *The Goon Show* inspired many humourists who followed. Although its surreal nature could not really be matched, its fast-paced celebration of illogic and its penchant for satire opened the doors for some of the edgier comedy that came to light in Britain in the Sixties, such as *Beyond the Fringe* (an internationally successful cabaret featuring Peter Cook, Jonathan Miller, Alan Bennett, and Dudley Moore), and the television series *That Was the Week That Was* and *The Frost Report*.

But while *The Goon Show* demonstrated how broadcast comedy could bend convention, it was the passionate satire of the rising talents from university revues that forced satire – typically a literary exercise – into the vernacular of the day. If a map were to be drawn of the comedy universe in the late Fifties and early Sixties, its centre would assuredly comprise the halls of Cambridge and Oxford; between them, they produced a flood of talented writers and performers who were to raise the comedy standard, extending from stage to recordings, magazines, television, and film.

Among the many illustrious figures who began their careers in the Cambridge Footlights comedy troupe or in revues at Oxford were Humphrey Barclay, David Frost, Tim Brooke-Taylor, Bill Oddie, Graeme Garden, Jo Kendall, David Hatch, Jonathan Lynn, Tony Hendra, and Trevor Nunn. Also from this rich training ground came five writer/performers of deft talent: Graham Chapman, John Cleese, Eric Idle, Terry Jones, and Michael Palin – five-sixths of what would become the most successful comedy group in film and television, Monty Python.

Leading up to their first collaboration as Python in the spring of 1969, these five Cambridge/Oxford university graduates were working separately or in teams for several radio and TV shows at the BBC and at independent television (ITV) companies. They soon recognized similar tastes or aesthetics about how comedy should be written and performed. It was partly magnetism and partly luck which brought the group together, and the result was a programme that reinvented television comedy, launched a successful string of films, books, and recordings, and turned dead parrots and Spam into cherished comic icons.

## I MEAN, THEY THINK WELL, DON'T THEY

**TERRY JONES:** Mike and I had done a little bit of work together when we'd been at Oxford. I first saw Mike doing cabaret with Robert Hewison, who later became a theatre critic. Mike and I and Robert all worked together on a thing called *Hang Down Your Head and Die*. It was in the style of Joan Littlewood's *Oh, What a Lovely War*, and it was a show against capital punishment, which we still had in this country at that time. That was the first time Mike and I worked together. And then we did an Oxford revue called *Loitering Within Tent* – it was a revue done *in* a tent – and he and I worked out a sequence called the 'Slapstick Sequence' [in which a professor introduces demonstrations of various laugh-inducing pratfalls]. As far as I remember that was the first real writing collaboration we did, and in fact that sketch was later done in the Python stage show.

I did a bit of writing with Miles Kington (who was a columnist for *The Independent*), and then when Mike came down (I was a year ahead of Mike) he worked on a TV pop show for a while. By that time I'd got a job at the BBC, so I kind of knew what was happening, and Mike and I started writing stuff for *The Frost Report*. We were contributing little one-liners for Frost's monologue and sketches, and then we got to doing these little visual films which we actually got to perform in. Little things like, 'What judges do at the high court during recess'. We just filmed a lot of judges with their wigs and gowns in a children's playground, going down slides.

We weren't being paid very much for the writing; our fee in those days was seven guineas a minute – of course, that's a minute of airtime, not how long it takes to write! We were kind of lucky [if] we got two or three minutes of material on the show, so by letting us appear in our little visual films, it meant that they could pay us a bit more.

**MICHAEL PALIN:** Terry and I worked together since I left Oxford, which would be 1965. Terry by that time had a job in the BBC in a script department, and we worked together very closely. We saw each other on an almost daily basis, and that was true from that period right up to the Python times; we wrote for all sorts of shows, tons and tons of stuff.

*Apart from your collaboration with Terry,*
*were you also writing on your own?*

**PALIN:** Not really, there wasn't time. We had to make money in those days, too. We'd just got married and [were] having children and all that sort of thing. I probably had days when I thought, 'Today I'm going to start The Novel,' or whatever. And then we'd be offered by Marty Feldman a hundred pounds a minute for this new sketch (that's between the two of us). 'A hundred pounds a minute? I don't believe that, that's *fantastic*, so we better write something for Marty!' So that day would be spent writing something for Marty Feldman. So yeah, we were real genuine writers during that time, we worked as a team. Although the mechanics of writing were not necessarily that we would sit in the same room with a giant piece of paper and say, 'All right, now we're going to make a sketch.'

**JONES:** Originally when we'd been writing for *The Frost Report* and for Marty Feldman, Mike and I would go and read them through, they'd all laugh, the sketch would get in, and then you see the sketch on the air and they fucking changed it all! We'd get furious. There was one sketch Marty did about a gnome going into a mortgage office to try to raise a mortgage. And he comes in and sits down and talks very sensibly about collateral and everything, and eventually the mortgage guy says, 'Well, what's the property?' And he says, 'Oh, it's the magic oak tree in Dingly Dell.' And the thing went back and forth like that. Everybody laughed when we did it, and when we saw it finally come out on TV, Marty comes in, sits cross-legged on the desk, and starts telling a string of one-line gnome jokes. This wasn't what the joke was at all.

What happens is that people (especially someone like Marty) would start rehearsing it, and of course after you've been rehearsing it a few times people don't laugh anymore. And so Marty being the kind of character he was, he'd throw in a few jokes, and everybody would laugh again. And so that's how things would accumulate. It was things like that that made us want to perform our own stuff. We sort of felt if it worked, you wanted to leave it as it was.

Humphrey Barclay[*] asked if Mike and I would like to get together and do a children's show with Eric Idle. We'd seen Eric in Edinburgh in my final year in the Cambridge revue, a young blue-eyed boy; he looked very glamorous on the stage as I remember! So we knew of Eric, but we'd never worked with him. The three of us wrote *Do Not Adjust Your Set*. It

---

[*] A Footlights veteran and director of *Cambridge Circus,* Barclay became a producer at the BBC and later head of comedy at London Weekend Television.

was basically a children's TV show but we thought, 'Well, we'll just do whatever *we* think is funny, we won't write specifically for children.' And we had the Bonzo Dog Doo-Dah Band in it.[*] And then at the same time we were doing the second series of *Do Not Adjust Your Set*, Mike and I were also doing *The Complete and Utter History of Britain* for London Weekend Television.

**PALIN:** *The Complete and Utter History* had a narrative [like] a television news programme. You had someone in the studio describing events that were going on, and then the camera would go out 'live' to, for instance, the shower room leading out to the Battle of Hastings where all the teams were washing, cleaning themselves off, and talking about the battle, as if it were a current affairs show in 1066 or 1285 or 1415. It was a very simple set-up. So we could parody television a little bit, but on the other hand we had to accept the convention of a television show, which made it a much more regular shape.

**JONES:** My big hero is Buster Keaton because he made comedy look beautiful; he took it seriously. He didn't say, 'Oh, it's comedy, so we don't need to bother about the way it looks.' The way it looks is crucial, particularly *because* we were doing silly stuff. It had to have an integrity to it.

One time on *The Complete and Utter History*, we were shooting the Battle of Harfleur, the English against the French, and we wanted to shoot it like a Western. It was parodying Westerns where you see the Indians up on the skyline; when you come closer they're actually Frenchmen with striped shirts and berets and baguettes and bicycles and onions, things like that. And then the Frenchmen breathe on the English: 'They're using garlic, chaps!' And the English all come out with gas masks. All pretty stupid stuff. But it was very important that it should *look* right.

---

[*]   Its members included Neil Innes, Vivian Stanshall, Rodney Slater, Larry Smith, and Roger Ruskin-Spear.

Anyway we turned up on the location to shoot it, looking around with the director, actually it was a nice gentle bit of rolling countryside amongst the woods. I said, 'Where's the skyline? There isn't a skyline, doesn't look like America, it looks like English countryside.' We were there, we had to shoot it, but it wasn't the thing we meant to be shooting. It wasn't a Western parody – that element was missing from it – so it looked like just a lot of silly goings-on in front of the camera. And it was at that moment when I realized you can't just write it, you can't just perform it, you've actually got to *be* there, looking at the locations, checking on the costumes – *everything* was crucial for the jokes.

Curiously, we thought *Complete and Utter History* was wiped.[*] The only things that existed of that were the 16-millimetre film inserts which I collected, but in fact a couple of years ago somebody turned up a whole programme that had been misfiled. All the stuff filed under 'Comedy' had been wiped, but this was filed under 'History' and so it was still there! But it was quite odd seeing it again, after all those years, and how Pythonic it was, way more so than *Do Not Adjust Your Set*.

---

[*] A typical, short-sighted economy move on the part of broadcasters, so that video-tape could be reused.

*Terry Jones in* The Complete and Utter History of Britain.

## NOW WHICH ONE OF YOU IS THE SURGEON?

John Cleese and Graham Chapman met in the Footlights club at Cambridge, where they were studying law and medicine, respectively. Cleese had originally gone to university for science, but upon realizing it wasn't for him, he found his choices limited to archaeology and anthropology ('which no serious-minded boy from Weston-super-Mare would waste a university education on'), economics ('which I couldn't think of anything much more dreadful to study'), and law.

**JOHN CLEESE:** Graham and I met at Cambridge when we were both auditioning for a Footlights show, which would have been 1961, and we both auditioned unsuccessfully. And we went and had a coffee afterwards and the funny thing is I remember that I quite disliked him, which is not a reaction I have to most people. But it was odd that that was my first reaction to him. It was purely intuitive.

What I liked about Footlights (which numbered about sixty) is there was a wider cross-section, so you got English people but you also got scientists, historians, and psychologists. Also, there was much more of a mix of class. A lot of the other clubs tended to have a predominant class or predominant attitude; the Footlights crowd were very mixed and very good company, very amusing, and a lot less intense and serious and dedicated than the drama societies, who (it seemed to us) took themselves a bit seriously.

At the beginning of the following university year, a number of us arrived back at Cambridge and we went to the Footlights club room and in bewilderment we saw a notice board informing us that we were now officers! We had been in the club for such a short period of time that we'd not realized that almost everyone in the club had left the previous year. So I found myself registrar, Tim Brooke-Taylor was junior treasurer, Graham was on the committee, we all had these jobs (without having

*Chapman and Cleese and friends.*

the slightest idea what they entailed), but it meant that we got pushed together because we had to run the club.

So I got to know Graham. And he and I (and I don't remember how) started to write together, and most of the things I wrote at Cambridge after I met Graham were written with Graham.

And then at the end of that year he went to London to continue his medical studies at St Bartholomew's Hospital. He used to do some moonlighting, a late-night revue (which I never saw) with a guy called Tony Hendra, in a little room above the Royal Court Theatre. Graham used to come up to Cambridge occasionally and we continued to write a bit. And then when the Footlights Revue of 1963, *A Clump of Plinths*, started, Chapman used to come and watch and I used to make him laugh!

Then on the opening couple of weeks two very nice men in grey suits, Ted Taylor and Peter Titheradge, turned up at Cambridge. They'd noticed that I'd written a large portion of the material and they offered me a job. I was never very committed to being a lawyer, so when these guys offered me £30 a week when I was facing two and a half years in a solicitor's office where I was going to get £12 a week (which was not much money even in 1963), I took the BBC job. I wasn't at all sorry to say good-bye to the law; it was easy to convince my parents that it was okay because this was the BBC so there was a pension scheme – it was almost like going into the entertainment branch of the civil service.

Later when the Footlights Revue (which obviously didn't have Graham in it) transferred to London, Anthony Buffery did not want to stay with the show very long, and his place was taken by Graham.

---

*Cambridge Circus*, directed by Humphrey Barclay, was a smash in the West End in August 1963. The show featured Chapman, Cleese, and Bill Oddie and Tim Brooke-Taylor (who would later form two-thirds of the Goodies), David Hatch, Jo Kendall, and Chris Stuart-Clark. Cleese followed the stage show with a knockabout radio programme, *I'm Sorry, I'll Read That Again*, which Barclay produced for the BBC. It borrowed not only material from *Cambridge Circus* but also several of its stars: Oddie, Brooke-Taylor, Hatch, and Kendall.

---

**CLEESE:** That's what I did for a time until Michael White, the guy who put *Cambridge Circus* on in London, got in touch with us all about the middle of the following year and said, 'Would you guys like to come to New Zealand and probably Broadway?' So we all gave up our jobs and joined up.

Graham interrupted his medical studies. He always had a nice story that the Queen Mother came to St Bart's around this time to take tea with some of them, and he actually put his quandary in front of her, and said, 'Should I go on being a medical student or should I go off to do this show in New Zealand and Broadway?' And she said, 'Oh, you *must* travel.' So he came! We had fun in New Zealand, which was a strange part of the Empire: very refined and very well mannered and sort of stuck around 1910. I remember [in] one town you could not find a restaurant that was open after eight o'clock!

**DAVID SHERLOCK:** Graham was training at St Bart's Hospital at the same time that Cleese was still training as a solicitor. A Footlights-type revue was brought every Christmas to the patients in the wards, with all the people Graham worked with – Cleese, Bill Oddie, Jo Kendall, all the cast of *Cambridge Circus* – moving from ward to ward. Graham often directed; later on, he worked with other young doctors who were equally talented.

*Cambridge Circus* had so many elements of Python – the anarchic humour, sketches which had no punchline. The New York show was produced by Sol Hurok, who was better known at that period for bringing ballet over to New York (the Royal Ballet, etc.). It turned out these almost-schoolboys were brought over specifically as a tax loss, and on the first night they were given their notice – which is a hell of a way to open in New York, particularly as I think Clive Barnes absolutely raved.

**CLEESE:** We were always puzzled because it got such good reviews, with the exception of Howard Taubman of the *New York Times*, the former sportswriter (which I always add!), and it got this terrific review from Walter Kerr, who then – when he heard we were coming off – wrote another to try to boost the audience, which was marvellous. We could never figure out why Hurok had bothered to bring us to New York and put us on, when after we got such good reviews he didn't bother to publicize the show. Somebody said he was looking for a tax loss and I don't know whether there was any truth to it, or whether it was the *exact* truth or whether it was a rumour.

After Broadway, we went and performed at a small theater club off Washington Square called Square East. And after a time we put together a second show, but Graham said, 'I must be off.' So he went back to England to continue his studies.

I stayed on, got invited to do *Half a Sixpence* with Tommy Steele for six months, and tried to have a journalistic career at *Newsweek*, but my mentor disappeared to cover a crisis in the Dominican Republic so I sort of resigned before I was fired. I did one more show which took me to Chicago and Washington, and then came back to England in the beginning of 1966.

The threads start to come together at the end of 1965. David Frost had called from the airport and said, 'Would you like to be in a television show? There are two other guys who are very funny but they're unknowns – Ronnie Barker and Ronnie Corbett – and there's me, and it's a sketch show and I'd like you to be in it, and it starts in March.' And I said, 'Yes, please!' I mean, I was astonished, it was just absolutely out of the blue. David was the only person in England who knew my work at all and who was in any position of power to give me a job, so it was very lucky.

While I was in America doing these other things, that's when they got *I'm Sorry, I'll Read That Again* together on a regular, organized basis, and they did one or two series with Graeme Garden, and when I got back in 1966 they asked me to join the team, and I was very happy to do it. But the big thing was the television show, *The Frost Report*, for a number of reasons: one was I had never been particularly picked out or noticed as being especially good on stage. The moment I appeared on television something else happened, and I can only assume that some of the acting stuff I did worked better in close-up than it did from the tenth-row stalls. Because the moment I appeared on television there was a bit of a rustle of interest, and I'd got used to there *not* being a rustle of interest. Because when *Cambridge Circus* started most of the reviews were garnered by Bill Oddie (who was singing songs which he did very, very well, and he also had a couple of very amusing parts like a dwarf in a courtroom sketch), and the next most successful guy was Tim Brooke-Taylor (who had two or three big funny set pieces). I picked up a few reviews along with David Hatch, but I was not singled out.

*Did Graham write outside of his partnership with John?*

**SHERLOCK:** Graham wrote links for Petula Clark when she was doing her early Sixties television show over here. Petula Clark, while being a wonderful singer, could not ad-lib at all. She was very frightened about opening her mouth on stage and not knowing what to say. So *everything* had to be scripted, all the links between the songs. So he had a close rapport with Clark, which is very funny, particularly when you see some of the Python sketches later on which reference her.[*]

**CLEESE:** So I'd got *The Frost Report,* and sitting at the scriptwriter's table were five future Pythons: Mike and Terry tended to write visual, fill-in items, which we used to shoot during the course of the week and then they would be edited into the show. And Eric typically used to write monologues which Ronnie Barker often did. So the show frequently consisted of a filmed item by Mike and Terry, one or two sketches by Graham and me, occasional Ronnie Barker pieces by Eric, and then a lot of other material from another dozen scriptwriters, of whom the leader was Marty Feldman. Graham didn't perform; Mike and Terry would probably say that he turned up in one of the filmed items at some point, but I don't remember him.

We did these half-hour shows every week for thirteen weeks, each on a theme. Tony Jay, who founded Video Arts and has been a friend of mine for thirty years, wrote a theme each week – advertising or education or transport. Everybody used to read the theme paper because it was actually insightful and original, and then we completely ignored it! Then, because it had gone well, David Frost said to Tim and me, 'Would you like to do a show together?' And we said, 'Yes, we would,' and we immediately said we'd do it with Graham, and then we said to Frost that as the fourth member of the team we would like to have Marty Feldman.

---

[*]   In the 'Historical Impersonations' sketch, Cardinal Richelieu impersonates Clark singing 'Don't Sleep in the Subway'.

I remember that David was quite thrown, a little embarrassed, and said, 'Well, people would be put off by his appearance.'

So Graham and I, along with Tim and Marty, did *At Last the 1948 Show*, which was very much more way-out than anything we'd done. Some of it was *very* bizarre and very funny, it was a good little show, done on no money at all. I remember we used to edit the videotape with a razor, literally.

So in my first two years of television, between *The Frost Report* and *At Last the 1948 Show*, I did forty television shows, which is quite a lot when you're contributing as a writer. It was pretty busy. And then I got married to Connie Booth (whom I'd met in New York), and I thought it was not fair for me to spend time in the studios until she got used to London, so I forswore acting, which cost me nothing at all. I've never been that attached to acting, and I can easily live without it, it's just that it pays much better than writing – that's the problem. And I didn't in fact perform for really quite a long time, something on the order of eighteen months.

And during that time Graham and I wrote various things; at one point for some reason Graham, Eric, and I wrote most of a special for a very good English comedian, Sheila Hancock. We just did one show – I've no idea in retrospect why. And we got to know Peter Sellers. Graham and I wrote two or three screenplays for Sellers, the only one of which that got made was *The Magic Christian*. We came in on about draft nine of that, did I think a good draft on which they raised the money, and then Terry Southern came back and rewrote it again, and – we thought – made it worse. A certain amount of our stuff survived that, including my scene at Sotheby's, cutting the nose off the portrait.

Graham and I towards the end of Thursday afternoons formed a habit of turning on the television to watch *Do Not Adjust Your Set*, which was much the funniest thing on television; although it was thought of as a kids' show it was really funny stuff. We knew these guys although we had not spent that much time with them, and I picked Palin out as a performer and asked him to be in *How to Irritate People*, a special produced by Frost.

Mike and I got on very well. I wrote a lot of that with Graham and one or two of the sketches with Connie, like the upper-class couple who can't say, 'I love you'; they have to say, 'One loves one'.

I didn't enjoy the experience. The recording of it was a nightmare; *everything* went wrong. I remember starting one sketch and then we had to relight it, we stopped in the middle of the sketch and then started again, and again stopped it and relit it. And the audience had been there so long, about halfway

*The cast of* Do Not Adjust Your Set *(clockwise from top left: Idle, Palin, David Jason, Denise Coffey, Jones).*

through the recording they started leaving to be able to catch their buses home. I remember standing in front of the camera reading something and thinking, 'I don't think I want to do this again as long as I live!' It was an awful experience. Maybe that helped put me off the acting!

## WITH A MELON?

Eric Idle, who was also in Cambridge (and as president of Footlights allowed women in as full members for the first time), appeared on-stage in *Oh, What a Lovely War*, contributed to *I'm Sorry, I'll Read That Again* and *The Frost Report*, and helped create (with Palin and Jones) *Do Not Adjust Your Set* and *We Have Ways of Making You Laugh*.

*How familiar were each of you with the other*
*Pythons before the group was formed?*

**ERIC IDLE:** We weren't new to each other at all. I met Cleese in February 1963 at Cambridge; Jonesy, Edinburgh 1963; Palin, Edinburgh 1964; Chapman, also Cambridge, summer 1963. We had all worked together as writers and actors. Jones, Palin, and I were perhaps the closest, having written two whole seasons of *Do Not Adjust Your Set*, but I had written six episodes of a sitcom with Graham, and we had all worked together on *The Frost Report*. So we weren't new to each other at all, but were actually very familiar; what was new was being free to decide what we wanted to do.

## HAVE WE SHOWN 'EM WE GOT TEETH?

The lone American of Python – a native of Minnesota and a product of Los Angeles – Terry Gilliam fled the land of his birth in the late Sixties by turning the advice of Horace Greeley on its end and heading east, first to New York, then London. He worked in magazines as an illustrator and designer, most notably for *Help!*, published by the creator of *Mad* magazine, Harvey Kurtzman.

**TERRY GILLIAM:** I always drew when I was a kid. I did cartoons because they were the most entertaining. It's easiest to impress people if you draw a funny picture, and I think that was a sort of passport through much of my early life. The only art training I had was in college, where I majored in political science. I took several art courses, drawing classes, and sculpture classes. I'd never taken oil painting, any of those forms of art, and I was always criticized because I kept doing cartoons instead of more serious painting.

My training has actually been fairly sloppy and I've been learning about art in retrospect. In college I didn't take things like art history courses. I didn't like the professor and it was a terribly boring course, so I didn't really *know* that much. But I've always just kept my eyes open, and things that I like I am influenced by.

Once I had my little Bolex camera, every Saturday with a three-minute roll of film we'd run out and invent a movie, depending upon what the weather was. I remember doing animation that way as well; we would go around the dustbins and get old bits of film and then we'd scratch on them, each frame, make little animated sequences; it was pathetic! But you were kind of learning something in the course of all this – *anger,* I think, is what I was learning, hatred for society, and wealth, and powerful people who I've never been able to deal with subsequently!

I spent about a year and a half in advertising in Los Angeles. My illustrating days were becoming less and less remunerative, and Joel Siegel (now the famous television critic) was an old friend, in fact the very first cartoon I ever had published was an idea by him. He was working at an ad agency and got me in because I had long hair – the agency needed a longhair in the place – so I became an art director and copywriter. The last job we had there Joel and I were doing advertisements for Universal Pictures, and we *hated* the job. Richard Widmark did a film called *Madigan*, and the kinds of things we were throwing back at Universal were: 'Once he was happy, but now he's MADIGAN!'

**CLEESE:** I'd got to know Terry Gilliam in New York a little bit.[*] He turned up in England out of the blue – must have been 1966 – and I remember having lunch with him when I was doing *At Last the 1948 Show*. I introduced him to one or two people, including Humphrey Barclay, who was producing *Do Not Adjust Your Set*. So Humphrey used him on a London Weekend Television show called *We Have Ways of Making You Laugh*. Terry used to do little sketches, caricatures of guests appearing on the show.

---

[*]  In a photo-comic by Gilliam for *Help!* magazine, Cleese portrayed a man who succumbs to his sexual obsession for a Barbie doll.

*How did you start with animation in England?*

**GILLIAM:** That was just a fluke, really. When I was in London, still drawing these fucking cartoons, I was on a show doing caricatures of the guests, and they had some material they didn't know how to present. I remembered seeing somewhere years earlier, projected on a sheet in somebody's flat, a Stan VanDerBeek cartoon. It was the first time I'd ever seen cutout animation, and it was Richard Nixon photographed with a foot in his mouth, trying to get it out. I thought it was *outrageously* funny. So on the show I said, 'Why don't I make an animated film?' And they let me. And overnight I was an animator.

I had two weeks to do it in, and four hundred pounds. The only way I could do it in that time was using cutouts. I just did these silly things with these cutouts and nobody had ever seen that before on British television. And the result was instantaneous; within a week I had all these offers to do all this other stuff. That's the power of that going out there and millions of people seeing your stuff.

❂    ❂    ❂

# BIRTH

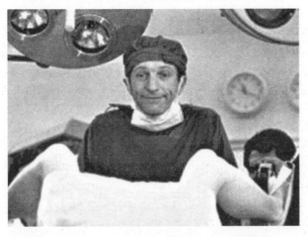

*Chapman in the delivery room, from* The Meaning of Life.

## LEAVE IT ALL TO US, YOU'LL NEVER KNOW WHAT HIT YOU

*How did the grouping of Python come about?*

**BARRY TOOK, BBC AND INDEPENDENT TELEVISION PRODUCER:** Marty Feldman and I were sitting in an Indian restaurant. He had been working on *The Frost Report* with John Cleese and Graham Chapman, and I'd been working at Thames Television with Michael Palin and Terry Jones, and I said, 'I'll put my two Oxford chaps against your two Cambridge chaps.' It started as a joke – hah hah hah – so I got home and I thought, 'Hey, that's not a bad idea.'

So I put it to Michael Palin, and he said yeah, he thought it'd be fine by him, but if it came off could he bring Gilliam and Eric Idle because they'd been working together at Thames on this children's show, *Do Not Adjust Your Set*. And I took it to Cleese and Graham Chapman, and we got together and talked about it, and I went to the BBC.

**CLEESE:** So what happened – and I am fairly clear that *my* account is fundamentally right – after Graham and I had been laughing at *Do Not Adjust Your Set* every Thursday, we said, 'Wouldn't it be fun to do something with those guys, because they are the funniest people around.' Connie had now been in England for a year and a half and had found her feet, so I didn't feel guilty about going off to the studio for rehearsal. We rang them up – I rang them up, because when I say 'Graham and I' rang them up it always meant *I* did; Graham didn't do that kind of thing, he'd sit there sucking on his pipe – and I suggested it to them, and they were a bit cautious. They didn't say, 'What a wonderful idea!'

I was told later that they'd had an offer from Thames Television, so they were making up their minds how to proceed. And then about two weeks later they rang back and said, 'Okay, we've thought about it and we like the idea.'

Marty Feldman's writing partner was Barry Took, and they'd written hundreds of very good radio shows together of which *Round the Horne* was the best known. Graham and I wrote a certain amount of stuff for Marty during that period when we weren't performing, so I knew Barry a little and I'd always liked him, and I knew he was some kind of comedy advisor to the BBC. I spoke to Barry and said, 'Look, I've talked to the *Do Not Adjust Your Set* people and we'd like to do something.' And my partly constructed memory is that Barry said, 'I'll speak to someone.'

**PALIN:** I can remember John ringing me up and saying that he'd seen *The Complete and Utter History of Britain* that Terry and I did, and saying, 'Well, you won't be doing any more of those!' – John's estimation of *The Complete and Utter History*, which had been a partial success (or partial failure, according to which way you looked at it)!

Terry, Eric, and myself had all been contributors to *The Frost Report*,

[but] I had worked as an actor with John and Graham on a thing called *How to Irritate People* which was made in 1968. I think this was the first time that I'd actually acted with John in sort of long sketches. John was pretty much a star in the television comedy world by 1968 because of *The Frost Report* and then *At Last the 1948 Show*, and I was very flattered that I was asked to go and do this show, because John was the best around – by far he was the most interesting, the most effective television comedy writer/performer around, as far as I was concerned. I think it was doing that that we realized that we enjoyed working together, we had a similar sense of humour, but also a similar attitude to comedy performing: playing it straight for laughs rather than to handle it too obviously. So that really brought John and myself together. I don't think John had worked with Terry Jones, but he knew Terry Gilliam of course because he worked with him on that magazine in America.

So anyway this phone call came and I think it must have been early in '69, John saying why don't we do something together. I think not just because *Complete and Utter History* was over but [also] I don't think John wanted to do any more of *At Last the 1948 Show*. I think he had had enough of those for whatever reason. Marty Feldman had gone on to be a big star, and I think John saw his future with a style of writing that Terry Jones and myself were doing being compatible with his and Graham's writing.

**TOOK:** By then I had become the advisor to the comedy department at the BBC on what they called cheerfully a 'peppercorn rent', meaning they paid me nothing but I was allowed to steal; I didn't steal because I'm not that sort of person, but I desperately wanted to get some shows together. Things were pretty flat [at that time] because David Frost had gone elsewhere, the Marty Feldman series was finished, and they had a show called *Broaden Your Mind* with Tim Brooke-Taylor and Graeme Garden which was a bit flabby.

I had seen Barry Humphries, the Australian, in a one-man show and thought he would make good material for television, and I had this idea of putting this Cleese/Chapman/Palin/Jones together. So I arrived at the BBC and they said, 'Well, Barry Humphries was a female impersonator.' I said, 'He's not, he's a very broad, interesting comedian, he does all kinds of things, and Edna Everage was just one of his jokes' – it came to overwhelm him in the end, but I mean in those days he had several characters. And they said, 'Oh, this Palin and Jones, all that is much too expensive.' I said, 'You must do it, you've *got* to. Why the hell have you employed me? You said come in, bring us new ideas, I bring you new ideas, you say: *We can't do it. Too expensive.*'

I thought, you can't fiddle about with these guys, you've got to go for the throat, you've got to say, 'You've *got* to do this!' So my boss at the time, an eccentric man by the name of Michael Mills, said, 'You're like bloody Barry Von Richthofen and his Flying Circus. You're so bloody arrogant – Took asks you a question, halfway through you realize he's giving you an order.'

So it was known internally as *Baron Von Took's Flying Circus*. It was then reduced to *The Flying Circus* and subsequently *The Circus*. All the internal memos said *'The Circus'*: i.e., 'Would you please engage the following people at these prices dah dah dah.' I have a copy of the memo somewhere which predates anybody else's claim to have invented the name, it's something I'm fairly jealous about – I mean, I don't give a damn, but I *did* invent it.

When they wrote their first script, it was called *Owl Stretching Time* or *Whither Canada?* and Michael Mills said, 'I don't give a damn what it's called, it's called *The Circus* in all the memos – make them call it *"something Flying Circus."'*

**PALIN:** Pretty soon after we decided to do something together, John and Graham went off to finish a film they were doing with Carlo Ponti or somebody like that and then take a holiday in Ibiza, leaving Terry and myself and Terry Gilliam to think more about a shape for the show. That would have happened during May or June of '69; when they came back we actually started writing.

**IDLE:** I remember sitting on the grass in some London park idly discussing what we should do. Mike, me, Terry G., and Terry J. already had an offer to do an adult version of *Do Not Adjust Your Set* on ITV, but not for another year. John and Graham came with an offer to go straight ahead in the autumn. John was keen to get Mike, and we had him. John was not keen to do a show on his own that the BBC had offered him, therefore he came to us. Our decision was to blend the two shows: *At Last the 1948 Show* and *Do Not Adjust Your Set*.

Mike said Cleese was interested. We met up with him and Graham in this park somewhere, [and] said, 'Let's do it.' [We] went to the Beeb, who said, 'Right you are, thirteen on air in September,' and that was it.

It wasn't like US TV at all! We didn't have to do anything as stupid as selling a concept. There was no executive structure. They just gave us thirteen shows and said, 'Get on with it.' Executives only spoil things and hold back originality – that is their job.

**CLEESE:** The worst problem we had with the whole show was finding a good title for it. We had the first show written and we didn't know what to call it, and we had a whole lot of fanciful titles: *A Horse, a Spoon and a Basin*, which I really liked; *Bunn Wackett Buzzard Stubble and Boot; Owl Stretching Time; The Toad Elevating Moment.* In fact, the BBC had started to call it *The Flying Circus*. They'd started writing it into their schedules, in *ink*, and so they said, 'Well, could you call it *The Flying Circus?* Because otherwise we'd have to write out new schedules.'

Then we couldn't decide *who*. We thought it might be *Gwen Dibley's Flying Circus*, because she was a name Michael had pulled out of a newspaper, and then somehow we went off Gwen Dibley, I don't know why – she could be famous now, you know? But somebody came up with Monty Python and we all fell about, and I can't explain why; we just thought it was funny that night!

**TOOK:** I fended off the BBC, who were constantly whinging about how much it was going to cost. They just thought there was too many of them, they knew the animation would be very expensive, and they knew these guys had a lot of imagination and they'd rush off into the fields and film, they would have elaborate sets and all that, and they knew the whole bag of tricks would be very costly, as indeed it was. I said, 'How much is in the budget for scripts?' And they said such and such, and I said, 'Well, split it in six and give them a sixth each. And how much for performing? Do the same thing. It won't cost you any more.'

'Well, we can't because John Cleese gets *more* than Michael Palin.'

'That's irrelevant; if they're going to do it they're going to do it.'

I was about ten years older than the Pythons were and was regarded by them as a man who had a track record which was quite respectable, and I looked a fairly cheerful person. I could be objective. We used to have these meetings at my home in the study, and they used to come in, have tea and cakes and chat and discuss ideas, and they would argue and discuss and they would all agree, and then they would go home. An hour later, the phone would start: 'Is this a bad move for me, is it worth doing?' And I said to all of them, anybody who would ask me that, 'Well, if it's a success, it can't possibly hurt your career, and if it's a failure it'll be off so fast that nobody within six months will remember it, so it won't hurt your career at all.'

*Were they confident in being able to carry the show by themselves?*

**TOOK:** Well, yes, they'd been given free rein. They were told by the BBC, 'Yes, you can do whatever you like, within reason, as long as it's within the bounds of common law.' I made the BBC make that statement to them so they wouldn't feel threatened. And that was my role, then I got out of the way!

To see people with real talent using that talent to the full, it's terrific and if I've been involved in somehow helping to shove that along I'm even more pleased. I suppose I remember my own struggles and how you need patrons and people who help you along in the beginning.

The only criticism that I actually had to face head-on was [from] the head of Light Entertainment, a man called Tom Sloane, [who] came into my office one day and said, 'Excuse me, Barry, I've just been looking at a playback of *Python*. Does John Cleese have to say "bastard" *twice?*' I said, 'Yeah, if he wants to.' He said, 'Well, I'm just *asking!* I'm not trying to –' He shut the door and went away. And that was that!

They were sort of a bit scared of me, and a bit scared of them because they're a pretty high-powered bunch, as time has revealed.

### Did the BBC know what they were getting with the Pythons?

**PALIN:** I think probably something like *Dad's Army**\* was more up their street than *Python*, because we couldn't tell them what we wanted to do – we didn't know ourselves. Barry Took was very much involved in introducing us to the BBC as a group. Barry at the time was very interested in exporting British comedy to America, because *Laugh-In* had just come to England and made a big impression on BBC2, I think. And Barry knew George Schlatter, who was *Laugh-In*'s executive producer. They wanted to produce comedy shows in this country that would have that sort of effect in America. Which was ironic, because they said, 'Well, we can't show this at all' (for the first few years anyway). And the BBC were not particularly committed to *Python* in the sense that 'we need this sort of show'. They had lots of shows going on at Light Entertainment at the time.

So Barry just had to present us as decent, responsible young men who could produce this sort of wacky new show that we couldn't quite describe but was going to be something very fresh.

The BBC did have a certain amount to go on: John was a big name for them, one of their new great discoveries of the Sixties, so whatever John wanted they considered that to be significant. The rest of us, I don't think they particularly cared; we were journeymen scriptwriters. We'd done

---

\* Jimmy Perry and David Croft's long-running sitcom about the Walmington-on-Sea platoon of the Home Guard.

most of our shows for independent companies: *Do Not Adjust Your Set*, *The Complete and Utter History*, and for that matter, *At Last the 1948 Show* were all made for ITV companies, so we hadn't really worked for the BBC except for *The Frost Report*. So their attitude was [to] take a gamble, saying, 'Well, you know, you could do more good than harm letting these people produce a series.'

But the early steps were very faltering. For a start they gave us thirteen shows, which was quite a commitment, and then they immediately started trying to strangle us financially by offering pitiable money. And they regarded Gilliam as something quite unnecessary: 'An *animator*? Who wants an animator? There's no animators in programmes, what's an animator going to do, for God's sake? That's Walt Disney, we can't afford that!' So they showed their confidence in Terry by giving him about a hundred quid a week extra to make these animations, and Terry couldn't afford an assistant – he had to do them all himself.

## ALL BRONTOSAURUSES ARE THIN AT ONE END, MUCH MUCH THICKER IN THE MIDDLE, AND THEN THIN AGAIN AT THE FAR END.

### – (MISS) ANNE ELK

**CLEESE:** When I was working on *The Frost Report* I felt quite frustrated – not in a desperate, emotional sense, but held in – by the format of sketches, by the tyranny of the punchline, by the fact that more surreal things would be suggested and all the writers would laugh, and the producer/director Jimmy Gilbert (a man I liked hugely) would smile and be amused himself, and say, 'Yes, but they won't understand that in Bradford.' So we were straining against conventions.

I do know when we sat down for *Python* that we were convinced we were not going to do something in a conventional format. On *At Last the 1948 Show* we managed to parody the format without breaking it;

in other words, between sketches we would cut to this delightful girl, Aimi MacDonald, and Aimi would say with this extraordinary voice of hers – it was like someone had escaped from a cartoon and had elocution lessons – 'Well! *That* was a funny sketch, wasn't it?' We were already beginning to play with the form; it was definitely a step towards *Python*.

I had a gut feeling that the sort of thing we were going to do on *Python* was all the things that made the writers laugh on *The Frost Report* but which we weren't allowed to put on. But of course we didn't know how, and if you look at *Python*, the first few are much more conventionally constructed (although to my taste the humour is very, very good; I think a lot of the early stuff is very odd and very funny). And what happened was the material in some cases got rather less funny, but we began to package it more skilfully as we played with the format.

*How was the format or shape of the show ultimately decided upon,*
*as it was quite different from what had come before?*

**JONES:** We never really discussed it that much. John, Eric, and Graham weren't particularly interested in the *shape* of the show; they were just interested in funny material, making sure the sketches were funny. I was much more concerned – and Terry and Mike also felt a bit more like I did – that we needed to find a new formula, a new format, really. Apart from the sketch material, the earliest meetings were mainly discussions about the *name* of the show! But I remember I really had this feeling that this was going to be an absolutely crucial time, that we had to get this one right, this is our chance.

So I was thinking quite hard about the shape of the show, and I saw [Spike] Milligan's *Q5*, and I thought, 'Fuck! Milligan's *done* it!' He did a show [where] one sketch would start and drift off into another sketch, things would drift into one another; he made it so clear that we'd been writing in clichés all this time, where we either did three-minute sketches with a beginning, middle, and end, or else we did thirty-second black-outs – one joke with a blackout – so it was still very much the shape of a traditional English revue. Milligan was messing around with this and doing something totally different.

I can just remember walking upstairs at my parents' home in Claygate and suddenly realizing that Terry Gilliam had done an animation for one of the *Do Not Adjust Your Set*s called 'Beware of Elephants'. He'd been a bit diffident about it; he'd say, 'Well, it's sort of stream-of-consciousness, one thing leads to another, it's not really *about* anything.' He'd done another one called 'Christmas Cards'. And so I was going upstairs and I suddenly thought, '*That's* what we could do: we can do what Milligan's done with breaking up the sketch format and just do a whole thing that's stream-of-consciousness, and Terry's animations can go in and out and link things, and the whole show would just flow like that. And I phoned Mike, I suppose, and Terry G., in great excitement. [They went,] 'Yeah, yeah, yeah, yeah!'

And then as far as I remember, we put this to the group and they were grumbling: 'Yeah, all right, well anyway, let's get on with the *sketch*.'

So the first series was very much a fight between the Oxford contingent, if you like, trying to push this stream-of-consciousness into the thing, and the Cambridge group. The Cambridge side weren't particularly interested; they weren't *against* it, but they weren't particularly interested.

**IDLE:** We had already tried something like this on *Do Not Adjust Your Set* and also *We Have Ways of Making You Laugh* with Gilliam. It was the natural way to go. We were essentially avoiding doing anything that was like the shows we had already worked on or were on the Beeb at the time. Cleese was tired of formats, Jonesy the keenest on experimentation – or at least the loudest in praise of it. But Gilliam was keen to experiment and Graham always anxious to push the envelope: 'Can we make it a little madder?' he would say.

**GILLIAM:** My memory of the first meetings was in John's flat in Basil Street in Knightsbridge. I just remember sitting up in John's room a lot and talking and arguing. I think by loosening it up as we did, it then freed us up so that we could have everybody write what they wanted to do, and then we start filtering it through the group's reaction to the stuff.

## DIRECTOR: CLOSE UP, ZOOM IN ON ME

Ian MacNaughton was an actor before becoming a director at the BBC in 1961. After several years toiling in the trenches of the Drama Department, he was offered a chance by the then-head of comedy to direct programming for the Light Entertainment Division.

**IAN MACNAUGHTON:** I asked the head of comedy why did he ask me and he had a very funny answer: he had been in Studio 3, where they were doing a Light Entertainment show, and someone came to him and said, 'Do look into Studio 2, where they're doing a drama series called *Dr Finlay's Casebook* – they're getting more laughs in there than you're getting out here!'

*Dr Finlay's Casebook* was a very turgid drama, it was *too* dramatic, and I arranged with the script editor to write something funny, a small scene before the end in which we have a bit of funny to heighten the tragedy at the end of the piece, and so this came about that way. The head of comedy did look in, and the next day he asked would I like to do the funnies? And I said, 'Yes, very much!'

And so I joined the Light Entertainment branch and was immediately handed a Spike Milligan show, *Q5*. Now Spike Milligan is a rather eccentric comic clown, and I don't think anybody else was very happy to work with him – he was a very undisciplined man – but we did the show and it was a reasonable success, and the Python boys had seen this show going out and they asked the BBC if they could have me direct their first series. The BBC said yes, and so that's how we started together.

**IDLE:** In fact, I hardly remember Barry Took being involved at all; the key meeting was with MacNaughton. He was directing Spike and we all liked the mad direction those shows were going in, so we met him and he seemed loony enough, so we said, 'Okay'. He couldn't do the studio direction for the first four (though he did do the exterior filming), so John Howard Davies did those. He was more in control and a bit less of a loony, and I found him very helpful on the early acting because he was an actor – indeed, he was Oliver Twist in David Lean's movie!

Ian's great brilliance was that he didn't get in the way.

**PALIN:** We had a few battles over a director, because in early meetings some of us had found John Howard Davies to be completely wrong for the ethos of *Python*; he represented the most conventional, conservative side of BBC comedy. And there was this mad cat Ian MacNaughton, who seemed to represent the free spirit that we wanted. I remember a couple of fights over that – not fights, but sort of *polite disagreements*; there were some tensions over that. John Cleese was very much a John Howard Davies man; in fact, he used John Howard Davies for all of *Fawlty Towers*. And Cleese was guarded about Ian MacNaughton; he didn't like Ian because he drank, he was sometimes out of control, he was a mad incomprehensible Scotsman, and Cleese saw him allying with the sort of wild, passionate [Pythons] on the other side. But in the end we got Ian MacNaughton.

I think probably we did need somebody like that who was going to be responsive to our ideas. John Howard Davies was a nice man, and he did four shows (although Ian always directed the film sequences). Davies found that it wasn't a natural sort of programme for him to do, whereas Ian was very responsive to all our ideas, especially if we had him do something different. He would be at home with the anti-authoritarian aspect of it, which was something he liked and rather identified with, whereas I think John Howard Davies was much more identified with BBC structure as it was then. He wasn't the kind to be taking risks; he was an organization man.

Ian would take some risks. Ian was always somebody outside the organization, probably because of his lifestyle: he was a Scottish actor, he didn't see himself as a metropolitan London man at all, which helped, because *Python* was never metropolitan. As Barry Took once pointed out (which was very acute), all of the Pythons come from the provinces and none of us were Londoners. We all saw London in a sense as slightly the enemy, a citadel to be conquered, and of course Ian was definitely from Glasgow – he had this anti-metropolitan attitude, which helped us.

**CLEESE:** Well, I suspect my view on this is rather different from the others', because I thought John Howard Davies was very good. But he wasn't as skilful with his cameras as Ian was; Ian was a very visual director. John was a very, very good judge of comedy. He wasn't a tremendously verbal person, but his instincts were extraordinarily good, and he was very good at casting. So I had a lot of respect for him to do comedy, but I know that the more visually oriented people felt that the show took a big step forward (from the point of view of form as opposed to content) when Ian took over. And I thought Ian was pretty good, but I never thought he was particularly expert in the direction of comedy. He was always more bothered by how he was going to shoot it than he was about whether the sketch was really working or not, whereas John Howard Davies' focus on just those first four shows he directed was more towards the content, even if he didn't actually shoot it so well.

**GILLIAM:** Ian had worked with Spike Milligan, that's why we liked the idea of Ian coming in. He wasn't forced upon us; we lucked out. Ian worked, because he *put up* with things. Everybody pushed him around. I like Ian a lot, I mean just his personality.

Ian held it together, but we would be constantly going, 'Shit, why is the camera on *that*?' But I think anybody would have been beaten up by us in the same way. He trotted on, he *did* it. If it had been left up to us, we couldn't have done it, there's just no way. We *thought* we could, but I'm sure we couldn't have!

*Ian MacNaughton directing Palin in 'The Cycling Tour'.*

❈    ❈    ❈

# TAKE-OFF

## LET'S GET THE BACON DELIVERED

As the group prepared for the first series of *Monty Python's Flying Circus* (which began recording in August 1969), the notion of applying a stream-of-consciousness style to the show's content and execution was accepted.

**PALIN:** Certainly Terry Gilliam provided an example of how you could do stream-of-consciousness comedy in his animations, which he'd done on *Do Not Adjust Your Set*. We thought those were remarkable and a real breakthrough; there was nothing like that being done on British television. We loved the way the ideas flowed one into another.

Terry Jones was very interested in the form of the show, wanting it to be different from any other – not only should we write better material than anybody else, but we should write in a different shape from any other comedy show. And probably Terry Jones and myself saw (or were easily persuaded) that Gilliam's way of doing animation maybe held a clue to how we could do it. It didn't matter if sketches didn't have a beginning or end, we could just have some bits here or there, we could do it more like a sort of collage effect. I remember that everyone was quite enthusiastic about this, but it would have almost certainly come from Terry Gilliam, Terry Jones, and myself.

**GILLIAM:** I think it was more like saying 'no' to certain things, and the first thing was 'no' to punchlines, which is a really critical thing. We'd seen Peter Cook and Dudley Moore doing so many really great sketches where they traditionally had to end with a zinger, and the zinger was never as good as the sketch. The sketch was about two characters, so in a sense it was more character-driven than plot-driven, [but] time and time again you'd see these really great sketches that would die at the end – they wouldn't *die*, but they just wouldn't end better [than] or as well as the middle bits. So very early on we made a decision to get rid of punchlines. And then Terry Jones was besotted with this cartoon I had done, 'Beware of Elephants', [in which] things flowed in a much more stream-of-consciousness way. Terry thought that was the shape that we should be playing with.

Spike Milligan had been doing some amazing things just before; his *Q* series in a sense really freed it up, playing with the medium of television, admitting to it *being* television, and commenting on that. We just continued to do even more of that than he had done, but once we agreed on the idea of not having to end sketches, and having things linked and flowing, it allowed us to get out of a sketch when it was at its peak, when it was really still good; we would laugh when it was funny and it would move on when it wasn't funny. That also immediately made a place for me; it sat me in the middle, connecting things.

**IDLE:** We were young, and doing a show we would be in charge of for the first time. There were no executives. This freedom allowed us to experiment without having to say what we were trying to do – indeed, we didn't have a clue what we were trying to do except please ourselves. This was the *leitmotiv:* if it made us laugh, it was in; if it didn't, we sold it to other shows.

## THIS YEAR OUR MEMBERS HAVE PUT MORE THINGS ON TOP OF OTHER THINGS THAN EVER BEFORE

**JONES:** The way we went and did the shows is, first of all we'd meet and talk about ideas. And then we'd all go off for like two weeks and each write individually or in our pairs. Mike and I tended to write separately and then get together, read out material to each other, and then swap over and mess around like that. So at the end of two weeks we'd all meet together, quite often downstairs in my front room or dining room, and we'd read out the stuff. That was the best time of Python, the most exciting time, when you knew you were going to hear new stuff and they were going to make you laugh.

**GILLIAM:** And so you get a sketch where John and Graham had written something and it got that far and it was really good, but then it just started dribbling; well, either you stop there, or maybe Mike and Terry would take it over with some ideas to patch it up. I always liked the fact that there was just a pile of material to start with all the time, because everybody would go their separate ways, come back, and there would be *the stuff,* [sorted into] piles: we all liked that pile of stuff, [we were] mixed on *that* one, we didn't like *that* one.

You had to jockey for position about when and where a sketch was going to be read out, which time of the day; if it came in too early it was going to bomb. And you knew that if Mike and Terry or John and Graham had something they wanted to do, they wouldn't laugh as much [at the others' material]. And I was in a funny position, because I was kind of the apolitical laugh; I was the one guy who had nothing at stake because my stuff was outside of theirs.

**IDLE:** It seems to me since all comedians seek control we were a group of potential controllers. Obviously some are more manipulative than others, or cleverer at getting their own way. Cleese is the most canny, but everyone had their ways. Mike would charm himself into things. Terry J. would simply not listen to anyone else, and Gilliam stayed home and did his own thing since we soon got tired of listening to him trying to explain in words what he was doing.

The writing was the most glorious fun. We would go away and write anything at all that came to mind for about two weeks, then get together for a day and read it all out. Then, what got laughs was in, and people would suggest different ways of improving things. This was very good, this critical moment. Then we would compile about six or seven shows at a go, obviously moving things too similar into different shows, and then noticing themes and enlarging on strands of ideas and then finally linking them all together in various mad ways that came out of group thought. This, as far as I know, was an original way of working which hasn't been tried before (or since) and was unique to *Python*. Gilliam was there, too, as an individual non-writer, and whenever we were stuck we would leave it to him to make the links, which he would do.

**PALIN:** By [the time *Python* started] Terry and I were working separately; there'd be a couple of days just writing ideas down and then we'd get together, talk about things, so some of the sketches that were Jones and Palin would be entirely Jones or entirely Palin, but the other would add lines here and there. So it was good in that way; we were writing separately perhaps more than we had before.

I think we were all (certainly to start with) anxious to be generous to each other, and give each other time and due consideration. You know, it was important that everybody write something that was funny, otherwise it would have been very difficult, and generally I think everybody did. Spirits were pretty high. It was not difficult for some of those sessions to be happy at the way things were going because the material was fresh; we could chop stuff around and not be confined to the shapes of previous comedy shows; we were really getting some very nice, new, surreal stuff together.

The best sessions I remember were when we were just putting the whole lot into a shape, into a form. Certainly there would be some sketches that were still very conventional, and others would just be fragments. We'd have read the stuff out and then we'd try and put them together, follow this by that, and then, 'Why don't we introduce that Gambolputty character and then try to say the name "Gambolputty" later in the programme,' something like that. 'Yes, that's right, he can come in and we do this, and then the Viking can come in and sort of club him or something.' The idea of having characters in quite elaborate costume just coming in to say one word – 'So' or 'It's' – in the middle of a bit of narration, all that seemed very fresh. We enjoyed that feeling of being able to clown around the way we wanted to. And the material coming in was (we felt) pretty strong and really unusual. Things like the man with three buttocks seemed just wonderful, especially because it was done in this very serious mode – bringing the camera around to see this extra buttock, and he'd say, 'Go away, go on!' – this man who'd agreed to go on television because he's got three buttocks then getting rather sort of prudish about any talk about buttocks! Really nice ideas.

*How did your own work habits change as you*
*started working as part of a larger group?*

**PALIN:** I wasn't used to working like that, but basically I have such respect for the other writers. I mean, Graham and John were just writing the best sketches around at that time, so to be able to give them [something] they would then take away, one had absolute confidence. And the same usually with Eric; we'd worked together on *Do Not Adjust Your Set*. There was really, as far as I can remember at that early stage, very little wastage. I mean, sketches didn't just disappear if someone screwed them up; it would happen: someone would take something away and it just didn't work out, and we would similarly take other people's ideas. It didn't happen that much. And in the early shows John and Graham were still writing 'sketchey' sketches; 'The Mouse Problem' or 'The Dead Parrot'. They came fully formed, four or five minutes of stuff which didn't need to be changed, so very often it was just the links that would be our group. There wasn't an awful lot of cross-writing.

If anything strengthened Terry and myself as a team, I think we felt this was highly competitive in a way it hadn't been before. We'd send sketches to Marty Feldman or *The Two Ronnies* and someone somewhere would take a decision and you get the word back – 'We love this, we don't like this' – we wouldn't be in the room at the time, we wouldn't be part of that process. Here, because we were writing the whole thing and performing it ourselves, the atmosphere was quite competitive. We felt we really had to get our ideas really *right* before they were read.

That was an interesting thing. We'd have a discussion the day before: 'Shall we read this, shall we read that?' Terry and I always wrote more than anybody else – a lot of it was of a fairly inferior quality – but we didn't want to read the group too much because there was a certain point where you could see people getting restless: 'And what have *you* got?'

'Oh, we've got another six sketches!'

'[*Huffing*] All right, we'll have some coffee and then read these next *six sketches* for Mike and Terry!'

You had to be a bit careful about how you sold your stuff!

> *Were you at a disadvantage because you didn't have*
> *a writing partner helping to 'sell' your material?*

**IDLE:** No, no. The other teams had two people to laugh. But I had the advantage of working with myself, a far more interesting partner!

Comedy writing is done often in pairs, but I always found it boring. I occasionally worked with John ('The Bruces', Australian philosophy professors with a passion for beer and a distaste for 'pooftahs'; 'Sir George Head', the mountaineering expedition leader with double vision) and a bit with Mike. But I like writing by myself.

Last time I looked, writing was always largely a solitary occupation. I like to write first thing in the morning and then stop when I feel like it. I don't like to talk. I don't much care for meetings. My favourite form of collaboration is with a partner on email who bounces back my day's work. I think you need partners for shape, notes, and criticism.

**CLEESE:** I was the one who was having to write with Graham. Now I thought early on, before Graham's drinking was any sort of a problem, it would be much more fun if we occasionally broke up into different writing groups; we could keep the material more varied. To some extent there was a Chapman/Cleese type of sketch (which was usually somebody going into an office of some kind and probably getting into an argument in which there would be quite a lot of thesaurus-type words), whereas Mike and Terry would nearly always start things where some camera would pan over Scottish or Icelandic or Dartmoor countryside and afterwards would get into some sort of tale. And Eric's was largely one man sitting at a desk talking to the camera and getting completely caught up, as they say, disappearing up his own arse.

The result of this switching was that Eric and I wrote 'Sir George Head', and Michael and I wrote about Adolf Hilter standing for Parliament in Minehead. I thought those were rather successful. But there was a general resistance to that switching around, and maybe it was partly that nobody else wanted to write with Graham. I think he was regarded as my problem, which naturally I thought was a little unfair. But I think that Terry was always very keen to write with Michael, that it was quite difficult for him to let go of that. And Eric liked to write on his own because it gave him such autonomy – for instance, he could write when he wanted to. There are many good things to be said for that, because if you write with someone else it becomes an office job.

So I guess Terry wanted to reclaim Michael, and Eric maybe liked being on his own, and Graham was my problem; I guess that was the dynamic.

*Did you and Terry 'perform' your sketches*
*for the group at these meetings?*

**PALIN:** No, no, no. I used to read our stuff, and John used to read the stuff that he and Graham wrote. I can't really give you a reason for that other than Terry was happy that that's the way it was, and Graham was quite happy that John should read his. I think we were perhaps wary of selling this as a complete sketch. In a way by just one person reading it would be like reading *notes* for a sketch, it wouldn't be taken too seriously – you know, this wasn't a full performance you were being judged on, this was just a way of gauging whether it was funny or not. You could also read it much more quickly, it was much easier to get the essence of it quite quickly.

**CLEESE:** The great joy of the group was that we made each other laugh immoderately. We had dinner together quite recently, all of us except Eric, and we all said afterwards we don't really laugh with anyone else the way we laugh together – we really make each other laugh more than anyone else makes us laugh. And so the great joy of the meetings, one of the totally positive things that kept us ticking over and happy for a long time and probably helped us when things weren't so easy, was the fact that we laughed so much.

But if you read something out at a meeting and people became hysterical with laughter, whatever was read out next would always be anticlimactic. So there was a certain amount of very careful stage managing going on during meetings, because I would come in with the material that Graham and I had written, and I would be very aware that approval would vary according to certain extrinsic factors. The usual psychological factors were at work, such as don't read your best stuff out first. Also, the first couple of things read out were unlikely to produce enormous laughter.

While I was reading material out, I was often adjusting the order because you could sometimes sense the energy of the group start to slump after a couple of hours; and if Mike and Terry just read out something *screamingly* funny, I would not try and read out something terribly funny after that; I would read out something that was sort of interesting and clever and witty.

**JONES:** We just read out material, it wasn't performing it. Quite often there might be two or three characters, so it'd be difficult to actually perform it. Mike's the better reader of the two of us, in the same way that John was the better reader. And I always felt if I read something it wouldn't do it justice – partly because of my reading, and partly I think I didn't quite know what kind of mood John would be in – he might sort of take against something if he felt it was partly mine!

**PALIN:** And also it was the sensitive area of casting. If you cast it already, even if it's just the two writers, you in a way staked a claim on those characters, which was difficult for the others to take. We would not make suggestions [on casting]; it was done really quite democratically. We'd actually rather people say, 'I'd like to do that' or whatever, or then we'd say, 'This is a sort of Eric-type character.' Sometimes it was clear, it didn't need discussion. Sometimes very often the people who'd read that sketch had read a character so well that there was no point in putting it out to tender, as it were. But then casting would come slightly later because you'd have to assemble the show first. Once the show's assembled, then the casting could really begin because we wanted it to be fairly equal; one didn't want one person to dominate, and everyone wanted to perform – everyone was dead keen to get up there and do the sketches. We were aware without ever saying it absolutely, as a sort of rule, that there should be a balance in casting. When we had all the sketches together, we would say, 'Actually you can't put those three together because they're all three John characters; so let's put this sketch in show eight, and then bring an Eric sketch from show eight to this one. So you have John, Eric, then the thing which Mike and Terry are doing, then one for John and Eric should come nicely there.' So casting would very much depend upon the actual shape of the show itself, so everyone got time on screen.

**JONES:** If you'd written it, you tended to get the first say-so if you really wanted to do it. People would tend to come up with what they wanted to do. And then it would be thrown around; there would be a discussion if somebody else wanted to do it.

**IDLE:** Casting always came last in everything. That was the brilliance of it being a writer's show. Once we were happy with the text, then we cast. It was usually fairly easy, like the John parts were obvious – people who shouted or were cruel to defenceless people or animals. Mike and I were usually the ones who could play each other's parts. Usually people spoke up if they felt they were a bit light in a show; they might sulk until some-one noticed, but it was swings and roundabouts, really. Also, we had no girls to sulk or feel left out (i.e., *Saturday Night Live*) and we would hap-pily grab most of the girls' parts for ourselves. Serve 'em right, too. Get their own bloody shows! How many men are in the Spice Girls?

*Did everyone have an equal interest in performing? Did you all consider yourselves writers first and then actors, or writer/actors?*

**PALIN:** Writer/actors I think, yes. Everybody loved performing, absolutely. Everybody wanted to go out there and put the dress on or whatever! I rarely heard an instance where someone said, 'Well, I don't want to do that.' The great thing was, because we were all brought up in the university cabarets, to get out there and show your own material was all part of it. Writing was merely 50 per cent; the other 50 per cent was the performing of it.

**IDLE:** Sometimes I enjoyed performing more. In film, I loved the scene in *Grail* where the guard is told not to leave the room till anyone, etc., because the first time it went right and it's there on film. It just felt funny – all one take. (Well done, Jonesy. I have to say I love filming for Jonesy.) And likewise in *Brian* with me as the jailer and Gilliam as the jailer's assistant. I loved playing both these Palin-created scenes. I wish he had written more. He has an effortless grasp of character for an actor, especially scenes where all three parts are funny. Graham only hiccoughs in the guard scene, but it just adds a wonderful pleasant madness. In *Brian,* Terry Gilliam makes dark, grunting noises where I stutter away and Michael is this very pleasant lost man who is somehow in charge of these lunatics. It is pure Palin at his finest. They are delightful scenes and my personal acting favourites.

**PALIN:** Personally, I always enjoyed when you were able to flesh the character out a bit, even within a sketch. I mean, I loved playing the man in the 'Dead Parrot' sketch or the 'Cheese Shop', because you can give them some sort of character – they're not just somebody saying, 'No, we haven't got this,' 'No, we haven't got that.' It isn't just the words, it's the evasiveness and the *degree* of evasiveness, and *why* a man should be that evasive, and what's going through his mind [that] appeals to me. I really enjoyed getting to grips with characters like that, even within a fairly short sketch.

**CLEESE:** I remember once that I particularly liked a sketch that either Mike or Terry had written about one of those magazines that is just full of advertisements, so if you wanted to buy a pair of World War II German U-boat commander field glasses or a mountain bike or a garden shed you went to this magazine. And I liked the sketch so much I asked if I could do it – very unusual for me. And Mike had slight reservations about whether I should do it, but they let me. And I didn't do it particularly well, and I remember discussing it afterwards with Mike, and it was because I was trying to go outside my range – in other words, I didn't do it as well as *he* would have done it because he's better at doing the 'Cheerful Charlie' salesman.

But similarly if you'd given Mike that scene where I go on about the Masons and start that strangely aggressive and resentful speech, I think Michael wouldn't be so good in *that* area. But it's much more complicated than you might think because it is not that *I* am happy about shouting at people, because actually I'm extremely *unhappy*, I've almost never shouted at anyone. I've found it almost impossible to do, but I seem to be able to do it on screen. So it's not like saying, 'In character you're the same as you are in everyday life'; that would be utterly simple-minded and untrue, but it just seems to be the case that some people are more comfortable portraying some emotions; I don't mean that it isn't utterly connected with their ordinary life, but that it's not *as* connected with it as you might think.

*Which of the Pythons did you think was the prettiest in drag?*

**GILLIAM:** Prettiest woman, goodness! I don't know. John was actually pretty nice when he played in 'The Piranha Brothers', he's wonderful sitting in the bar: 'He knows how to treat a female impersonator.' John was fantastic in that. John loved it so much I was beginning to have concerns there! The most *convincing* woman? I think Eric was the best woman. I'm not sure 'pretty' came into it. Do you have another adjective?

*'We could have it any time we wanted.' Chapman and Idle as the Protestants in* The Meaning of Life.

### *'Least unattractive'?*

**GILLIAM:** I think in *Meaning of Life*, Eric as the Protestant Wife was spectacular. I just thought that was an extraordinary, wonderful performance. Terry and Mike were always very broad, and Graham was also very broad, but I actually thought the Protestant Wife that Eric played was amazing. Eric's father died when he was young, so his role model was his mother, and maybe *that's* why he was good.

# THAT'S *MY* FLANNEL

*Once the shows were assembled, was it easy to see it as*
*a group effort, or was there still a sort of jealous, protective feeling:*
*'This is* our *sketch, that is* their *material'?*

**PALIN:** I'd like to think we naturally were rooting for every sketch [rather than] anyone wanting their sketches to go down better, although there probably was a little bit of that, but basically you just wanted the show to have laughs all the way through. Putting together that show involved decisions which we'd all taken – the choice of the material, the casting, the links, all that – as part of the group. So if something didn't work, then yes, it was seen as a failure of the group: 'We shouldn't have put that in or cast it that way, set it up in such a way.' It was very much all group decisions.

And quite interesting, because early on John was undoubtedly the most well-known, [yet] he was very happy to be part of that group – he didn't want it to be in any way *The John Cleese Show,* and I would have thought if there was going to be a possible area of difficulty, that would have been one of the problems. John was the 'star' before Python; he wasn't necessarily the star *of* Python, although he probably was – he was the best known and possibly the best performer. But John didn't see it that way; John saw it as a group, and Python [assumed] responsibility for everything that went up there, rather than your individual responsibility.

I'm sure at the end of the day there was a bit of, 'Terry and Mike . . . *ehh!'*

**SHERLOCK:** Graham and John did a bizarre murder sketch for David Frost whereby I think the murderer turned out to be the regimental goat mascot that belonged to the guard who was a suspect: 'It was the Regimental Goat wot done it!' It was new in terms of off-the-wall wacky humour. At the time we thought it was hysterical, but most people wondered what the hell the sketch was *about.* Some of the more surreal sketches they

# Portishead Library
## Tel: 01934 426040

Borrowed Items 18/07/2019 14:55
XXXXXX5347

| Item Title | Due Date |
| --- | --- |
| Monty Python speaks! | 08/08/2019 |
| Goodbye Christopher Robin | 06/08/2019 |
| A. A. Milne and the making | |
| of Winnie-the-Pooh | |

Indicates items borrowed today

were doing [for Python] had been rejected by every other thing they worked for.

**JONES:** One of the first sketches was about sheep nesting in trees, which John and Graham had offered to *The Frost Report,* and the producer Jimmy Gilbert had said, 'No, no, no, it's too silly. We can't do that.' John's thing was always, 'The great thing about *Python* was that it was somewhere where we could use up all that material that everybody else had said was too silly.'

> *Did you and Michael also use sketches you had*
> *written for other comedians?*

**JONES:** All ours was *original* material, squire!

> *Was there EVER any consideration given during the writing*
> *process to how an audience would respond to the material?*

**IDLE:** None whatsoever.

## PERT PIECES OF COPPER COINAGE

**JONES:** I think our budget was £5,000 a show. It had been kind of a tight operation. Everything was planned very rigorously. We'd do the outdoor filming for most of the series before we started shooting the studio stuff. We had to write the entire series before we even started doing anything because we'd be shooting stuff for show 13, show 1, or show 2 while we're in one location, so that while you're at the seaside you can do *all* the seaside bits.

**PALIN:** A lot of the early arguments were just over money; we were paid so incredibly little. So in a sense the BBC committed a lot, they'd given us thirteen shows (which was nice), but they'd taken away with one hand what they'd given us with the other. But on the other hand they let us go ahead and *do* it!

**MACNAUGHTON:** Because I was the producer as well as the director, I was able to speak as a producer, so I could say [to the Pythons], 'That is impossible, we have only got so much of a budget; can we alter this slightly to allow that we don't go too far over?' Because you know at the BBC in those days if you went too far over budget the people got rather anarchic. Unless you were exceptionally successful.

**PALIN:** We presented a script to Ian, we knew what we wanted to do on film and what should be done in the studio, and Ian didn't really get involved in that aspect of it. On the other hand when we were discussing things like *where* we would film and how we could best get the effect of a piece of film he would have quite a bit of input. And we'd actually film in Yorkshire and Scotland – that was very often Ian saying, 'Let's go out and *do* that.'

**MACNAUGHTON:** We used to plan about eight weeks in advance of the series. We knew we wanted an average of, say, five minutes of film per episode (in the first series anyway). The series was thirteen, so we needed time to [shoot] an hour and a half of film. We would plan what sketches or what sequences were better filmed than done in the studio, etc. And as the Pythons went on, they got more interested in the filming side than in the studio side.

Nothing was too ridiculous for us to try. You have a silly sketch like 'Spot the Loony' and you happen to be up in Scotland shooting 'Njorl's Saga', and you suddenly think, 'Wouldn't it be good to have the loony here in the middle of Glen Coe leaping through the thing?' These kinds of things happened. They enjoyed all that kind of thing. And it was not particularly more expensive than filming, say, in London because the permission and the fees we had to pay in filming in Glen Coe or Oban or whatever were much less than what we had to pay at the Lower Courts or Cheapside. So the expense was not so great, [and] the opulence of the locations was *there,* you didn't have to build them!

**GILLIAM:** We weren't doing drama, we were doing comedy, which fell under Light Entertainment, and *light* seemed to be required constantly so that you could *see* the joke! *Feel* the joke! And I just always had a stronger visual sense than [what] we were able to get on those filmings. There would be all these times I'd get in there: 'The camera should be *there.*' Terry would do the same thing; we were always pushing Ian around! I think we were just frustrated because we wanted to film this, too; we were convinced we could do it better. But the BBC didn't work that way. They would put a producer/director on the thing. And there was a kind of Light Entertainment direction at the BBC which was very sort of sloppy.

I was always frustrated because it didn't look as good as it should; the lighting wasn't as good as it should have been. Everything was done so fast and shoddily, there was very little time to get real atmosphere on the screen, or to shoot it dramatically enough or exciting enough. But you churned it out; it's the nature of television.

We wanted it to look like Drama as opposed to Light Entertainment. Drama was serious; that's where the *real* talents hung out!

*They ate at a separate canteen?*

**GILLIAM:** It's almost like that, it always felt like that; they had more money, they can light this stuff. If you've got something beautifully lit and the costumes are really great and the set's looking good and then you do some absurd nonsense, it's *funnier* than having it in a cardboard set with some broad lighting. And especially since a lot of the stuff would be parodies of things – if you're going to do a parody, it's got to *look* like the original.

So when we were able to do *Holy Grail* and direct it ourselves, it looked a lot better. I think the jokes were funnier because the world was believable, as opposed to some cheap LE lightweight. I mean, we approached *Grail* as seriously as Pasolini did. We were watching the Pasolini films a lot at that time because he more than anybody seemed to be able to capture a place and period in a very simple but really effective way. It wasn't *El Cid* and the big epics, it was much smaller. You could *feel* it, you could *smell* it, you could *hear* it.

**JONES:** Poor old Ian had me [to deal with]. I insisted on going on the location scouts with him and then when we were filming was really sitting in and seeing what Ian was doing all the time. And it was *awful* for me, too; I used to go out with this terrible tight stomach because we'd see Ian put the camera down and I'd think, 'It's in the wrong place, it should be over there!' So I'd have to go up to Ian very quietly and sort of say, 'Ian, don't you think you should put it over *there*?' or something like that, and then depending on Ian's mood at the time, because if it were morning when he hadn't been drinking he would be very good, but sometimes he got a bit shirty.

Obviously when we were in the studio on the floor you can't do very much, so Ian had his head then. But in the editing I'd always ring Ian up and say, 'When's the editing?' I could see Ian going, *Jesus Christ!* Sort of tell me between gritted teeth, and then I'd turn up.

*Did he ever purposely tell you the wrong time, to put you off?*

**JONES:** I get the feeling he wanted to do that, but he was too honourable a man! Especially at the beginning, I'd turn up and he'd say, 'Look, we've only got two hours to do this in.' And I just had to shut out of my head everything about that and say, 'Well, let's just see how long.' We'd end up doing the whole day. I'd see something and I'd think, 'Ian, we have to take that out, there's a gap there.' Usually it was cutting things out, and closing up the show so that it went fast. But it was very hard, because every time I wanted to change something, my stomach would go tight because I *knew* Ian would go, 'We've nearly had two hours now and we've only done ten minutes!' So we got on a bit like that. And then at the end of the day I'd ring everybody up to have a look at the show. But then as it went on Ian really got very good, actually, because although it was a bit sticky in the first series – and it shows, I think; the first series is not edited as tightly as it could have been – as it went on, Ian got really good at it, and realized that I wasn't trying to muscle in on his thing; we were just trying to make the best show possible, making sure the material actually came over. So it was very hard for him, but eventually the relationship got really good, and Ian and I worked really well. Ian got very creative, and once you relaxed he got very creative about it, and then came up with a lot of different stuff.

## TEN, NINE, EIGHT AND ALL THAT

**CLEESE:** My memory is that on the whole Ian did not, let's be polite, *interfere* much with the acting! We tended to watch each other's stuff – not all the time because a certain amount of rehearsal is just practice, but we would keep an eye on each other's sketches, and at a suitable moment somebody might suggest an additional line, or we might come forward and say, 'I think that bit isn't working.' But there was such an instinctive understanding within the group that you probably didn't even have to say that because people would already *know* it wasn't working. It was very much a group activity – not that we were all sitting around desperately focused on each other's sketches, because people sat around and read the paper and wrote up their diaries.

**MACNAUGHTON:** We did the usual BBC style of five or six days' rehearsal. On the sixth day there would be a technical run-through for all the lighting, etc., and then we were one day in the studio. And of course all the stuff we had filmed we showed to the audience in the studio as we did each episode.

*Cleese and Idle in rehearsal, c. 1971.*

From the beginning I had no problem working with them because they're extremely disciplined as actors, as comic actors.

We honestly had a very good working relationship. I have never from the beginning had one problem with any of them. I felt myself to be a part of the team anyway.

I can remember one time John looking at me after a sketch had been done and saying, 'Why aren't you laughing?' And I said, 'Well, there's something not quite right with this sketch.' He said, 'You hear that, gentlemen? Let's do it again.' They did it again, and he said, 'No, I think we'll find a new one,' and did a new one the next day.

I can't remember any explosions. Come the second series there was one moment and that was quite fun: we were making the film 'The Bishop', and I'd set up the opening shot with a lower-level camera. The bishop's car raced up to the camera, stopped, out jumped all the mafia bishops, etc., and ran up to the church. Now Terry Jones said to me, 'No, no, you must do this in a high angle.' And I said, 'No, I think the low angle's better for this opening,' knowing what had gone before. 'No, no, no!' We had a bit of a row, and we walked off together, Terry kicking stones right and left. And I said, 'Look, Terry, just leave it for a moment – anyway, I haven't got a cherry picker with me and can't get the big high angle that you're looking for.' We came back and did it. We then went on another location in Norwich I think it was, and where we saw the rushes from the previous week, up came the rushes for 'The Bishop' – and this is what's so nice about the whole group: Terry Jones turned around in the hotel's dining room where we were watching the rushes, held his thumb up to me, and said, 'You were right, it worked perfectly.' And that is I think the biggest row we ever had, and it's not a very big one, you must admit.

**JONES:** In studio, we tried to do it sequentially as much as we could. It was a bit stop-and-starty sometimes, but we tried as much as we could to rush through the costume changes. We only had an hour and a half recording time anyway, so you had thirty-five minutes of material to record. We very often did it as a live show with just a few hitches, try and keep the momentum going to keep the audience entertained. We didn't want to stop the show because it meant the audience going off the boil a bit.

**MACNAUGHTON:** We had a studio audience of 320; that was a BBC policy, to have a studio audience. And you know, never had we laid a laugh from a laugh track on *Python*. It was a kind of policy, because we thought if the audience don't really like it, they won't laugh anyway, and there's nothing worse than listening to shows that have laugh tracks on and the audience is *roaring* with laughter at something you've found totally unfunny yourself.

**JONES:** For me, when we came to the editing the audience was always the great key – we always had that laughter to go by so you knew whether something was working or not. And if something didn't get a laugh, then we cut it. A lot of the time we were actually having to take laughs *out* because it was holding up the shows.

I remember one show that didn't seem to work in the studio, and that was 'The Cycling Tour'. Everybody came out very disappointed, all the audience and our friends going, 'Eh, that wasn't very good, didn't really work, that.' And of course the trouble with that was that it wasn't shot sequentially, or even when it was shot sequentially it was very stop-and-starty. Like all the stuff in the hospital, the casualty ward, was very quick cuts – a sign falling off, a trolley collapsing, a window falling on somebody's hand – that all had to be shot separately, so they didn't seem very funny at the time. But when you cut them in very fast, that made it seem quite funny.

**MACNAUGHTON:** At the beginning they *all* wanted to come to the editing, and I said, 'That's no use, we can't have five guys standing around me standing around the editor.' So in the end only Terry used to come to the editing. We'd sit together and we'd say, 'Yes, I think cut there,' and 'No, I think it should be cut later,' and 'No, I'm sorry, I think it's quicker' – the usual thing. There were honestly no problems.

**GILLIAM:** Terry tended to be the one to be in the editing room, sitting looking over Ian's shoulder, and keeping an eye on things. I popped in occasionally, John, different people. Terry was almost always there.

Ian dealt with the BBC, basically; we didn't have to. That's the great thing about the BBC, it's not like American television; once they said 'Go', they basically left. It was a real, incredibly laissez-faire operation. That was the strength of the place, because it just allowed the talent to get on to do what it did. And in the end the talent ended up producing more good material than all these meetings are producing now. I don't think the batting average is any better now than it was then, it's actually worse, and they all end up sitting around talking things to death. It was very simple: you've got this series, we want seven shows now and six later and you do it, that's it.

We had freedom like nobody gets now, basically. And the only time we started getting some involvement from them was later on, I think it was probably the third series, because as we'd become successful they felt that they had to interfere in some way, to be involved in this thing.

## WHY DON'T YOU MOVE INTO MORE CONVENTIONAL AREAS?

**PALIN:** I think there was always a conscious desire to do something which was ahead of or tested the audience's taste, or tested the limits of what we can or cannot say. I think it's probably strongest in John and Graham's writing; they enjoyed being able to shock, whereas Terry and I enjoyed surprise more than shock. For us it was more putting together odd and surreal images in a certain way which would not *offend* but really jolt, surprise, and amaze. John and Graham took some pleasure in writing something which shocked an audience. I think this came from within, but John never seemed to be totally happy or centred – there was always something which John was having to cope with. And that desire to shock I think came from the way Graham was, too. Graham was a genuine outsider, a very strait-laced man who was homosexual and an alcoholic at that time and therefore found himself constantly in conflict with people, and so he would fight back. And the two of them would put together things like the 'Undertaker Sketch' purely because they knew it *was* outrageous, and yet they did it in a way none of the other Pythons would have done, so it was quite refreshing. When we first heard that we thought, 'Well, we just *can't* do it.' But then you think about it: this is a really good, refreshing view of death, talking about it that way. In that particular case I think yes, there was a desire to shock an audience by talking about something that was *not* talked about.

Terry and I were not quite so interested in taboos.

*Was it because, having been journeymen scriptwriters for hire,*
*your previous experience did not allow for taboo material?*
*If you had written taboo material for others,*
*you wouldn't have got hired again.*

**PALIN:** No, I don't think that's it, I think it just wasn't in our nature to write deliberately shocking material; we couldn't make it very funny. We could surprise, we could amaze. It was personal, it was nothing to do with our writing; in fact, quite the opposite: the writing that we had to do in the Sixties made us *relish* Python and the freedom Python had. We utterly supported John and Graham and what they were writing, and for us it was all part of the freedom of Python: to do stuff we wouldn't have been able to do as journeymen writers. Great, someone writes a sketch about undertakers; it seemed shocking to start with it, you look at it and say, 'Okay, let's give this a go.' And that was part of the exhilaration of doing Python. But no, I don't think Terry and myself were particularly good about getting laughs [from] very abrasive material. There might have been instances, I can't remember, [but] we were more about human behaviour, moralizing.

**SHERLOCK:** Cleese as he's got older has become more conservative, but when they first started out Python was really quite left-wing; it was considered by some to be commie and subversive.

**IDLE:** Always we tried to *épater les bourgeois.*

Once when filming, a British middle-class lady came up and said, 'Oh, Monty Python; I absolutely *hate* you lot.' And we felt quite proud and happy. Nowadays I miss people who hate us; we have sadly become nice, safe, and acceptable now, which shows how clever an Establishment really is, opening up to make room inside itself.

# FRANKLY I DON'T FULLY UNDERSTAND IT MYSELF, THE KIDS SEEM TO LIKE IT

**MACNAUGHTON:** Now Terry Gilliam was meanwhile working on the animation links for all the shows; sometimes Terry's film would arrive on the day we were recording that certain episode. No one had seen it beforehand, but everybody trusted everybody else. Which was a very good thing.

**GILLIAM:** [In story meetings] I always had the most difficulty because I could never explain what I was doing; whenever I did, there would be these blank faces. I was in maybe the best position because I had the most freedom. The others had to submit all their material to the group and get rejected or included or changed; mine, because I couldn't *explain* it, and because we were always revising at the last moment, was pretty much never touched.

*What was the actual process like for you?*

**GILLIAM:** Sometimes I had an assistant working on *Python*; Terry's sister-in-law Katie Hepburn assisted me for a while. Basically it was me on my own, with books.

I'd always start: there were the scripts, they go from there to *there,* and I just sort of had an idea, an image to start with. A lot of times I had a *lot* of ideas, a lot of things I wanted to get into the shows; I just had to stick them in between and find connecting tissues to get from there to *there.* So I would use these little storyboard sketches, then I would start looking for the artwork; whether it was stuff I had drawn myself or pictures that I got from books, I'd start getting the elements together.

And in the end the room is all these flats full of artwork. It became like a scenic dock for a studio: I'd have the ground, and I'd have different skies, and I could build a background very quickly after a certain point, and then I just started, totally a magpie approach, things that I liked I

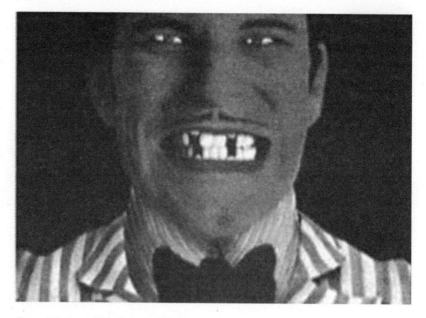

*Conrad Poohs and His Dancing Teeth.*

use and chop up. If it was photos I needed, I'd send the books in to the photographic place and blow them up to the sizes I want and start cutting them out; usually they wouldn't be complete so I'd have to draw or airbrush part of it.

So I'd have all this artwork and I'd go to the BBC's rostrum camera, set it up, and just start pushing the stuff around. You'd find at three or four in the morning the papers arranging themselves after a while! The stuff kind of made itself. You pile all these things there and they start forming patterns, a thing lands on top of that; *ooh,* that's an idea. It was really free, because even though I had storyboarded and set out with a very specific look or an idea I was after, if I couldn't find it I'd grab something that was just as good or it would be a little bit different than I expected but I could make it work, and it would flow in *that* direction.

And I would always shoot long; a lot of the work was done in the editing room afterwards, because I never knew quite [how long] somebody

*Cannibalism, Gilliam-style.*

would talk. I would just wiggle the mouth up and down – leave it open for twelve frames, close it for ten – and then later I would chop frames out to try and get it vaguely to [match] whatever was being said. And then for voices I either do them myself, or I'd run and get the guys in the corridor, or in rehearsal. I just stand there with a tape recorder and say, 'John, say this, say that; okay, good, thank you. Terry, say that . . .' And the BBC had a great sound effects library which is all on discs, [but] a lot of times I'd just sit at home, a blanket over my head, with a tape recorder, making noises with kitchen utensils, and just record this shit. And then I'd get down to the editing room and we'd start sticking it all together. I was working seven days a week, it was just crazed. There'd be at least one all-nighter in there.

All the underground press were convinced I was an acidhead, they thought all of us were on drugs but me in particular, and we *weren't* – it's all *natural* stuff!

And it's not like a Disney cartoon where everything's planned and drawn; it's using things around me, and just incorporating and letting it grow organically.

I was producing this stuff in two weeks [for each show]. Some of the [location] filming I wouldn't get to because I was desperately trying to get ahead. I'd have to keep up with the shows, so by the end of the series it was always a mad rush. It was weird.

When you sail in a race, you just go out on the ocean, and you come around a buoy and all the boats are there, and before you get to the next marker everybody disperses and goes a different way; suddenly you're alone. And then you come to the next marker buoy and *Oh!* Everybody converges. And it was kind of like that in doing the shows; we'd have the meetings, I'd be there as part of the group, then I'd go off into my world, and we'd only get together the days the shows were being recorded. So they were always together, they were always at rehearsals. My problem was there was one side of me that wanted to be a performer as well, but I really didn't think I was in their class, so I'd just turn up on the days we were recording and take that little part there, put on a costume, do something silly there, just to keep myself both from being bored and feeling more a part of the thing. Because they were having all the fun, and I felt I was doing all the work!

*In story meetings, would you ever bring a fully devised sketch to be animated, such as 'The House Hunters' [in which two hunters armed with 'condemned' posters track a wild building]?*

**GILLIAM:** I wouldn't have brought it in as a sketch – I would bring it as an idea. 'I want to do this whole thing about house hunters, it's a *literal* thing.' And again they didn't know quite where to put those things because they couldn't imagine them; that was part of the problem. If I wanted to do that little story, in a sense it was up to me to find the right spot to slide that in. I'm trying to remember whether I would actually say, 'I've got a thing that's probably going to run about three minutes.' I honestly can't remember whether I was ever that specific. Because we'd

*A typical magpie approach.*

try to work out a thirty-minute show, so I'm sure I must have been saying 'a big chunk'. 'I've got a *big* thing to do here,' something specific!

Terry always loved what I was doing, and Mike. It's so weird because Terry and Mike are much more visually oriented than the others, but it may just have been my inability to explain things. John I think was constantly bemused by my stuff, he was so – 'intimidated' is probably too strong a word, but he didn't know how to criticize it, so he never criticized it except for this one thing where he could actually go, 'Well, that's blasphemous,' or 'That's offensive.' [*See page 146.*]

That was the bad side of it: I felt at times I wasn't getting any of the benefit of the criticisms of the group. We all had to be self-criticizing, saying, 'That doesn't work,' 'That's not good enough for the shows.' But a lot of times I never got a sense that they knew whether [what I did] was good or bad, whether it worked or didn't work, because it was another language that they don't understand. John didn't understand the language.

In the English language there's no word for 'visual illiteracy'. You have 'illiterate', but visual? There's no term for it; it's the idea that visual things are not a language. There *is* a visual language, and yet people who invent words don't invent *that* word. I want to use 'ivvisualites', people who are visually illiterate.

It's a thing that intrigues me, the information you get from images; they're saying things and they're telling these stories and they don't necessarily have to be words. Being down with these kids at the Royal College's Animation Department, some of the stuff they're doing is just wonderful, but if you sit down and go, 'Tell me the story,' they can't do it. A splotch of stuff here, a funny little noise happens there, what's *that*? And yet it's fantastic – at least it is for me. I look at some of their stuff and I'm not sure that John Cleese would find it funny, I don't think he would know what to say about it. Sounds like I'm picking on John, but he was the most visually illiterate; I think it's that. But I wish the others would have been able to come up and say, 'Terry, that's pretty weird.' They didn't!

*Was any animation ever rejected out of hand?*

**GILLIAM:** There was this thing that Ian MacNaughton just completely fucked up because he didn't understand it, and Terry hadn't been in the editing room that day. It was a strange abstract thing – it's really hard to describe! I mean, it was like trees growing and reaching barriers in space you can't see, and then they go around and did all sorts of really strange and interesting things. And I don't know what he was thinking when he did it, he just didn't get what it was and he cut it. That was a big mistake, [but] that wasn't like somebody censoring.

## BUT IT'S MY ONLY LINE!

**CAROL CLEVELAND, ACTRESS:** I had been doing a fair amount of work at the BBC, doing what I call – I think this is my own definition – a 'glamour stooge', working alongside people like Ronnie Corbett, Ronnie Barker, and Spike Milligan.

When the Pythons were starting, I hadn't met any of the fellas at all, though I knew a little of their work. They'd written five episodes of the original thirteen, and they were looking for a female. Somebody at the Beeb suggested my name and John Howard Davies saw me and cast me. I hadn't realized at that stage that my contract wouldn't go further than four episodes; I only discovered that when my agent got in touch with the Beeb. By this stage we'd got going and I got on extremely well with the guys, they thought I fitted in beautifully. I think they were more than happy with my contribution, and when Michael came up to me when we were doing episode three and said, 'Oh, we have got something great for you coming up,' – because already they felt that they weren't quite utilizing my talents enough and they wanted to give me something more to do than just giggle and smile, as I did in the 'Marriage Guidance Counsellor' sketch – I said, 'Well, it sounds great but I'm not in episode six.' And he said, 'What? What?' And he went over and spoke to the others, John came over and said, 'What's *this*?'

So they said, 'Absolutely no way – we want you with us for the rest of the series.' So that's what happened. I really owe it to the fellas that I became the Monty Python girl because they put their foot down.*

By now Ian MacNaughton was doing the directing. Ian wanted to have different ladies in each episode and he wanted to be responsible for the casting, so the fellas put their foot down and said, 'Uh-uh.' They came to the agreement that if Ian wanted someone to just literally stand there and say nothing and just look pretty, fine, he could cast that, but if there was any sort of acting involved, the fellas wanted me. And that was the agreement they came to and that was how I came to be in the series.

---

\* No doubt an unintentional pun.

*How was working with the Pythons different
from working on other comedy programmes?*

**CLEVELAND:** Working with Spike Milligan was almost traumatic – an amazing experience but exhausting because you never knew what this man was going to do next. But the other people I worked with were all fairly sane – I mean, very funny but it was all fairly sane stuff, you knew what was going on; there wasn't quite such a lunacy with those. With the Pythons I really didn't know what to expect. It's just a wonderful combination of looniness and great wit and intelligence and foresight. When I first joined them, I didn't honestly quite know what to make of it to begin with. I remember the first two or three days of rehearsal thinking, 'I don't know if this is going to take off,' because they were sort of all over the place. It was fairly manic.

*Carol Cleveland, steadfast straight woman to the group, in* Monty Python Live at the Hollywood Bowl.

We didn't actually do a lot of rehearsal. If anything, it was *under*-rehearsed to keep it fresh and fun. Lots of people say to me, 'How much of that was improvised?' Because it came over so fresh, they felt a lot of it was being improvised. And I say, 'Well, none of it; none of it was improvised. It was all scripted, everything.'

There wasn't a lot that went on in the first few days of rehearsal; because they had written it themselves, they knew exactly what they wanted, so they knew just what was going to happen.

Once they knew exactly what they were doing, in order to keep it fresh, we'd just stop rehearsing and the rest of the time was mucking about. Once we'd done our little bit of rehearsal we'd go, 'Right, that's good now, we don't want to sort of louse it up,' we'd do something like play football. So all of the furniture would be moved aside and we set up a couple of goals at each end and we'd have a football match. I was always a goalie! And we had a great time at rehearsals mucking about, I have to say, much to the amusement of passers-by. When we were in the BBC Centre rehearsal rooms (which are great, big, vast rooms), all the doors have little peek-through windows, and it was wonderful – as people pass by, you'd see them come back and take a double take, and not know what to make of it. They thought we were rehearsing a football sketch that went on day after day after day.

*What allowed you to work so well with the group as their foil?*

**CLEVELAND:** Well, certainly I was very prepared to have a go. There was very little they could ask me to do that I would ever say 'no' to. I was willing and able, and I'd throw myself into it with great gusto. I guess there's a fair amount of lunacy in me, there *must* have been to get into things the way I did, and I think that was very appealing to them. I could do the sort of 'glamour dollie bird' bit and put that across very well but at the same time send myself up on that. I was quite happy to go over the top with anything and I think that was the other thing that they liked. And obviously they felt I had quite a good comedy flair and I looked good as well, which was a combination they wanted.

It still irritates me that I meet Python fans and their recollections seem to be of me without any clothes on! I never took my clothes off in *Python*, not entirely. There was a lot of me in underwear and showgirl outfits and bathing suits and lingerie, but never without *any* clothes. The nearest I came to that was when we were filming 'Scott of the Sahara'. In that I'm being chased by a man-eating roll-top desk, having my clothes ripped off bit by bit by cacti. I'm running towards the camera on each occasion, and on the last one my bra comes off and I'm still meant to be running towards the camera and I was feeling a little bit shy about all sorts of things, and certainly the fact that we were filming on a crowded beach and there were masses of people milling about, so I did feel a little bit inhibited about that. I wasn't happy about running towards the camera with my bra coming off so in fact they did change it. The last shot is of me topless running *away* with my back to the camera as I pass John sitting at his desk facing the camera. But that was the only time I think I ever resisted. And the funny thing is that I suppose if they asked me to do it now, I'd say, 'Yeah, great, I'll do it!' But it's too late now, they won't ask me!

> *Was there difficulty in that there were Python wives and girlfriends who also appeared in the shows but not as frequently as you?*

**CLEVELAND:** I suppose if I had been a wife or a girlfriend I wouldn't have got the job! Connie Cleese appeared occasionally, and Eric's then-wife Lynn Ashley appeared, but only occasionally. Neither of them would have actually wanted to be involved, I think; it was only because they were wives that they were brought in.

I don't think I would have got the job if I had been heavily involved [with one of them]. And I remember very early on Terry Gilliam did ask me out on a date – when I think how things might have turned out if I'd said 'yes'! I said 'no' for two reasons: first of all because I actually had a boyfriend who was an extremely jealous Italian, but I think I would have said no anyway because business and pleasure don't mix. As it turns out Terry dated a make-up girl on the show, Maggie, and they're now married and very happy.

> *What were your impressions of the Pythons?*

**CLEVELAND:** Individually they were all as they were collectively: brilliant, clever, fun, very nice men. The only one I never really felt close to was

Eric. All the others treated me like one of the boys, and I never quite felt that with Eric. Eric always seemed a little distant, rather aloof. He in my opinion was the most serious of the lot, and the most businesslike. He was the one that always had his head together as far as the financial side of *Python* was concerned. If anyone started getting a little bit too wacky he would be the one to say, 'Well, yeah, but this one is going to cost such-and-such.'

Terry Jones: very excitable, being a Welshman very emotional, quite fiery at times. I was never present at the writing sessions or the business meetings but I'm told that he was the one that had been known to throw things. And he, along with Terry Gilliam, were the two looniest of the lot, who would cause the most havoc and confusion during the rehearsal period.

Terry Gilliam, also very excitable, very visual, very loud! And you never quite knew what was going on in his head, until you actually saw the animations – and when you saw the animations you really got quite *worried* about what was going on there!

Graham always did everything to excess, everything he did: obviously his drinking, and the way he flaunted his homosexuality, which wasn't the done thing in the early Seventies certainly, and caused a certain amount of embarrassment at the time. Personally I felt quite embarrassed by some of his behaviour. I don't know quite how to describe Graham; I sort of describe his behaviour rather than his personality. He was a lovely man. I think because of his drinking and his homosexuality, everyone felt they needed to take care of Graham a little.

John: the most logical, definitely moody, like all comic geniuses a complex man but he was the only one who really changed during the course of Python. When he was going through his questioning period with his psychoanalysis, he was actually at times quite unpleasant to be around. He was unfriendly and difficult – certainly that's what I noticed. Fortunately, by the time we were doing *Life of Brian* he was back to being his fun self.

And as for Michael, well, Michael has never changed. He's the one that's never changed at all, and he remains the same charming, shy, sweet, helpful person that he is, and he is of course the only one who's actually quite shy, and that's very appealing, which is why all the women *adore* Michael. He was always the ladies' favourite.

## IF THEY CAN'T SEE YOU, THEY CAN'T *GET* YOU

**MACNAUGHTON:** This was a very strange thing because when I'd done four or five *Monty Python* shows which had not yet gone out, I was called to the head of entertainment, who said to me, 'I don't think we'll be renewing your contract.' I had a year's contract. So I said, 'Oh, really? Why not?' He said, 'Well, this *Q5* show of yours was a bit of a cult success, but only on BBC2. [!] And who really wants to see the Monty Pythons?' They were ready to drop me. It wasn't that they were going to drop the Pythons; they just didn't think that the way we were doing it – which meant me as producer and director – was what was wanted. Fortunately I think their public became of a different mind – the Pythons went out and became a cult success.

> Promotional item in the *Radio Times*:
> ***MONTY PYTHON'S FLYING CIRCUS***
> is the new late programme on Sunday night.
> It's designed 'to subdue the violence in us all'.

The first *Python* show, broadcast on October 5, 1969, demonstrated quite clearly that the group was after something quite uncategorizable. It presented a surreal mix of violence (Wolfgang Amadeus Mozart hosts a programme depicting famous deaths); television parodies ('We find that nine out of ten British housewives can't tell the difference between Whizzo butter and a dead crab.' 'It's true, we can't!'); occasions where all propriety is ripped to shreds (an interviewer proceeds to address his guest as 'sugar plum' and 'angel drawers'); some intellectually tainted comic bits (Picasso paints while riding a bicycle, followed by Kandinsky, Mondrian, Chagall, Miró, Dufy, Jackson Pollock, '…and Bernard Buffet making a break on the outside'); and a loopy premise allowing for both some slapstick *and* social commentary (the tale of the World's Funniest Joke, appropriated by the army as a weapon against the Nazis, who fail miserably at developing a counter-joke of their own). Running throughout the programme were gags and animations about pigs.

In the weeks that followed, the programme became more fragmented, more surreal, more violent. Sheep nesting in trees gave way to a man playing the 'Mouse Organ' (namely, some rodents trained to squeak at a certain musical pitch accompanied by a pair of heavy mallets), to a cartoon of a pram that ingests the doting women who lean too closely. Kitchen-sink melodramas were turned on their heads, as when a young coal miner returns home to his playwright father, who rants about his son's values ('LABOURER!'). A scandal-mongering documentary examines men who choose to live as mice ('And when did you first notice these, shall we say, tendencies?'). And a confectioner is investigated for fraud in labeling his latest product, Crunchy Frog ('If we took the bones out it wouldn't be crunchy, would it?').

---

### *How was the series sold originally by the BBC?*

**TOOK:** Well, it's this 'new wacky series, these wacky kids, these bright new Cambridge graduates and Oxford lads who delighted us for years with their merry antics, now together at last in a brand-new series'. I suppose that's what they did. That's what they do about everything else!

**GILLIAM:** The BBC I think were constantly uncomfortable with us. They didn't know quite what we were, and I think they were slightly embarrassed by it, and yet it was too successful, it was making all this noise out there. When they took us off after the fourth show (this was the first series), we were off for a couple of weeks, I think there was a serious attempt to ditch it at that point. But there was too much noise being made by us. The most wonderful thing was everybody tuning in when *Python* was supposed to run and it was the International Horse of the Year Show; in the middle of it, they were doing their routines to music, it was Sousa's 'Liberty Bell' – *our* theme music. It was like *Python* was even *there,* you couldn't keep it down!

But in the beginning they would put us out at all these different times, and change it, but somehow the word got out and they kept us on.

**TOOK:** The BBC split up into different areas, and the option was to take the show or not to take the show, and half the regions didn't take the first series. So if you lived in London you'd get it; if you went down to Southampton on the south coast you wouldn't be able to see it because they put on *Herring Fishing in the North Sea* or something. It was very irritating that the regions had that kind of autonomy; there was nothing you could do. But the word started to go around that this was very good and very new, and something they ought to have. So one after another came back into the fold, and by the time the second series was done, the complete network had it.

**CLEESE:** I had a friend who was trying to watch the series, and he sat down in his hotel room in Newcastle and switched it on and there was this hysterical start to *Monty Python* about this guy wandering around being terribly boring about all the ancient monuments around Newcastle. And he watched it falling about, and said it's real nerve to do this, it's really terrific and what a great start to the show. And about twenty minutes in he realized it was the regional off-time.

The nicest thing anybody ever said about *Python* was that they could never watch the news after it. You get in a certain frame of mind and then almost *anything's* funny!

# HE WANTS TO SIT DOWN AND HE WANTS TO BE ENTERTAINED

*How was the public's response to your work different
from what you'd experienced on your previous series?*

**PALIN:** I suppose the difference was that, partly because of its programming and the time it went out, *Python* clearly was seen as very much for
an adult audience, which is very interesting because nowadays the spirit
of *Python* burns on in ten-year-olds, twelve-year-olds, thirteen-year-olds.
So many children love *Python*. But at the time it was seen as an adult
show. I'd never really been involved in an 'adult' show, kind of X-rated
comedy show, and this seemed to be the image of it.

And also we became sort of the intellectuals' darling for a bit, written
up in *The Observer*, things like that, which was again quite different from
anything I'd done before. The word 'cult' was quite soon applied to *Python*,
though we weren't quite sure what a 'cult show' *is*. It applies to something
that is the property of only a very few select people. I'd never been interested in doing that before. *Frost Report* was a very popular show; *Do Not
Adjust Your Set* was aimed at a popular audience. But *Python* seemed to fit
into this niche of daring, irreverent, therefore only accessible to those of a
certain sort of intellectual status, and that lasted for a long time.

So much in television depends on when programmes go out. The
BBC labelled the programme – without meaning to – by the time we
put it out. We were put out so late at night and people who had to work
early next morning couldn't see it; there wasn't videos, you couldn't tape
them and run them the next morning if they were put out late at night.
Insomniacs and intellectuals were the only people up!

**MACNAUGHTON:** You do know about Spike Milligan's remark on the radio
once when somebody asked him about the success of the Pythons? 'Oh,'
he said, 'my nephews are doing very well, aren't they?' Which is a very
reasonable thing, because they loved Milligan.

*Python would not have been what it was had it not been for*
*The Goon Show or the Q series.*

**MACNAUGHTON:** Precisely. But would *The Goon Show* have been what it was were it not for the Marx Brothers? And then would the Marx Brothers have been the way they were were it not for burlesque, and would burlesque have been the way it was were it not for music halls? And so it's got a wonderful progression, I think.

The trouble is, since *Python* I haven't seen anything come up yet that takes its place. And I'm very pleased, because quite honestly I don't think you can. I guess that's one of the big pluses for *Python,* in that nobody can really copy their style – it doesn't work. I mean, *Morecombe and Wise* can be copied. But how do you copy [these] guys? I think it would be very difficult to do it again.

**CLEESE:** My experience is that critics recognize what is *slightly* original, but very frequently miss what is *very* original! And if you look back at the reviews of *Monty Python's Flying Circus,* they were really not particularly noticeable – nothing remarkable about the reviews for quite a long time. I suspect you would probably get to show nine or ten of the first series before anybody was really writing that something remarkable was happening. A few people got it right away. But critics on the whole did something that they do when they're insecure: they describe what the show was like without really committing themselves to a value judgment.

**GILLIAM:** We'd rather be making films that people are passionate about than, 'Oh, that's a nice film.' And Python's always managed to do that; people are *passionate* about Python. I think that's where we've always been good. That's probably the area we should stay in. It's like comic books; comic book artists and people who deal in comic book all feel like outsiders, they're never given respect. There's an amazing skill involved in making a good comic book. The artwork in comic books is brilliant, some of the writing is brilliant – comic books is a really great art form, but it's not [considered] *art*. Not literature. It's this bastard thing hanging out there. And they complain, [but] I keep saying, 'No, you're *lucky* that you haven't been accepted – keep being angry and outside and doing stuff.' Because if you become a Keith Haring or Basquiat or any of these people who get drawn into the Establishment, they die, they just freeze up. What's Keith Haring? His stuff is nice and it's sweet and it's cute, it's all right, but I don't think when they look back a hundred years from now they're going to say, 'He nailed it.' Except maybe they *will*: that's how *infantile and silly* things had got, that in fact he captured the essence of the whole thing doing just nice, sweet stick figures and nice colours. I don't dislike his stuff at all, I think it's nice, but I don't think it's *Wow!!*

I think certainly with comedy, comics, and all that – comics/comedy, we're stuck with sounding very similar! – that's outside, and it should stay outside.

**MACNAUGHTON:** They were quite surprised by the positive reaction to the Gumbys, these daft people with the handkerchiefs tied on their heads. When they walked into the studio one time, what happens but the whole front row of the audience had handkerchiefs tied around their heads! Gumby just had to appear and there was a roar of laughter.

**GILLIAM:** I'm the luckiest one because I'm the least known, the least recognized. And it's nice to be recognized occasionally. I get enough, somebody saying 'Hi,' just to assuage my fading ego: 'That'll keep me going for a month or two.'

And the whole thing is so ephemeral, it's just incredible how thin the line is between being known and not known. There was one day after we'd done a chat show here after one of these series, my wife, Maggie, and I were shopping somewhere, and someone all excitedly started shouting, 'Hey, hey, look who's here!' *Oh fuck*. It's this piece of meat that is being attacked by all these excitable people who had just seen you on television the night before. And then you realize, 'Thank God I'm not John.' It's an awful job to walk down the street and be John Cleese, because you can't escape from it!

**CLEESE:** You know when you do something and it catches on, and everybody likes it, then for the next eight years as you creep out of your house at half past eight in the morning: '*Oi, do your funny walk there, John!*' Just so painful!

# THE PYTHONS THROUGH THE LOOKING GLASS

## APART FROM THAT HE'S PERFECTLY ALL RIGHT

I asked each of the Pythons what they thought the greatest contributions were of their fellow members to the group, and then to describe how the disparate personalities (sometimes in conflict with one another) merged to become a thriving whole which in many ways was far greater than the sum of its parts.

*Cleese, the icon.*

# THE CONTROL FREAK

### It Certainly Wouldn't Be Worth Your While Risking It Because I'm a Very Good Shot; I Practice Every Day ... Well, Not Absolutely *Every* Day

**PALIN:** Well, John's quality, apart from just being very, very focused and disciplined as a writer, was a great economy in his writing – very funny and very tight – and that I think comes from his legal background.

Apart from the superb sense of comic timing – the ability to deliver a line – John was able better than any of us (apart from perhaps Graham) to show this wonderful process of an Establishment character undermining the Establishment. The rest of us could be dismissed as being your sort of irritants, the smaller person getting in the way; or the way our characters were played could sort of be dismissed. [But] the great thing about John's characters was he epitomized the ruling establishment of Britain; he looked like the bishop or bank manager, a man of authority. He looks just right, and to be able to undermine it as successfully as he did from that perspective was really wonderful and I think the greatest strength of John. It meant that people were really genuinely taken aback when John would be in full blow of invective. His is not just a purely comedic character; this is an archetypal English, respectable, responsible person physically attacking from within. It seemed to me that was an ability that John had, because we all felt he wasn't acting the part, he *was* it. That's the best analogy – he was a headmaster who had gone mad.

John is a very strong, forceful character and within the group he was probably the one who would have the most obsessive desire for structure, both within the sketches and in the *way* we wrote, the way we worked. John would want to know when we were going to finish, what time we were going to do this, how we were going to do that. We needed that structure, so that was good, as it gave the others who were perhaps more languid something to react against.

As well as having a great time, you had to be businesslike. Not that we were unfocused, but for instance the rest of us were far more likely to say, 'Let's stop now and go out and have a nice lunch.' And John would have to meet somebody, he'd go out and do that and be back at *exactly* 2:15. So in a sense John forced us to organize ourselves pretty thoroughly, which I think was a good thing, but it didn't impinge on the comedy. There was never a sort of feeling of, '*God*, here he is, Mr Bossy Boots.' I mean, he *was* bossy, but he delivered.

**GILLIAM:** John's a hard one. John loves manipulating and controlling; he's only comfortable when he's doing that. When he lets go of control and just starts hanging out, he can only do it for a short while and then the panic sets in, it really sets in. I mean, after we did *Holy Grail* we were in Amsterdam all together promoting it, and we went on a pub crawl one night, and we were having a great time, all of us. And we were getting drunk and speaking openly, all the things that a group can never [otherwise do], and it really was getting funny, and we were saying a lot of things that needed to be said in a really jolly, drunken way. And at a certain point John just had to pull back from it; he was relaxing, he was letting down his guard too much, and he went back off wherever he went. It was really weird. And it was a pity because we were having a good time, and *John* was having a good time, and he couldn't allow himself to not try to be in control.

After the first series, John had taken a house down in Majorca, and said, 'Come on down.' There was one night we went into Palma and we were sitting there having this silly time, like two guys – 'Yours isn't so good looking,' you know, like two kids laughing, trying to pick up girls and failing miserably and all that – and we were driving back and the sun was setting, and there was this castle on the hill. I said, 'Oh, shit, let's drive up there!' *VVrrmm!!* Knocked on the door of the castle, it was locked, it was after hours. I said, 'Let's break in, let's climb in.' So we went around, climbed over the wall and eventually got in. There were sheep grazing in the middle of this castle and we chased them around, it was like really, really good fun – and then John closed down again. It was like one of the few times I've seen him just totally relaxed. But he can only do it for a limited period, and then he's got to get back in control.

I think his attempt to try and control things gave a sense there was always something one could go against – his need to control [versus] our need to *not* be controlled, and that's such an interesting dynamic. I don't know if that's exactly the *best use* of everybody in the group!

But John, as I said, was the one we could all struggle against all the time, one thing we always agreed on: 'He's going to try this.' 'Oh, fuck him!'

### Did he serve as a substitute for the BBC, or a potential audience, that you had to win over?

**GILLIAM:** No, it wasn't about that he represented anything larger than himself, or that he was right or wrong. It was about him trying to get his own way. And that's why he and Terry were at opposite ends, they *both* wanted their own way. They were these two poles, sort of psychic emotional poles that were at opposite ends – Terry's passion and John's intellectual need to control – and that set up this really weird and interesting dynamic.

**JONES:** When we first started I remember John saying, 'We don't want to have personalities in this group, it's going to be *the group*.' Which is why we didn't sort of have our names and faces up at the end of the show. It was a group undertaking, and that very much came from John's feeling, I don't know quite why. He had just come out of *At Last the 1948 Show*, where somehow Marty Feldman had been perceived to be the star, and Marty had gone on to do his own series, and it was somehow some sort of reaction, against the cult of the individual kind of thing. But nonetheless I think the original offer was from the BBC to John to do a show, and then he came to us and it sort of grew up around him like that.

John was useful to have as your front man; he could deal with the bureaucracy, though there wasn't that much bureaucracy in those days. John's contribution was always being kind of a rallying point, a spokesperson. He always had the authority; when it came to dealing with the BBC, we always felt they took John seriously. Partly because he was best known; it's partly his personality as well. Everybody always feels that John's really the prime minister in disguise.

*Colin 'Bomber' Harris wrestling Colin 'Bomber' Harris, from* Monty Python Live at the Hollywood Bowl.

# SPLUNGE!

### I'd Like to Answer This Question If I May in Two Ways: Firstly in My Normal Voice and Then in a Kind of Silly, High-Pitched Whine

**JONES:** I always loved Graham as a performer, from when I first saw him in *Cambridge Circus* and then in *At Last the 1948 Show,* because you could never quite see what he was doing. I mean, John I dearly love as a performer, but from the moment you first see John you know where John *is;* Graham was always very intangible.

I think Graham always played everything as if he didn't think anything was funny, [as if] he didn't see the joke in anything, really, which was just wonderful. Which was why he worked for the leads in *Holy Grail* and *Life of Brian*, because he played it so straight and sincerely and seriously.

**PALIN:** The characters that Graham played were again great Establishment characters. He would play a colonel exactly right and add this wonderful mad streak throughout. I think Graham took more risks than John, and I think when they wrote together, although John I'm sure put together 80 per cent of their sketches, the 20 per cent that Graham put in was the truly surreal and extraordinary. Graham had a wonderful gift with words; I'm sure 'Norwegian Blue' for a parrot would be Graham's. There's something about it: a Norwegian Blue parrot – that just *sounds* like Graham.

Graham as a performer had a quiet intensity which, if you look at all of his performances, quite unlike any of the rest of us, is very convincing whatever he does. That's why he was so good as Brian, so good as Arthur; here was a man who genuinely suffered, you know, trying to get through this world – he just *happened* to be a king, it wasn't his fault – he was trying to do his best, and all these people around him were just mucking him up. One really felt for him. Graham could portray that very well, partly because I think he was a little nervous as a performer, because he took to drink at one time. By *Life of Brian* he had given it up, and he didn't need that, but he was always slightly nervous about it. There's a concentration in the way Graham does things which looks good, it comes across as very natural and very right.

**CLEESE:** Graham was fundamentally a very, very fine actor. He could do very odd things, like mime, and he did a very funny impression of the noise made by an espresso machine, things like that. He was a really, really good actor. But to understand Graham you have to realize he didn't really work properly. If he was a little machine, you would take him back and somebody would fiddle with it, and then it would come back working properly. So he was a very odd man; he was in many ways highly intelligent and quite insightful, in other ways he was a complete child, and not someone who was really any good at taking any sort of responsibility and discharging it.

His best function, and the reason that I wrote with him all those years, is that we got on pretty well. We laughed at the same things, we made each other laugh. And he was the greatest sounding board that I ever worked with. When Graham laughed or thought something funny, he was nearly always right, and that's extraordinary. For example: when we were writing the 'Cheese Shop' [sketch], I kept saying to him, 'Is this funny? Is this funny?' And he'd go, [*puff puff on his pipe*] 'It's funny, go on.' And that's really how the 'Cheese Shop' [sketch] was written as opposed to just being abandoned, because I kept having my doubts. He was a wonderful sounding-board.

And the other side of that was that he was very disorganized – I mean we were all a bit disorganized, but he was *really* disorganized, and really fundamentally very lazy. His input was minimal; I remember working with Kevin Billington on a movie that turned out to be called *The Rise and Rise of Michael Rimmer*. After a couple of sessions, Kevin said to me very quietly, perhaps on a lunch break when Graham had gone to the bathroom, 'Does Graham usually make so little contribution?' And I remember being quite surprised by the question, because I'd got used to the fact that he made so little contribution.

He didn't say very much, but when he did say something it was often very good. But he was never the engine; someone had to be in the engine room driving something forward, and then Graham would sit there and add the new thought or twist here or there, which is terribly useful. But I remember saying to somebody once that there were two kinds of days with Graham; there were the days when I did 80 per cent of the work, and there were the days when he did 5 per cent of the work.

To give you a real example of how bad it could be: when we finished the first series of *The Frost Report* in 1966, David Frost gave us £1,000 to write a movie script. With the money we went off to Ibiza, and we took a villa for two months and decided to write there, and a whole lot of friends came and stayed with us and passed through, and that is when Graham met David Sherlock. I remember that I would sit inside at the desk writing, and Graham would literally be lying on the balcony outside sunbathing, calling suggestions into the room as I sat there writing.

And the funny thing is I don't remember being cross about it; I think I just accepted that writing with Graham I was going to have to do 80 per cent of the work and sometimes more. And it always slightly annoyed me when people used to come up to me on *Fawlty Towers* and say, 'Well, how much did Connie Booth actually write?' And I wanted to say to them, 'Certainly a lot more than Graham ever wrote.' That used to annoy me, the assumption that because Graham was a man he was obviously making a bigger contribution than Connie as a woman.

**SHERLOCK:** Graham would have been a very good shrink, because if nothing else he understood what made people tick. And if he couldn't understand, he would make it his job to find out. And his interview technique, if he was looking for prospective interesting people wanting to join his coterie, within five minutes he could sum somebody up and sort them out.

However, I think he was far less astute financially than Cleese, who had a great many friends who were accountants – hence a lot of the sketches! – but he learned from them. Sadly those sort of people bored Graham, I don't think he was even interested [in connecting]. That's why he lost money while others were gaining.

One of the most delightful sounds I've ever heard was Graham and John writing. This was in the days when we lived in Highgate in the Seventies. I would often be preparing food for our large nuclear family (who could be anything from three to four to ten on an evening sometimes, depending on who Graham invited back from the pub or whatever). Part of my life consisted of keeping the household kicking over. I didn't do it very well, but it was fairly Bohemian anyway, so it didn't matter too much. But in the morning if I was making coffee for them, I would often hear a delighted shriek as they hit on some outrageous idea, often followed by the thudding of bodies hitting the floor, and the drumming of feet like a child with a tantrum, only this was the sheer delight of the *idiocy* of the idea, which would absolutely floor either the people at the BBC or the watching public. And they would howl screaming with laughter before they could even get back to finishing the sketch. Sometimes Gray [Graham] would go off to the pub for lunch, and John would say, 'No, I'm not coming,' and he would do his Alexander technique exercises[*] on the floor and would want to borrow a couple of books to put under his head. I often wondered in fact whether he needed that technique to get over the stress and strain of rolling about and falling to the floor!

Graham's work with John would start off with apparent normality and then slowly chaos starts to seep in; all the time they try to drag the character back to reality or they try to keep control of whatever it is, but eventually it ends in chaos. I always see most of their classic sketches to be about that. One thing that was very important to them was a concrete time and place – even the maddest sketch had to have solidity, a reality. The sets were as realistic as the budget would allow and so were the costumes.

They had some extraordinary ideas when they were working to pressure; everyone knew they had so many sketches to bring to the table at the end of their writing time, half or two-thirds may be completely scrapped. Well, in their case, they would often flip through a paper while starting a very, very late morning. Mornings would be very testy because sometimes there would be nothing done at all other than playing with crosswords, making umpteen coffees, and searching for an idea for that very first thing. Once they'd got an idea they were off and they could finish the sketch in record time. On a good day, when they were working happily together, they would work from eleven in the morning, have a proper lunch break of an hour, and then work through till four in the afternoon, sometimes six.

But of course Cleese was a great perfectionist; Graham is on record saying that John could spend a day worrying about a single word that

---

[*]    A method of releasing muscle tension, focusing on the head, neck, and spine.

was placed in each sketch; as far as he was concerned a sketch was not finished until that word was placed or removed.

Cleese was definitely extremely disciplined. Graham was often seen as a loose cannon. But that's not entirely true. When I was working with Graham he would be very disciplined, but he could do six things at once, which was pretty amazing. When working at home he could often answer the telephone in the middle of writing a sketch with a line half-finished or not even written down, and I often as the scribe would find myself pen poised. He could come straight back to that line having had an extremely complex conversation with an agent or whatever, and yet the whole shape of the sketch so far (even though it was very often with three wheels) was [still] in his head.

But very often it was Graham who would absolutely throw John by turning a sketch on its head or literally introducing some extraordinary character or even an animal. It's very interesting, many of the more bizarre sketches such as the 'Pet Conversions' sketch, where they'd be doing absolutely hideous things to small furry animals ('Terriers make lovely fish. Legs off, fins on, stick a little pipe through the back of its neck so it can breathe, bit of gold paint . . .'), have been Cleese and Chapman.

**GILLIAM:** Graham's contribution was greater than I think John pretended in a sense; he was so frustrated writing with Graham, yet Graham would make those leaps that nobody [else] John has worked with has done. Graham was just on another planet at times. Suddenly he'd say, 'Splunge!' What, *splunge*? And after that, you had to then *deal* with it; [it became] part of the comedy equation: $E = mc^2 splunge$.

Graham was *there* and he had to be *dealt* with in some way. And that's what was so interesting in the end, becoming the best leading man of the group. He was the one on films who was the straightest in a sense, he just had a really interesting presence there.

**SHERLOCK:** I think in his biography [*A Liar's Autobiography*] it was plain that he was this extraordinary mixture. He came from a very dedicated family. Their devotion to duty – it's a very old-fashioned term, and it's almost died out as a human quality – was (and still is) very strong. In some ways it was something [the Pythons] sent up.

Graham was a darn good sportsman. He was a good runner, he played rugby, he loved climbing mountains particularly. Graham was a very different mixture altogether from this rather reflective [image]. My mother was terrified of him. She said, 'He just sits there smoking his pipe not saying much and I *know* he's taking it *all* in, every word! I know it's all going to come out on the television.' So that's your average sort of middle-class attitude to what Graham was like. But yes, there were definitely two sides to his character, and the Jekyll and Hyde side, if you like, was very pronounced; it's one reason why he drank as much as he did, because he was very shy, and he knew that his shyness could totally override everything unless there was some way of dealing with it.

Graham was fairly notorious as a boozer through the Seventies, and yet he could often start work eleven in the morning with a large tumbler of gin and tonic beside him and work through the whole day apparently sober, absolutely totally undetectable. He was a gentleman drunk, rather like Jimmy Stewart in *Harvey,* sort of gentle. The whole fun of that movie is that Jimmy Stewart is actually drunk all the time and yet you're never quite sure. That was the same with Graham.

### When did his alcoholism affect his work?

**SHERLOCK:** It did affect his work, recording *Python* shows. It's an aspect which really bothered the other guys. One of Graham's best friends, who was at St Bart's Hospital with him, became the medical officer (or one of them) at the BBC during the time that *Python* was being made. He remembers the set for the show – you know how a TV studio works: you've got one set and it's all built so that one doorway leads through into another which is a totally different set when viewed from the right angle – behind the flats, the actual scenery, very often there's a ledge which held the thing together, on which at the end of a recording he could find behind each set at least one tumbler full of gin and tonic still bubbling away. Because there were one or two occasions when Graham's terror of losing his lines, forgetting them completely, would be so much that he would freak out. It is after all every actor's nightmare, this thing of losing lines. Graham did it once so spectacularly that I think he had something like forty-eight takes. Now in a TV studio that is not funny; with an audience, it's even more frightening.

*When did you first recognize that Graham's drinking was a major problem?*

**CLEESE:** I have one very, very, very clear memory, and it was the day we were shooting the 'Upper Class Twit of the Year' at some big sports arena in North London for *And Now for Something Completely Different*. Graham for some reason wasn't there, and we all wanted to check a point in the script, and none of us could find a copy, and Michael said, 'Oh, Graham's got a script in his briefcase.' And Michael opened the briefcase, took the script out, and then did a double take, because there was a bottle (I think of vodka) in the briefcase. And Michael looked absolutely stunned, and somebody said, 'What's the matter?' And Michael said, 'That was full when we left this morning,' and it was like quarter past ten, and the bottle was half empty. That was the moment when I realized that instead of needing a bit of a drink now and then, he was seriously into it. But my recollection is that his performing began to get affected in the second series.

**JONES:** When he was drinking the worst thing would be he couldn't remember his lines, and Ian would be quite remorseless with him like in the studio shows, and make him go over and do it. I remember doing one sketch where we must have done about twenty-four takes of something, and then we had a problem because when Graham eventually got the line right, the audience *cheered*; [just listening to it], you don't know *why* there's cheering! We tried taking the cheer off [in the editing room] but we couldn't quite do it. That was a bit awkward.

I remember one time we were filming out in Glen Coe and Graham had a long speech to do and you *knew* he wasn't going to get it. And instead of doing Graham's bit *before* lunch, Ian broke for lunch, and of course it was a disaster. You say, 'Please, you want to do Graham's bit first.' But no, no, no, he *had* to break for lunch. And Ian was also drinking, and so you knew after lunch you weren't going to get a lot of sense out of Ian, either. And they came back and both were a bit squiffy. Graham couldn't quite remember his words, and Ian couldn't think of how to do it without just ploughing on. But instead of just doing little snatches, Graham insisted on doing the whole thing together. It was a nightmare. I think in the end I had to hold my script up so Graham could read.

**CLEESE:** Certainly by the third series there was one sketch that we had to abandon because he literally couldn't get through it; he literally couldn't remember a line. He used to always get more nervous than the rest of us, and then he would drink to kill the nerves, so the chances of his memory functioning got damaged by that. And then he got so worried by the fact that he was going to have to perform his words in public that I think he got to the point where he didn't even learn them properly, maybe so then you couldn't really say that he'd *forgot* them. It's an extraordinary kind of defence, but my intuition tells me that's what was going on.

   And later we were very careful in casting; although we would give him things on film because he could have several goes at it, we used to keep any parts away from him in the studio. But I do remember his shooting one piece in Devon dressed as a naval commander or something, and it was take after take after take. I think the director decided instead of letting him off he would keep at it, and he did so many takes that it got embarrassing. I mean, we got to slate one take seventeen, and I think they then made it 'slate two take one' so it wouldn't look *so* embarrassing.

   By the end Graham was really not able to remember in the afternoon what we'd written in the morning. He was sipping very early on and simply just got vaguer and vaguer – I'm really talking about the time when we were writing *Life of Brian,* that was the very worst.

   Then on Christmas Eve 1977, Graham fell over in a drunken state and gashed his head pretty badly on a fender by the fire. And he did an extraordinary thing: without ever going to AA, he *stopped* drinking, and that's remarkable. For all his vagueness and laziness, and the complete complacency with which he would take the same money as everyone else while doing considerably less work, for all that he was capable of this great act of will.

And he *wanted* to clean up. I think he realized he had just reached a point where he just had to, but also he very much wanted to play the role of Brian, and he knew he couldn't do it. If you watch him playing King Arthur you can see he's drunk quite a lot; his face would get puffy and he would squint his eyes. So he got himself together. The infuriating thing was that in about six months he was in better shape than anybody! If you look at him in *Life of Brian,* he was in very, very good shape.

But writing *Life of Brian* was probably when he was at his worst, and that's when he literally could not remember in the afternoon what we'd worked on in the morning. I remember I would go up and write at his place quite a lot – I used to go up there because it was the only way of getting started on time!

*Did you ever just refuse to write with him?*

**CLEESE:** I don't think so, because we were very incapable of any kind of real confrontation. Later I did sometimes suggest we should write on our own, and I did write some things on my own. But when you have a group – and I was as guilty as everyone – where the basic ethos is that nothing causing the group any difficulty is really confronted, it becomes pretty problematic.

**MACNAUGHTON:** BBC Light Entertainment used to have a party every Christmas and all the LE directors and actors used to come. We were all standing in this party one day, and suddenly up came the boss, Michael Mills, and he said to me, 'For God's sake, get Graham Chapman out of here.' I said, 'Why?' 'Why, he's crawling about the floor biting the ankles of everybody in the room!' Okay. I went to him, I found him, and I said,

'Graham, can you just select *whose* ankles you bite?' Graham said, 'I get the picture, old boy,' and he stood up and that was it. That was a typical Python thing!

**GILLIAM:** Graham to me was the guy that wherever we went, he was the one who would come back the next morning with tales that we all wanted to hear, because he was *out there*. Whenever you go into a public restaurant suddenly he'd disappear. You look around; he'd be under somebody else's table, licking the girl's feet while her date is there. It's like, what the fuck is this? That was the real thing; he was genuinely mad. And it's funny because he was really in a sense the shyest and most conservative. He pushed himself right out there all the time.

He was probably the only one who was really living at the edge in some strange way. We just played at it, we just wrote it; he *lived* the stuff.

In Torquay we were all in this huge dining room, and he was telling us about this guy that he'd met, this date he was really looking forward to. This monstrous buildup about this guy he'd met and he was 'Oh wow,' and then I guess the waiter'd come over and said, 'There's someone waiting for you, Mr Chapman.' He makes this long, long crossing of the dining room, long pause – eventually, longer – then he comes back in, and he's got a really unpleasant-looking guy in a wheelchair, wheeling him in. And *this* is Graham's hot new date? Because he'd been telling everybody, 'This is really going to be a night!' And I thought, 'What the fuck have you done now, Graham? This is really getting sick here!' And it turned out *he* was shocked because he had got somebody's number mixed up – this guy who he *thought* was going to be his date that night with this *other* guy who was just a fan, a desperate guy who's crippled and everything – I don't know, Graham had sent him a picture or something – and he'd mixed the numbers up. And Graham just went out and had his date. He was amazing; he didn't bat an eyelid, it was quite extraordinary. But *we* didn't understand the story until the next day, so all of us were wondering what this evening was all going to be about!

*Pawin from* Wife of Bwian.

# THE NICE ONE

### Well, I'm Afraid We Don't Get Much
### Call for It Around These Parts

**CLEESE:** Michael is immensely likable and for me the best performer. I enjoy performing with Michael more than anyone else. I *loved* performing with him because I thought he had the biggest range, and also he and I had a certain rapport as performers which was greater than I had with the others.

Michael's great aim in life is to be affable. And this makes him enormously pleasant and enormously good company, but infuriating if he doesn't want to do something, or if he disagrees with something, because it's almost *impossible* for him to say so at the time. And you find out about it slowly. I used to, for example, try to put the Amnesty International shows together, and I'd ring up Mike and I'd say, 'Do you think you'd be able to do it?' And he would say without any apparent hesitation in his voice, 'Oh yes, yes, yes.' And I'd ring up again and say, 'Are you still on?'

He'd say, 'Yes.' And when I'd start to get specific, then suddenly I'd get a call saying, 'You know, I've got to do *this* there and *that* there . . . ,' and it would be much easier with Michael if he would say, 'I don't like that', or 'I disagree with that', straight off. But when he does that he risks his affability. So that's the main problem with Michael.

*Could he do that easily on a creative level, if he didn't like material?*

**CLEESE:** Yes, I think he could do that creatively. But we were *all* cowards; we'd all avoid confrontations about anything that wasn't to do with the material. Those kinds of things never got spoken about; we were very English in a sense that any kind of direct confrontation about anything emotional was impossible. For example, I don't think we ever spoke to Graham about his lateness, which was absolutely chronic. I don't suppose Graham was on time two times in three years. I mean, he just couldn't do it. And Michael's joke at Graham's memorial service was, 'I'd like to think he's with us now – well, at least he *will* be in twenty minutes.'

**GILLIAM:** Mike's gift was his ease with dealing with things. Essentially I think Mike was the one that everybody liked, he was the one we all could agree on that we could like, because he was the easiest to work with.

**JONES:** I think Mike was the best performer in many ways, he was great. John is sort of the greatest comic persona and Mike as a character actor was best. And also I think Mike's writing was terrific. He'd come up with some of the most original concepts, like 'The Spanish Inquisition'.

When Mike read out 'Spanish Inquisition', I knew we had a terrific piece to work on. Mike's writing could be so off-the-wall it was magical – it was funny, but you couldn't see where it had *come* from. And occasionally it worked like that when we wrote together; for example, we had this hairdresser sketch which was funny but wasn't going anywhere, and then the two of us suddenly came up with the 'Lumberjack Song', which we wrote in about half an hour.

*Idle in* The Meaning of Life.

# THE CHEEKY ONE

### If You're Going to Split Hairs, I'm Going to Piss Off

**PALIN:** Eric was always a slightly cheeky chap. I don't think his characters were ever very complex, but they were really superbly performed. The man who talked in anagrams and all that: 'Staht sit sepreicly'. Well, I can't imagine *any* of us doing that in quite that way.

Eric's stuff was very popular in the sense that he could catch a tune which none of the rest of us could do at all, so musically he made a very strong contribution; but also with some of the sketches he was very [into] wordplay, very deftly performed.

I think he just did provide a source of energy coming from a slightly different direction which wasn't present from any of the rest of us; really cheeky characters is sort of what Eric's known for, but if you like less conservatively Establishment (which John or Graham were), less surreal than Terry or myself – somewhere in the middle ground there. I suppose something like 'Nudge Nudge' ('Is your wife a goer, eh? Know what I mean? Nudge nudge?') was a real masterpiece of a very straight sketch, in fact, very ordinary – it didn't have Vikings swinging through on the ends of ropes or anything like that – it just goes through and is superbly well played.

And also in group discussion he was very good. Not being part of the two writing groups (Jones/Palin and Cleese/Chapman), Eric was able to look at our material in a slightly more detached way and make very good comments about what worked and what didn't work, which was effective and important. I suppose he was more on our side, as it were, if you wanted to take sides up; more like Terry and myself than with John and Graham. He also crossed over a bit and wrote a number of things with John, for instance.

What binds Python together is a similar sense of humour, a general consensus about what is funny. If you'd written something that appealed to the group sense of humour, that would go right through the group. That's why we worked well as a group, certainly you didn't have to explain what was funny; there really was a unanimity deep down. And then there was that middle area where certain people thought something was funny and others didn't, and there Eric was good, because John and Graham tended to agree with each other, and I suppose Terry and myself tended to agree with each other, and Eric would provide (if Gilliam wasn't there) the third man, as it were. And he was extraordinary, very articulate and on the ball, and also extremely good at inventing solutions. I think in the way that material was moved around within the show, someone like Eric would be very good at that.

**GILLIAM:** Eric's strength is sharpness, I suppose; his quickness, his ability to do one-liners, fast things. That kind of fast precision is always interesting. He should have been the manager of the group, he was the one that got things started in a sense, ideas like the books. He was a good starter, is what he was. Not a good finisher – and in the middle he wasn't even there a lot of the time! Eric was great at starting the projects, then we need someone to take them over and finish them. But also in some weird way he was the contact to the outside world – he knew all the best people!

His chameleon-like quality is another thing. In many ways he's the least original as far as coming up with really original things, but he could pick up on what everybody else was doing. He could style his stuff on other people's work and be brilliant – sort of an extension of somebody else's idea, or a sketch that somebody else had done, Eric could then do a version of that sketch that would be taking those ideas and doing it in a really slick, funny, sharp, fast way.

Not only is he the one who's out there – 'Here's an idea, I think we ought to do a book' – he'd get an idea and he'd *want* to do it, and he'd start it off putting all the right kind of people together. And then all I remember is being up there doing it at the end and he was *gone*!

**JONES:** Eric developed as an actor and a performer as it went on, as it got better and better, and got more and more involved in the musical side of it, and he became our kind of musical authority.

**CLEESE:** Eric is much more of a loner than the rest of us, and it suited him to write on his own, although he quite justifiably used to complain that that only gave him one vote. I always thought that Eric was very good in the meetings. I thought his analysis of comedy – why a sketch worked or why it didn't work – was always very good, and I always found him very constructive in terms of how meetings can be run in an efficient way. I sense that in terms of him just getting business done – I'm not really talking about *business* business, I'm talking about *artistic* business – that Eric was the one I could work with most easily. We could kind of agree on things and come to a compromise or negotiate and make progress more easily with Eric than anyone else.

*Jones, at his most calm and complacent.*

# THE ZEALOUS FANATIC

### I'd Like the Blow on the Head

**PALIN:** I think more than anybody Terry Jones kept the group together and kept it going forward, because Terry's probably got more energy, sheer mental energy. If he commits to an idea, Terry will really follow it through. And right from the very first discussions we had about *Python*, Terry was always positive about what the group could do and what we could achieve. I think he was the one who worked most to get this new form, this new shape together. He was always hurrying the director in editing sessions and all that. When the television series was coming to an end, he was the one who was most keen to try and get a film together.

That was one side of Terry: he just would not let up, really concerned about getting perfection on screen (which I don't think you *can* get). Terry knew how it should be, which is why he used to have clashes with

John, because Terry's commitment sometimes came across as very dogmatic, and this would rile John at the other end of the spectrum.

*Was Terry most keen to continue the TV series*
*after John had departed?*

**PALIN:** Probably; I think both Terry and myself were quite keen and felt, as Gilliam did, we should do another one. Eric was the biggest doubter; he felt without John there it wouldn't work.

But Terry always saw the potential. He was always very positive about what Python could achieve. I always say Terry was like the conscience of Python. He was always pushing us to do something better, or get this right. Terry always saw it as a battle to be won, against the BBC or directors or editors or whatever.

*Did he have a more personal stake in the success of the group?*

**PALIN:** I don't know. I think Terry felt very concerned about and personally identified with *Python*. How the show looked was very, very important to him, where, again, I don't think John or Graham were quite as interested in that. The whole thing did mean something to Terry, yes. And I think he enjoyed very much working in a team, much more so than, say, John did.

Because he would not let things go, Terry had a doggedness which sometimes was very useful and sometimes could be an irritant to other members of the group, because I think in the dynamics of the group it's counterproductive. Terry argued for too long; I think he's probably aware of that himself. [There's] a certain point where your own view has to be compromised for the unity of the group, and if you're not prepared to do that, then I think very often the reaction against you is much stronger than it would be if you'd compromised in the first place – you actually lose more ground. I think that's true of all the members of the group at certain points, but I suppose Terry was the *most* dogged, the one who least accepted compromise. But then the strengths of that bring out something like Mr Creosote in *Meaning of Life* – just the conception of that was wonderful – and the 'Sperm Song', which Terry directed. That's the work of somebody who is determined to make this special and not compromise, to get it the way he wants it to be.

He fulfilled a role which always – day in, day out, day and night – seemed to be concerned at the whole.

And Terry made those Pepperpots,[*] the women he played, his own; he was superb at those.

**CLEESE:** Terry Jones and I were the most powerful personalities, or the most argumentative, or the most stroppy – you could put it lots of different ways, positively or negatively. On the one hand it probably did come out of a bit of excessive caring about the script, and the other side probably came out from the fact that we were the two most naturally argumentative. I mean, I *enjoy* arguing, not in an angry sense, but I love to test the strength of arguments. Because if someone can tell me something that I didn't know – an argument I hadn't thought of, or a piece of information I didn't have – I love it. And people sometimes interpret that – my ex-wife does! – as that I'm bullying people. And that's not what *I* think I'm doing. What I think I'm doing is testing the argument, because if someone can give me a good argument, I have no problem about taking it on board.

It's also that I need to *understand*. I get very frustrated when I don't understand something. When somebody knows something and I want to understand what it is they know and they can't explain it in a way which I can take in (which would be my fault), I get very frustrated.

So what I've discovered with Jones was that we very frequently argued before we really understood what the other one was on about. I then found that by asking more questions I could get a better idea in my head of what Jones was on about. And then I would frequently find that I *liked* it. But because we were such different character types, and he was all

---

[*]   Python's designation for their dowdy women characters, such as Mrs Ratbag.

about feelings and I in those days was all about intellect, it was very easy for us to get into these confrontations. But they were artistic confrontations rather than basic personal ones.

The hardest thing was that sometimes something would be resolved and Terry was taking an enormously long time to be persuaded out of something. It would take a very long time to argue Terry out of something, and then the next morning he would come in, 'You know, I was thinking about it and I *really* feel . . . ,' and we'd be off again. It was as though he really couldn't separate from some ideas. I used to say to him sometimes, 'Terry, look, Eric doesn't think that's right, Graham doesn't think that's right, I don't think that's right . . .' He'd say, 'No, but I *really* feel . . .' What I found with Terry – and I say this with great affection – is that he would sometimes sit down with me and would listen with great care and real attention to what I had to say, and would then almost invariably do the opposite!

Yes, we were very different temperamentally. We're good friends, but we will never be *great* friends because we're just too different.

I'm a great admirer of Jonesy if you look at the breadth of what he's done – on the one hand a programme about the Crusades, on the other hand directing the movies, and on the *other* hand writing children's books and writing an academic book about Chaucer's *The Knight's Tale*. He's got the widest spread of all of us. But I think that Jonesy's problem was that for a number of years he was quite insecure outside the group. He along with Graham accused me of – what was the word they used – 'betrayal' or 'treachery', when I didn't want to go on with the group. And I said to them, 'I joined you to work, I didn't *marry* you!'

But Terry and Graham's animus towards me for not wanting to continue with the TV series was that they didn't think they could function properly outside the group – they felt very insecure that they would achieve anything outside Python. For Graham it was pretty much the case, he didn't really achieve anything very good after that – the films *Odd Job* and *Yellowbeard,* pretty terrible – he was way, way over his head. But Jonesy didn't have any problem at all, that was just a confidence problem. And I remember somebody saying around about the time that he directed *Personal Services* how he had relaxed, and he seemed much less tense than he used to, and what a good director he had become. That was just a confidence thing; he felt that he was always going to do his best work within Python. And he didn't have any *need* to feel that.

**GILLIAM:** Terry's passion, his enthusiasm, his crusading zeal, that's so beside his writing skills. It's just his passion for things. When somebody is so enthusiastic and so convinced of something, I tend to think that's probably a good way to go.

Terry did it to me on *Jabberwocky*. In the beginning he's the poacher. I've set this crane up, it's a cherry picker [that's picking him] up off the ground. It takes a while to set up, and the sun is going down, and we've got to get it before the sun's gone – I wanted long shadows. And Terry goes, '*Eeeauuuewwwl,*\* there's a little place over there that I think might be better.' 'No, it's better *here*.' Terry's very persuasive, and the producer John Goldstone said, 'Well, why don't you just move the crane?' I said, 'If I move the fucking crane we're going to lose the light.' Terry says, '*Eeeauuuewwwl . . .*'

Fuck! 'Move the fucking crane.' (Just to show them!) So we move the crane, we get in there, and it *doesn't work*. Now I've got to move the crane *back*. So I proved my point, lost the light, all this because I know I'm right (because that's what I'm good at), and I don't have the time or patience to explain exactly *why* the shot is better here.

*It sounds like Terry is manipulating things, like John.*

**GILLIAM:** But Terry isn't manipulating. With John, it's him trying to pull strings like a puppet. Terry does it just [because] his *gut* is telling him, his passion, his enthusiasm. And I'm always a complete sucker for enthusiasm.

---

\* The closest to this Welsh squeal as is transcribable.

*Gilliam as the jailer's assistant in* Life of Brian.

# THE MONOSYLLABIC
# MINNESOTA FARM BOY

### Beanssssssssss!!!

**PALIN:** Terry Gilliam certainly in visual terms comes across as the most stylish of the group; he really gave the show its major style, which I don't think they really had otherwise. They were put together pretty roughly, but Gilliam always gave the show a bit of polish. I think Terry provided the element which made *Python* different than anything else.

The animation [gave it] a tight edge – it was well done, it was sharp. Like John, he was very economical with what he did with the images he used; his timing was brilliant, the images he used were pretty strong, his sound effects were brilliant, his choice of music was very good – just the images he had, like a cat stomping through London or a bus just being flipped over by a woman's leg. We'd all heave a sigh of relief when Terry's animations came to the show on the Sunday morning, and that was great – another three or four minutes in the can, good stuff.

None of us told Terry how to do his animations, which was interesting, whereas the rest of the scripts of *Python* would be all up for discussion. You could say, 'Well, John, I don't like this thing you've done here,' or Eric would say, 'Mike and Terry, I don't like what you've written there.' Terry did go his own way with his animations. And having worked with him on *Jabberwocky*, he had a very special vision as to how *Jabberwocky* was going to work. And he was always sort of, 'All right, I will show you something wonderful and then you can tell me whether you like it or not,' rather than, 'What do you want me to make? How should I do this? Please give me your advice. Tell me.' Terry said, 'No, I think I know what I want to do, and this is it.'

It was very good for us to have an American in the group. First off, he wasn't from our school background, so straight away he had a slightly fresh look at the way *we* would look at things. He'd say, 'God, you anally retentive English, you're writing this because of so-and-so . . .' He was an audience. Gilliam was a great laugher, too. At a writing session, once Gilliam started going it was just wonderful, and very infectious, too. And I think everyone respected Terry; I mean, anyone who seemed to have all the benefits of an American education and been successful both in California and New York and wants to come over and work for the BBC for a pittance, you know, deserves *some* respect! *Why should he want to do that?!* And John used to be very rude [to him], but John is only rude to people he actually quite likes!

But he would also muck in. Terry was intrigued by us English boys. I think he saw us as a strong group; I think university was the main thing which typified the way we worked. During the Sixties, Oxford/ Cambridge was a very, very strong source of comedic talents. It wasn't just us; there was the *Beyond the Fringe* group. I think Terry respected us in some way, so to act with these guys, just to do anything, he felt quite flattered to have a go at [it]. And we always put him in suits of armour to start with, really uncomfortable roles!

But then I think he realized later on, Terry's much better and much funnier than he'd given himself credit for, so in some of the films he had larger roles and he's just superb, like the jailer's assistant in *Life of Brian*.

That's Gilliam's contribution: the freshness and consistency of very good work.

**JONES:** I think Terry G. was a great fighter. He really loved the challenge and he always does; he survives on a fight, really. Doing his own animations really in the teeth of the BBC – the BBC was insisting that he had to employ one of their animators and they didn't really want him to touch material, and Terry was insisting that he had to do it himself. It was a really big fight!

**CLEESE:** Well, obviously on the occasions when he sat in the group his evaluation of the material read out could be taken very seriously. But for me it was always as though he was fundamentally operating slightly outside, and he would be given a job to do and take it away and do it almost always very, very well. So for example on *Life of Brian*, he was taking care of the look of it, he seemed to me to do a marvellous job, but I wasn't terribly aware of him being part of the group. He's much more like an artist in a painterly sense. He works in a studio, he doesn't work in a *team*, or didn't on *Python*; we worked very much in a team. He would often work very, very late whereas we were working office hours. And that was how he did his contribution. I vaguely remember him bringing in drawings and showing them to us, but he was always really a sort of semi-detached member of the group, but I didn't mind that.

*Did the others ever ask him to contribute to writing sketches?*

**CLEESE:** I don't think we expected him to write *words*. And although I'm quite sure he would have suggested a line here or there at script meetings, I can't remember his ever putting them down on paper, though he obviously did later on.

**IDLE:** Gilliam is one of the most manipulative bastards in that group of utterly manipulative bastards. Michael is a selfish bastard, Cleese a control freak, Jonesy is shagged out and now forgets everything, and Graham as you know is still dead. *I* am the only real nice one!

*Five Brits and a Yank combine to create one hilarious troupe.*

# THE GROUP DYNAMIC

### Yes! We Are All Individuals!

**CLEESE:** One or two people in the BBC definitely saw me as the mover of the group. The reality was that Terry Jones and I were probably the strongest personalities. The negative side of that is we were probably the two who argued the most, because we *cared* terribly about the material. You could say we were young and naive; writers are like this when they start. The funny thing was, we never argued about the acting. No one ever got into a snit because they hadn't got some role; all the arguments were about the material, and they would sometimes get quite intense and absurdly silly. I remember one sketch, we had a kind of taxidermized animal hanging from the ceiling with four light bulbs in its feet; we got into quite an acrimonious debate about whether it should be a sheep or a goat. And in retrospect it's *hilarious* that we could get cross with each other about

*A typical Python story meeting at Terry Jones' home, at which John Cleese displays his affection for his host.*

whether it should be a sheep or a goat! But we cared so much about the material that we fought quite a lot.

Jones and I would often lock horns and that would create a certain balance, and then the others could jump onto the scale on one side or the other. I didn't find Terry in those days at all easy, although I always liked him fundamentally as a person, because I always felt that he felt strongly about *everything*. And on the whole it's easier to negotiate stuff if people don't feel tremendously strongly about it; you might just say, 'Well, what do *you* think? What do *you* think?' Whereas Terry would forever say, 'Oh, I *really* feel, I *really* feel . . . ,' as though the *intensity* of his feeling was the strongest part of his argument. And I used to find that difficult.

**GILLIAM:** John and Graham wrote contained pieces; they tended to be very confrontational pieces – *bam bam bam!* Eric wrote again his tight things; wordplay was his speciality, I suppose. Mike and Terry tended to be more conceptual in the way they were approaching things, and I fit more in that group with what I was doing.

You've got John and Graham as the centre of one half of the brain, and you've got Mike and Terry as the centre of the other half, and Eric's the individual on that side, and I'm the individual on this side. It's like us on one side who thought in a freer way and those on the other who thought in this more aggressive, defensive way of writing sketches; they're much more the control freaks. I couldn't invent a better balance between us, this Cambridge/Oxford thing – or the tall guys versus the normal-sized guys. Whatever it was, the division was so clear. And Occidental [Gilliam's Los Angeles alma mater] starts with an *Occ* sound – even the first syllable is close enough to *Ox*ford!

Graham in a sense was like a fifth columnist in that group, because Graham was sort of floating out there, but he and John worked well. John always complained but they did work well as a team, because Graham balanced John's anal-ness.

Terry Jones would get incredibly angry about things because John was always trying to control. At the reading out of material, John was like the guy working in the Senate or the House of Commons where you get bills through. John was always very good at that! So there's John kind of manipulating people, and then Terry would get very frustrated because he could see we were being manipulated, and he'd be up in arms, and then the fights would start, and the rest of us could sit back and watch!

And then there's a weird dynamic between Eric and me because we were the two singles in the thing, and there was a sense that *we* shared something in common because we were both outside the two groups. And yet we don't really, we're very opposite, except I think Eric's love of music works well with animation – there's a musical quality in all his stuff and that kind of links [with me] in a strange way: we're the pop video section in the middle!

[You have] John's desperate need for control and Graham's kind of strange inertia floating around, or combination of inertia and chaos and anarchy all in one thing; Graham's *Splunge!* just gets in the way of John's need to control and manipulate. And then Mike balances Terry's passion and his belief [that] he's right; Terry's rightness is like a God-given right, a *righteousness* is what it is. And so Mike being the nicer, gentler guy balances Terry.

You've got the Zealous Fanatic and the Nice Guy, you've got the Control Freak and the *Splunge!*, and then Eric dances around them [as this] verbal chameleon, and then I'm doing this visual dance around it that connects the bits and pieces. I don't think you could invent a group that would work better than we did when we were working well. It's this amazing chemical balance, it's like a proper molecular compound – and Eric and I are the free radicals!

Those are the things that always intrigue me, how it came together – it's not like anybody *planned* it. The thing with *Saturday Night Live* was Lorne Michaels planned it, it's not a patch on *Python*, I don't think. I mean, wonderful, wonderful stuff, but it's much more of a packaged programme. And ours was this organic growth.

What was interesting about that chemistry was, after a while, you couldn't tell who wrote a sketch at a certain point. After a while Mike and Terry started writing things like John, and my cartoons were much influenced by what they were writing. Then suddenly the live-action stuff started looking like the cartoons! It was all blending in different ways, and that was really intriguing.

**IDLE:** I suspect these glib sub-divisions of Python. I like words, but John and Graham liked words, too – look at the 'Dead Parrot' sketch, which is pure Roget!

**JONES:** As we wrote on, we started parodying each other. Mike and I wrote a parody of one of John and Graham's sketches. Because of things like the 'Dead Parrot' sketch, which is basically straight out of the thesaurus, we wrote a parody of it, an 'Astrology Sketch' ('. . . the zodiacal signs, the horoscopic fates, the astrological portents, the omens, the genethliac prognostications . . .'). Mike read this out and everybody laughed and it went in, and we were just amazed because we'd written it as a *joke*, really. We thought they'd go, 'Oh come on! Get away! Making fun of *our* writing?' But we were quite surprised that it actually got into the show! They all thought it was funny, so we didn't say, '*Actually* it was just a parody of one of *yours*.' I kept a bit quiet, and it got into the Yes Pile.

And then John and Graham began writing slightly more visual things, so there was a bit of a crossover there. It became more difficult to recognize each other's material.

**IDLE:** People would begin to notice certain traits about each other's work, like Mike and Terry always starting off with long pans across the countryside, or a typical John and Graham confrontational opening. They would then parody [the others'] work in their own. This, too, was a useful form of criticism.

You must remember we were like a family. Sure, there were arguments and disagreements, of course we could say nasty things about our work, but this was the liberty: to be ruthlessly honest – we were not carrying any passengers. No allowance had to be made, or adjustments for people's feelings. By and large this worked; where there was a blockage or impasse, usually a third way would miraculously emerge. At these moments no one could ever remember who made the suggestion.

Jonesy is stubborn, John controlling, Mike affable, Eric suspicious of authority, and Gilliam incomprehensible, with the doctor as an emollient. It was a fine mix of good British chaps (and a Yank) who just got on with it. When we got to the States, we were amazed to find they assumed we wrote it out of our minds on drugs – as if anyone *could* successfully write stoned. (See *Saturday Night Live* and Hunter S. Thompson.) When you're stoned it's hard to find the keys to the typewriter. Actually we always worked office hours: nine to five with a break for lunch. Even in the West Indies!!

The criticism and encouragement was the best. I have never experienced anything like it before or since. It is still the standard by which I judge collaboration. You could say the honest truth about what other people had written; there were no polite solecisms. As Lenny Bruce said, 'You cannot fake a laugh.'

It was like a senior common room in this respect. The *métier* was taken seriously. We were very serious about our work, but we laughed like fuck.

*How did the group dynamic on Python differ from what you'd experienced working on other series?*

**JONES:** I suppose the great thing was that we all liked each other's work, so we all had a respect for what the others did. So therefore you really *wanted* to make the others laugh, and yet at the same time we respected each other's criticisms. So if they thought it wasn't funny, you'd think, 'Phew, that was a bit of luck, we might have tried to *do* that!' I mean, occasionally there was something you really thought was funny and you thought, 'They haven't *got* it.' I suppose the best example of that was a late one from *The Meaning of Life*, the 'Mr Creosote' sketch, the fat man in the restaurant, which was something I'd written. Mike and I both thought it was our funniest piece. And we saved it up for after lunch! Mike hit them with it first thing after lunch, and nobody thought it was funny; it got thrown out. And then about a month later, John rang up and said, 'Hello, this is something that will bring a little smile to your face: I've just been looking at that "Mr Creosote" sketch, I think it could be quite funny.' What John had realized I think was that the funniest part there was the waiter. And he and Graham came up with the idea of the 'wafer-thin mint'. So that got rescued. In a way it's the only real collaboration between me and John, in writing terms.

Generally when the group didn't like the thing, you felt, 'That won't be right then.'

**CLEESE:** You see, you become very pragmatic in comedy. I really mean this: comedy is what people laugh at. And if you come in with a piece of material you think is very funny and you read it out to the Python group and they didn't laugh much, you didn't think there was anything wrong with the group; you thought there was something wrong with the material.

I think we were much more tightly bound than the *Frost Report* group. When you read material out to *The Frost Report* there were so many more people sitting around the table, there wasn't the sense that we were a group, or a 'band of brothers', whereas there was in Python.

### *Do you recall a particular criticism of the group's that you didn't agree with?*

**JONES:** The 'Spam' sketch, the one in the restaurant with 'Spam Spam Spam Spam Spam . . .' and the Vikings. We read it out and everybody laughed, and then John and Graham said they'd like to work on it, they thought they could *improve* it a bit. And so they took it away and rewrote it, and they kind of rationalized it somehow – they made it more *logical*. And it lost the rhythm, it was a rhythm piece, really. Mike and I thought, 'This isn't as funny.' Actually there was no discussion about it – Michael and I just substituted our original sketch.

### *How was responsibility within the group taken or shared?*

**PALIN:** Terry J. was always incredibly keen to involve everybody in everything. He is the most open of people, and yet has this very strong feeling that he knows how to do it. So that makes it slightly complicated; he'd love people to come in and have a look, but basically, Terry had a very, very strong idea about how a thing should be, so he wasn't always as sort of altruistic as he was before. Yes, he was anxious that everybody should be happy with what was being done, but once you have that responsibility of directing, you end up doing much more of the work while the others go off and do their other things.

This had happened much earlier, on the records and the books. It was divided up as to who should do what; Terry Jones and myself went to records and almost exclusively were the ones who got those together, and

Eric was the editor of the books. If somebody didn't take on that role, things would never get done.

*Were those jobs taken on by choice, or by*
*default because no one else was interested?*

**PALIN:** Well, a bit of both: by default because no one else was particularly interested in doing all the work in putting albums together, but also by choice because there was a feeling where we knew how we could do it best. And I had a recording studio, I'd invested in Redwood Recording Studios with André Jacquemin, our engineer, so there was some interest there.

But I think it was largely again to do with commitment to the group. Terry was totally committed to the group, and I was working with Terry, therefore I was doing a lot of work in conjunction with Terry. John was not committed to the group; John didn't really care whether albums were made. I think he was very happy to contribute, and he was extremely happy when they were successful, [but] John was looking elsewhere; he had *Fawlty Towers* on his mind at that time. And Eric's interest was the book, and that was marvellous; Eric took on the editing, getting the material together, discussing with the rest of us what the book might be, suggesting an idea, getting sessions together, which would never have happened if he hadn't done it; again, that was Eric's choice.

But the feeling I had was it was always Eric and Terry and myself who could see the potential in Python, all the other things that could be done. I don't think John ever really believed it.

**IDLE:** The first Python book Gilliam wouldn't help at all, just grumbled, so I got a friend to raid his house and steal some of his illustrations. I then wrote up some of the sketches in other forms.

I enjoy working on my own on Python material. I love playing with form, putting different types of paper in the book and frightening the publisher. I would then send some of the stuff to the others, who would realize they had better actually contribute *something* or this book would go out without much of their stuff in, and then they would. Sort of the same thing I tried with the website, Pythonline. Will I ever learn?

*Why do you think Python humour is so idiosyncratic, even compared to the work done by its members away from the group?*

**PALIN:** I think there's a danger in Pythons analysing their own work. I think we shouldn't do it. Anyone else wants to do it, that's fine. I sort of feel we produced the material, it's out there; once one tries to sort of analyse *why* we're funny, I think it's – I think it's *impossible* to answer for a start, and also I think once we unpick ourselves and give guidelines, in a sense it takes away from the audience their choice of how they react to Python.

And also the joke is so many different things. In Python it isn't just the words; maybe 70 per cent are the words and maybe 10 per cent are a sort of look or gesture, something that just happened on that particular recording. There's the mystery of it. There were certain things which happened, you know. You do two takes of things, [and] there would be one which was funny and one which wasn't so funny, for the tiniest of reasons, the tiniest of reasons – just an edge more urgency in a certain one because we'd been told that there was a car coming and we've got to shoot the scene before the car passes, something like that, so there would be an edge to it which may just make it funny whereas if it were just the words it wouldn't have been.

*Despite your differing styles, did you find a common thread among the material that each one of you brought to Python?*

**PALIN:** A strand which I think is in a lot of Python humour, from all the various sources but perhaps particularly from Terry and myself, is human inadequacy – the fact that things don't always work out right. The grander, magnificent scheme which is set up by mere humans, you know, will go wrong. And in a sense the characters which John and Graham have written, like in the 'Dead Parrot' sketch, is just a man giving lots of excuses, and somebody who knows what he wants and not being able to get it. That's a similar kind of humour: you set something up and then some tiny little thing destroys it completely, because that's the way human beings are. I mean, you can be in a solemn occasion where trumpets play, something like that, [then] someone farts at the back, and *immediately* the atmosphere collapses. Because we are all on the edge of awareness of absurdity. It's just a nice vein we used to tap.

In *Holy Grail* that's constantly happening to Arthur and his troupe; they'd be very kingly and yet something would happen, they'll talk to some toiling peasant in this very hail-fellow way: 'Old man, tell us the way.'

'I'm thirty-seven, I'm not *old*.'

'Yes, okay, we don't want to get into that . . .'

I think that's a great strand of humour, which is dragging all those pretensions down to a certain level.

*Arthur's being inconvenienced, and has to come up with ways to deal with that.*

**PALIN:** Yes, I think we were quite fond of that, Terry and myself. But John and Graham also wrote that in their sketches, as did Eric. It was a very common Python thread.

But I think Terry and myself had a more visual sense – this is a slightly simplified way of saying it. John and Graham very much concentrated on a particular exchange: a war of words between characters was important to them, the wonderful logicality of it. John and Graham were not really interested in how you would build up a grand sequence. I *love* the start of movies, those magnificent tracking shots – so does Terry – the things you can do with a camera and a landscape and people and all that, and it seemed wonderful that we could do it with Python – more on the films than on the television series, because we had control – [where] we could play these wonderful jokes. We could have *boom!* '34 A.D.' comes up. 'Just after tea time.' '. . . Well, *almost* tea time.' Then things would be ~~crossed out~~ on the screen.

John and Graham were not particularly interested in *where* a sketch was set; it was usually an office or behind a counter of a shop somewhere. It would be a superb sketch, but the visual side didn't matter to them that much.

**JONES:** As soon as you start to try and analyse, ask why it works, why it doesn't work, you can't do it anymore. The only reason for Python is to be *funny*. I suppose if you have a consistent outlook and point of view, your attitudes come over even if you are writing nonsense, but there is certainly no conscious effort to put over a message.

✻ ✻ ✻

# AND NOW FOR SOMETHING COMPLETELY . . . THE SAME?

## I'VE HAD AN IDEA FOR THE NEXT MOVIE I'M GOING TO PRODUCE AND I WANT YOU BOYS TO WRITE IT

---

In 1970 the group formed a joint venture, Python Productions Ltd., with the intention to further exploit their material in other media and markets, including the cinema.

---

**CLEESE:** Victor Lownes, head of Playboy in London, called me and said, 'Would you like to come and have lunch?' And at the lunch, he said, 'I've just been watching *Python*' – these were the first episodes – 'I think it's the funniest thing I've seen on television for years, but American television is much too conservative to put this stuff out. But there are two thousand college cinemas and this stuff will be wonderful for American college students, so let's make a movie.'

Victor put half the money up and he found someone else to put up the other half.

**MACNAUGHTON:** I had to ask permission from the BBC to be allowed to take eight weeks off, unpaid leave, to do it. The BBC were happy to do that and that was quite nice. I was lucky.

All the studio work was done in an old milk depot in North London, and then of course there was lots of exteriors in and around London. It was not an expensive production by any means. And of course it got the boys all a tremendous liking for film.

Nobody had the time to write new material – they wanted the picture at *this* date – but there were a few sketches that were going into the second series which we incorporated into the script for the film. For instance, the 'Hungarian Phrasebook', which appears in the second series, appeared first in *And Now for Something Completely Different*.

I found it very interesting to do because film was different from television, totally different. I mean, the 'Hell's Grannies' on television is totally different-looking from the 'Hell's Grannies' in the film. You've got longer takes, you've got a wider screen, it was all very interesting to do.

The funny thing is at the same time Playboy was putting money into Roman Polanski's *Macbeth*. Now, I think Playboy is still making a little money out of *And Now for Something Completely Different*, but they're not doing a penny out of *Macbeth*, I don't know. That's nothing to do with Shakespeare, by the way!

*'The Upper Class Twit of the Year Show'.*

*The 'Dirty Fork' sketch.*

**JONES:** John's chum Victor Lownes put the money up to do the film on the condition that we'd put in sketches he'd seen on TV and knew were funny. The criteria that was sort of handed down to us was it should be stuff that Vic had seen and heard the studio audience laughing at. And in the end I thought it was not a very good selection of material, because you end up sort of John and Mike doing sketches across a desk from each other.

The sets looked a bit tacky, I thought, on the film. And the sound quality is a little bit odd at times, a bit echoey [because] we built these sets in an old dairy. I don't think the film is much of an improvement. But no, we were not trying to shoot it differently, very much the idea was to shoot this for the American audience. And Vic wanted to call it *And Now for Something Completely Different,* which we thought was a bit corny, but we said as long as it's not shown over here we don't mind. And then of course it came out over here, and it was all the old sketches that everybody had seen on TV, so we got a lot of stick for it – especially for *calling* it *And Now for Something Completely Different*!

**CLEESE:** I do remember an extraordinary experience: the first time we showed *And Now for Something Completely Different*, there was hilarious laughter up to fifty minutes, then the audience went quiet for twenty, twenty-five minutes, and then they came up again and finished very well. So we took all that middle material, put it at the beginning, and it all worked beautifully up to about fifty minutes, and then [the] audience got quiet! We discovered that whatever order we put the material in, at about fifty minutes they stopped laughing. And in order to get people to go with you past the fifty-minute mark they have to want to know what's going to happen next. In other words, you have to have characters that they care about and a story they can enjoy and believe in. There's a huge learning curve.

**JONES:** There was actually an instance where I can remember learning something – and that was when we had the 'Dirty Fork' sketch, the waiter comes in and commits suicide and everything. We'd done it on TV and it had been really funny, and we redid it – same sketch, same actors – and we showed it at some Odeon somewhere, and nobody laughed. I thought it was really weird, we'd *seen* people laugh before and it doesn't get a titter, and the only thing I could see was that Ian had put a muzak track over it, sort of posh restaurant muzak, and I thought maybe that's just filling in all the gaps and just obliterating the film. We took the muzak off and then, when we showed it, people laughed at the sketch again.

**CLEESE:** It was extraordinary because the movie was a complete flop in America; some idiot designed a poster with a happy snake with a funny hat on, and the adults looked at it and thought, 'Kids' movie', and nobody went. In fact, I believe the movie took in less than they spent on advertising – it was a total disaster. But it went well in England, where the sketches had already been transmitted, so it was all very scrambled!

In the second series of *Monty Python's Flying Circus*, the group was even more confident and daring than in their first series, as evident in both the tightness of the editing and the breadth of their material. From the first show broadcast in September 1970 (in which Idle moderates a discussion of public housing between Chapman – 'who is wearing a striking organza dress' – and a small patch of brown liquid), the second series avoided entirely the 'sophomore jinx', thus ensuring the Pythons' position as Britain's leading comic masters.

Among the highlights were Cleese's infamous turn as the Minister of Silly Walks; the Spanish Inquisition, whose diabolical members burst in on the scene to persecute heresy – which they do by banishing their victims to 'the Comfy Chair'; two Pepperpots musing about the penguin on top of their television ('If it came from the zoo it would have *Property of the Zoo* stamped on it'); figures from paintings going on strike to protest conditions at the National Gallery ('Dad, it's the man from *The Hay Wain* by Constable here to see you!'); and the infamous 'Undertaker' sketch. Among Gilliam's more surreal animated bits were 'Conrad Poohs and His Dancing Teeth', 'Killer Cars', and some wonderfully macabre examples of cannibalism.

## WENN IST DAS NUNSTÜCK GIT UND SLOTERMEYER?

In 1971, the Pythons produced the first of two shows for Bavarian television. Very close in style to the BBC series (except that both episodes were entirely shot on film, with no performances before a studio audience), *Monty Python's Fliegender Zirkus* was mostly original material with only a few hints of their BBC work (for example, Michael Palin sings 'Lumberjack Song' in German).

*Cleese and Palin on the same side of a desk, in* Monty Python's Fliegender Zirkus.

The lack of a live audience reveals how effective was the Pythons' skill in front of an audience, and that audience is missed here. But there are compensating pleasures, including a nod to the Munich Olympic games (featuring such track events as the 100-Yards for People with No Sense of Direction); a football match between Greek and German philosophers; a study of grizzled old men panning – Klondike-style – for chickens; and 'Little Red Riding Hood', featuring Cleese as the diminutive heroine. Some of the material has been screened during breaks in the Pythons' stage shows, and a fairy tale co-written by Cleese and his then-wife Connie Booth was included on *Monty Python's Previous Record*.

*The 'Bavarian Restaurant' sketch from* Monty Python's Fliegender Zirkus.

**MACNAUGHTON:** Michael Mills, who was head of comedy at that time, put a compilation of sketches from our first series into the Montreux Festival and it was reasonably successful. The only thing was that during this little film of ours with all the strange pictures of torpedoes coming out of ships and all that stuff over a supposed sex scene between Terry Jones and Carol Cleveland, the Italian delegation called it obscene and walked out!

And at Montreux that year was Alfred Biôlek, who was a producer from Bavaria Films. He phoned me up in London and said, 'What would you think of doing a show in conjunction with a Dutch group?' I asked the boys and they said, 'No, in conjunction with another group? We're not very happy,' and I said, 'I'm not either.' So I told Biôlek this on the phone, and he said, 'Can you come to a meeting at Bavaria Studios?' I had a weekend off and I went to this meeting and we agreed then that we would do our first *Monty Python's Fliegender Zirkus*.

The boys then came across the next time and we all went around in a bus, looking for locations and giving them – and me – a feeling of what it was like there, and then off we went home and they wrote. We didn't like dubbing, so they all decided to learn German themselves, and do the whole first show in German. So every night when they were filming we'd sit with Alfred Biôlek and parrot-wise learn the German for the English sketches they'd written, and we did it and were all quite happy with it. It *sounded* like Englishmen speaking German, but why not?

**JONES:** We sort of gaily said, 'Oh, we'll learn it phonetically.' It was only when we were doing the first shot when the full impact of what we were trying to do suddenly hit us, when Mike was having to be an Australian talking about the *hinterbacken das ein kangaroo* – the rectum of a kangaroo – and realizing you had to talk Parrot German with an Australian accent! We suddenly realized we had bitten off more than we could chew, that we were in for it.

We had no idea, either; we kept asking our translator, 'Was that all right? Is it *funny*, can you understand this?' I think only a certain amount was understandable!

**MACNAUGHTON:** And then they asked us to do the second one in 1972. They said, 'Would you please do it in English?' And I asked, 'Is it because the German was so bad?' And they said, 'No, but we couldn't *sell* it!' They only sold it to a couple of countries – England, and I think one other. So we did the next one in English and they sold it all over the place.

> *Did the producers place any restrictions on the material, or request that the content be specifically geared towards a German audience?*

**JONES:** Not really. I think we just did the same things that we do anyway. We were doing a little bit of German content, like the 'Bavarian Restaurant' sketch – that was because we were shooting it in Bavaria – and things about Albrecht Dürer.

**MACNAUGHTON:** They read all the stuff that the boys had put together and there was no objection. Biôlek was a great fan, and so the nonsensical things (such as the production of 'The Merchant of Venice' by the Cows of the Bad Tolz Dairy Herd), you know, a normal producer reading that sketch would have gone nuts! Biôlek knew the kind of thing we were doing, and he said, 'Go ahead,' which I thought was splendid, actually.

People here now say that it was much too soon for Germany. I don't know whether it was or not; it had the sort of response that we had at the very beginning in London. It was cultish, if you like; there was a certain group who loved it. But it's interesting that someone in England is now putting out a video of these two German productions, because they talk about them as the 'Lost *Pythons*'. Well, they never were *lost,* quite honestly. *I* have them!

# BE CAREFUL: YOU KNOW WHAT
# HE'S LIKE AFTER A FEW NOVELS

The challenge of adapting sketches to print form was especially attractive to Idle, who first suggested the possibility of a book, and who took the job of editor. *Monty Python's Big Red Book* (1971), whose cover was blue, was followed by *The Brand New Monty Python Bok* (1973), whose smudged cover fooled more than one into thinking the dirty fingerprints could be wiped off. (This hardcover 'bok' was later reissued as a 'papperbok'.)

The Pythons also adapted to recordings quite well. (After an initial recording with BBC Records of some of their first-series material, the group signed with Charisma Records.) In addition to some of their more memorable sketches from the TV show and highlights from their films, there were new effects-driven skits (revealing the sound of a cockroach sneezing magnified sixty million times) and musical numbers ('We Love the Yangtse', 'Eric the Half a Bee'). A memorable mix of effects and music was 'The Background to History', a lecture programme comprised of historians singing about medieval farming practices overlaid with diving aircraft. Another sketch demonstrated wonderful Python logic by featuring a news broadcast documenting a solar eclipse – not exactly subject matter best suited for an aural medium!

Conceptually, the most notorious record put out by Python was *Matching Tie and Handkerchief* (1973), the world's first three-sided LP (courtesy of a pair of grooves stamped on one side; however the phonograph needle fell determined which 'side' you would hear).

For the most part the records were engineered at Redwood Recording Studios, but not exclusively . . .

**GILLIAM:** André Jacquemin, who was the engineer involved with all our stuff, worked in his garden shed, and he had a four-track tape recorder and I had my two-track stereo, and we couldn't actually stand up all the way in his shed, so we were all crouching, and we were doing the whole thing like that.

*You recorded the album . . . in the shed?*

**GILLIAM:** In the shed! A lot of the stuff had been recorded in proper sort of things, but not all of it, we were still recording some of it in the shed and then piecing it all together. That's the great fun of Python: we were doing television stuff, we were doing records, we were doing books, we were doing stage shows, and we were able to teach ourselves all these jobs. And it was exciting because we didn't know where it was all leading, it was just good fun, and we were having a wonderful time just being silly, making ourselves laugh.

And it was strange because we'd been doing Python for so long in a sense before we really took off. When I met the guys who do the animated series *South Park* at Aspen a year ago, it was a couple of pieces of paper, and now they've got sixty animators working with them. That's what happens in the States: when suddenly something catches on, it balloons so out of control I think you burn out, you get destroyed. You may not get destroyed *economically*, you may become more famous and richer, but something dies. And with Python it was never like that, because we were just doing thirteen shows at a time. There was never a sense of 'Wow, it's happening, let's go and capitalize on this!' I think being in England allowed for our own unwillingness to be capitalized upon.

Talking about *Saturday Night Live,* as soon as one of the names became big, someone like Chevy Chase, he was popped out, he's got separate management, he's got his career. Then John Belushi and Danny Aykroyd pop out, and then Bill Murray, whatever, they're all divided up very quickly, shared out amongst many financial advisors and agents and lawyers [until] these shells, these organisms cluster around these little bits of talent, separate them from each other, and make millions and millions – and *they* die. They're totally neutered now, they're useless, they're not serving a function anymore because they're not outside, they're not angry, they're not attacking. At least John Belushi had the grace to get out!

We just stayed together, plowed on, doing the stuff and not churning it out too fast, and not being greedy, not wanting to rush off and make a fortune. I still think that's one of the great strengths of the group – that we did that for so long.

And then as life went on and we started separating and people were paid more money, they seem to get more greedy. That's what money does, it makes you want *more* money; it has this addictive quality.

Comedians should be kept outside of decent society. We'll scream and shout. I mean we're still doing rather well; you can't complain about this [*indicates his home in Highgate*], but *I* can!

❂ ❂ ❂

# FEAR AND LOATHING AT THE BBC

## I'LL DO WHAT I LIKE BECAUSE I'M SIX FOOT FIVE AND I EAT PUNKS LIKE YOU FOR BREAKFAST

In December 1971, the Pythons began recording their third series of shows for the BBC. The budgets for the programmes had risen, which was reflected in more ambitious location filming, including a Pepperpot selling tea and cakes to passing ships in a storm-tossed sea. More importantly, the Pythons reached for ever-further creative limits, taking greater risks in terms of subject matter and narrative development.

Series highlights included: 'Njorl's Saga', an Icelandic historical epic hijacked by small-town business interests promoting invest-ment in North Malden; 'Argument Clinic', where Palin is subjected to a variety of abuses (at a cost); 'Cheese Shop', where Cleese's customer is constantly thwarted from being able to purchase any sort of 'cheesy comestibles'; 'Dennis Moore', the misguided high-wayman; 'Fish Slapping Dance', a wonderfully nonsensical performance piece in which Palin and Cleese duel with fish; the 'Oscar Wilde' sketch, in which Wilde, James McNeill Whistler, and George Bernard Shaw trade *bons mots*; *Salad Days* as interpreted by director Sam Peckinpah, of *Wild Bunch* fame; and 'The Cycling Tour', a half-hour adventure in which a cyclist touring North Cornwall crosses paths with Soviet agents, Chinese bingo enthusiasts, and a man convinced he is singing star Clodagh Rodgers.

For purely surrealist ideas, there is little to beat the sketch of a city gent (Jones) who makes people laugh uncontrollably just by uttering a word. Let go from his firm because of the debilitating effect he has on his co-workers, he pours out his soul to his manager, even threatening suicide, while his boss is reduced to hysterical fits of laughter.

Despite the high level of quality, there were signs of disharmony both from within the group and from the upper strata of the BBC. Although John Cleese was still writing and performing, he had already indicated to the others that he was looking elsewhere, precipitating greater tensions in the group.

More germane to the success of the shows at that point, however, was the group's handling of the BBC's increased interest in what was being put out. Never an organization to intrude on the Pythons' creativity before, the BBC's management were now making their presence felt, resulting in censorship battles behind the scenes which descended at times into a sort of illogic most fitting for Python.

*Palin and Idle filming 'The Cycling Tour'.*

**CLEESE:** I loved the first series and thoroughly enjoyed it, and I very much enjoyed the first half of the second series. I was worried by the time we got to the second half of the second series that we were repeating ourselves, though it didn't seem to be a worry that bothered the others at all. I didn't really want to do the third series because I felt it was getting like a sausage machine; I mean we were just turning the handle and shows were coming out the other end, and I didn't feel anymore a sense of excitement or that we were really exploring new territory. And when I said this to the others, that I really wasn't very keen on doing the third series, they simply didn't take it seriously. It was as though they felt I was posturing – I don't know what that effect would be, but the real truth was I felt that we were just repeating ourselves. I agreed rather begrudgingly to do a half series, six or seven episodes. I didn't really want to do it but I felt since everyone asked me I would, and then I remember they really just ruthlessly put the pressure on me to do the whole series.

*Did they try to make you feel guilty for wanting to leave the group?*

**CLEESE:** Yeah, that sort of thing, and they were more or less going ahead rather as though I didn't have objections. Nobody ever sat down and said, 'What's really bothering you?' or 'Why don't you want to?' I just felt that I wasn't being heard.

But my strong feeling in the third series was that we'd really run out of original momentum. Quite by the middle of the second series, when people read out sketches (including those by Graham and myself), I would be able to say, 'Well, that sketch was show one of the first series plus a bit of that sketch from the other show for the first series plus a bit of that sketch from the second series.' I could see that they were beginning to derive from the material we had done previously, and in the third series I'm quite clear that there were only two really original bits that Graham and I wrote: one of them was the highwayman, Dennis Moore (which I thought was genuinely original), and the other was 'Cheese Shop'. Almost everything else I could point to and say, 'This derives from that.' And unless you're short of money, I don't see the point of doing that, it isn't interesting. But the others simply liked the process; you see, I didn't. Going into the smelly old hall that we used to go to every day and rehearse week after week after week. I get very easily bored; I need the sense that I'm learning or creating, and if I'm not doing one or the other I tend to get bored.

*'The Cycling Tour' was the first Python show to be comprised of one long extended skit. How did that develop?*

**PALIN:** I really don't know quite why something like 'The Cycling Tour' was as long as it was. There had been germs of that in some of the early sketches: for instance, the tennis-playing blancmange and the Podgorny family. What would happen is you have nice characters who then could crop up during the programme, so suddenly more and more seemed to revolve around these two characters. And I suppose that 'The Cycling

Tour' was a supreme example of stretching characters right out through a programme, which we then touch on all sorts of things – China, for one – so Mr Pither (who was the bicycle man) became almost like a linking device that took over the show. Linking devices were usually quite short; it'd be a colonel who'd come on and say, 'Right, stop that, very silly.' But with Mr Pither, he would appear at various moments during the show [and] these mentions would be much longer, they'd be little adventures in themselves. I'm not quite sure how that particularly happened; it might have been that Terry and myself had had a good writing week that week and John and Graham hadn't got the stuff; sometimes that happened. You go, 'This is show nine, you haven't got anything? Well, if we do the whole bicycle tour that's almost the [whole] show.'

And then of course 'Mr Neutron', that came in the series which John didn't write much on. By that time Terry Jones and myself were getting more keen on longer narrative, I suppose because 'The Cycling Tour' had worked well, but [also] because when you invent good characters it's a pity to lose them. Let's keep them going and weave the story around *them* rather than weave *them* around lots of sketches.

I understand why it happened; we were interested in the narrative for the films, because we took a conscious decision that films can't just be sketches – there's got to be some story, otherwise people would get bored stiff of just sketches. Certainly after fifty minutes you start to lose them; you've got to have characters that go through. That's a very conscious decision, which is why the Knights of the Round Table was something we thought to be an excellent vehicle.

# THE BBC WOULD LIKE TO APOLOGIZE TO EVERYONE IN THE WORLD FOR THE LAST ITEM

It seemed only a matter of time before the brazen Pythons would find themselves butting heads with the more conservative elements of the BBC. In the early-Seventies the BBC was facing a more spirited organized public outcry (from politicians and from self-appointed moral guardians like Mary Whitehouse, who formed the National Viewers' and Listeners' Association) against a seeming loosening of responsibility in the broadcast media. Eager to deflect criticism and to protect itself from the yoke of an outside overseer authority, the corporation began to take greater interest in programming before it was broadcast, engendering a more divisive atmosphere with creatives.

But while the spirit of pushing barriers of popularly accepted limits on good taste was a hallmark of the Pythons' work, the bureaucracy of the BBC that sought to reinforce those limits only demonstrated why constricting societal attitudes were such an evergreen target for the group's humour. As Robert Hewison

'*Sam Peckinpah's* Salad Days'.

noted in his definitive account of the group's censorship battles, *Monty Python: The Case Against*, 'Six angry, arrogant Pythons were usually a match for the BBC.' Indeed, engaging in internal censorship battles would merely toughen their skin for their future, more public confrontations against the moral police attacking their film *Life of Brian*.

**MACNAUGHTON:** One time Duncan Wood[*] said, 'Do come down. I want you to see an episode you've just done in my office.' We sat and watched it, and it was quite funny, I thought. It stopped, and Duncan said, 'How do you get away with this?' I said, 'I don't know, but listen to the audience in this studio, they seem to like it!' And it was that attitude – *I wonder how the hell they get away with it?* – which I think was a bit silly, quite honestly. They should have been happy to have an audience roaring with laughter!

**CLEESE:** You can always inject a bit of energy into something by introducing anger, shouting, bad language, or something shocking. Young comedians know this, and that is why very frequently they seem to be thrashing around, because if the material isn't very good you have two alternatives: one is you die, and the other is you thrash around – and on the whole, thrashing around is less humiliating.

David Attenborough, a man I much admire, said to me after the first series of *Python,* the best advice I ever had: 'use shock sparingly'. If you start using it too much, then it becomes the norm, and it isn't shocking anymore, and then you just seem to be thrashing around. The great thing is to use it very, very sparingly, like that wonderful conversation in *Life of Brian*, with all that stuff about, 'Tell us, Master, tell us!' Brian says, 'I'm not the saviour!' Somebody says, 'Only the saviour would deny his

---

[*]   A producer and one-time head of comedy.

own divinity.' So he says, 'All right, I *am* the saviour!' They all go, 'Ahh, he is the saviour!' And he says, 'Now, *fuck off!*' That's a wonderful use of real shock; we weren't using bad language before that so it really *hits* you.

We did one show where Michael, running in at the end dressed up in the 'Spanish Inquisition', was saying, 'Oh, bugger', when the end title went up. Michael Mills said afterwards that there was no way that he could ever have agreed to that in the script stage, but when he saw it on-screen it was so funny he knew no one would complain.

And in the particular case of the 'Undertaker' sketch ('I think we've got an eater!'), yes, there was on that one occasion a deliberate attempt to play with the idea of how shocking it would be. It was the thirteenth show of the second series, we'd been churning stuff out for seven months, and I think Graham and I had a feeling it was 'end of term'. We thought it would be fine to end the series on something fairly shocking, and I'm very grateful that the BBC let us do it.

**JONES:** Huw Wheldon, who was in control of BBC1, and David Attenborough, who was in control of BBC2 in the late Sixties, were both very enlightened men. I remember their saying that the BBC was very much an anarchic organization in a way, in that there was very little bureaucracy, very little personnel management. This tiny office was the personnel management, which now I think is a whole building!

In those days, the producers were the top dogs, and there were producer/directors; they decided what was going to go on the air and they took responsibility for it. I remember Wheldon saying the BBC takes great pride in not censoring itself; the producers are responsible, and the producers are all very carefully selected people who were tenured BBC staff. They would discuss projects with their heads of department, and they'd say, 'I want to do this', and they generally would be given a go-ahead. They then would make the shows and the heads of departments would deliberately not look at shows before they went out. They would see the shows when they were aired, and then there would be a weekly departmental meeting and the shows would be discussed at the meeting, and if somebody objected to something that had gone out, then the producer would be asked to account for himself and would be carpeted or something. But it was all *post*, there was no censorship at all.

This changed.

We started seeing it changing in *Python*. When the first and second series went out, nobody ever looked at the shows or anything until they went out. In the last episode we had the 'Undertaker' sketch, which was a gross breach of good taste! Ian didn't want to do it at all; we bamboozled him and persuaded him that if we had the audience revolting against the thing, then that would be all right, and he agreed to do it like that. Which is a bit of a pity; it ruined the sketch, really, because we had to do this shouting through the sketch ('Let's have something decent!'). And I think Ian really got carpeted for that. And then [for] the next series, they wanted to look at the shows *before* they went out.

**MACNAUGHTON:** I think we'd finished the last three of the third series. I was called in to the boss' office and told that these three episodes could not go out, could *never* go out. And I said, 'Why not?' And he said, 'Well, there are things in there we don't like. For instance, the "Prince of Wales and Oscar Wilde" sketch: in the middle of that somebody said, "Your Majesty is like a dose of the clap." We don't like any of that stuff, we don't want any of that in.' They made about eighteen points that they wanted to cut, and they said, 'We'll reedit the three programmes and you'll maybe get one or two [shows] out of it.'

**JONES:** That was when we got the list of things we had to take out [which became known as 'Thirty-Two Points of Worry']. One of them was in the 'Summarized Marcel Proust Competition', somebody saying his hobbies were 'strangling animals, golf, and masturbating'. And we had to cut out 'masturbating'! Very bizarre. I remember going to Duncan Wood – he was then head of comedy – and I said, 'Duncan, what's wrong with masturbating? *I* masturbate. *You* masturbate, don't you, Duncan?' And Duncan goes, *'Oh, uh, uh . . . !'* Anyways, it had to come out.

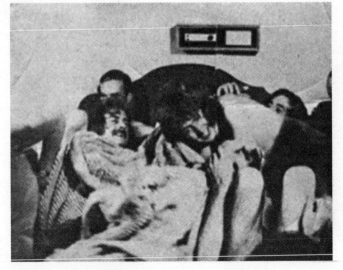

*Filming* 'Wife Swapping'.

Some of the other [demands] were things that they'd made up. They said, 'You must remove the giant penis that John holds around the door.' What on earth are they talking about? Had a look at it – it was actually a *severed leg* that somebody had to sign in the 'Curry's Brains' sketch. It was just they weren't looking very carefully!

**GILLIAM:** It was the most incredible demonstration, just shocking to see how their minds work, because they were truly sick people!

One [of their objections] was the 'Wee-Wee' sketch. Eric's offering Terry Jones some wine; he doesn't say it's wine, he just says, 'Will you taste this?' And he drinks what appears to be white wine: 'Hmm, that's a Talbot 1963?'

'Ah no, monsieur, that was wee-wee.'

It went on: 'That's a Chablis?'

'No, monsieur, that too was wee-wee.' It's just a very silly sketch – he's been laying down wee-wee for years!

And on the list of things, 'Now the scene where the man drinks menstrual urine –' *What the fuck are you talking about?* It was the 'Wee-Wee' sketch, because one of the white wines was a very light rosé!

And it went on like this. There were six of us in the room with Duncan, poor guy, and he just became more embarrassed, I think. He just looked more and more like a fool. This [list] had clearly been prepared by somebody else, and he was the one who had to go in and slap these boys down.

*On location shooting Sir Philip Sidney's fight against Tudor pornography.*

**JONES:** Yes, the 'Wee-Wee' sketch. John very much disapproved of the 'Wee-Wee' sketch. We defended it as being extremely silly, and in bad taste – and we couldn't think of anything else! We were running out of material by that time!

**TOOK:** They came to me and said, 'They've got a sketch about drinking urine, what do you think?' And I went, 'Oh God, that sounds awful.' They said, 'What can we do?' I said, 'Well, let them film it and then cut it.' Baron von Took strikes again!

So, they let them shoot the sketch and when it got to the editing, it was cut. You can't do *that* on the screen, anyway. But this was the reaching for the frontiers that had not been explored, the Terry Jones area.

**CLEESE:** I thought the 'Wee-Wee' sketch was a deeply embarrassing piece of material; I was utterly on the side of the BBC censor on that!

I was nearly always – while they would say 'conservative' I would say 'realistic' – about what you could put out on the BBC. I thought the BBC were *terrific*. I thought that the amount they messed around with censorship was absolutely minimal, but the others would probably tell you differently – particularly Terry Gilliam, who really does have a problem with any kind of authority of *any* kind; he would probably see them as insensitive monsters who were constantly fucking the show up. And I think that the number of times they insisted on an edit was very, very small, and most of those occasions I *agreed* with. On the whole of *Fawlty Towers* there were only two times Bill Cotton said to me that he was worried about something, and one of them I'd already cut. So I didn't have any problem with their censorship; I thought it was sensible and in tune with my own feeling.

**MACNAUGHTON:** I asked if the boss of BBC1, Paul Fox, had seen these three episodes. And they said, 'Why?' And I said, 'Well, I would like you to let him see them.' And they said, 'All right, but you can't see them with him.' I was very mistrusted!

So two days later came a note from Paul Fox through the head of comedy to me. It said, 'You don't have to cut the three episodes' – he made about four 'suggestions' for small cuts. And over the 'Your Highness is like a dose of the clap,' he wrote in his note, 'I don't much like a dose of the clap, but then, who does?,' which I think was rather a good way to put it. And so we managed to keep these three episodes, which turned out for me to be three of the funniest.

**JONES:** The BBC was changing – it was more sensitive to political pressure – but it felt like special attention was being paid to us because we were 'naughty boys'.

Certainly by the fourth series they wanted to read the scripts before we'd actually made them. So it had all gone full circle.

**TOOK:** I think it frightened the BBC to death, actually: they'd given the Pythons a lot of freedom and by God they'd *used* it! 'Won't do *that* again!'

**GILLIAM:** One time the BBC censored something [that] was on repeats, the 'Black Spot' thing. [*In an animated Gilliam fairy tale in the second series, a handsome young prince discovers a spot on his face. 'Foolishly he ignored it,' chimes the female narrator, 'and three years later he died of cancer.' In later broadcasts the word 'cancer' was replaced with 'gangrene', spoken by a male!*] What is that, gangrene? But it's extraordinary that the word 'cancer' was so frightening to them that they had to cut the word out.

On the *Derek and Clive* albums, Peter Cook and Dudley Moore did one whole sketch about cancer. Everything that was going wrong, he'd say, 'And then she went and it was –'

'Cancer?'

'Cancer.'

'And then the marriage broke up –'

'Cancer?'

'Cancer.' It became very, very funny.

*Gilliam's public service announcement for early detection of ~~cancer~~ gangrene.*

You can talk about cancer in any news programme, but with a cartoon, a comedy show, you can't say *'cancer'*?

To try and keep up with who got in and changed things at what point was always a problem.[*] Now we own all the stuff, so it's all right, except in Britain, where they probably show their version, I don't know. But there was always that kind of meddling that somehow went on there.

---

[*] Not all changes were for potentially offensive material. In the 'Penguin on the Television' sketch, Cleese and Chapman (as Pepperpots) mumble the song 'The Girl from Ipanema'. In repeats, the soundtrack was changed to a single Pepperpot mumbling 'I Dream of Jeannie with the Light Brown Hair'.

*What examples of Python self-censorship are there, apart from cutting something just because you didn't think it was funny?*

**GILLIAM:** There was the religious one where Christ ends up with a telephone linesman on the cross at Calvary. On the reruns John censored that. John really was worried about it; he was very sensitive it might be deemed to be blasphemous. And I can't remember how he was there and nobody else was to stop him cutting it out. Python always had a veto; we vetoed things that couldn't be used, and I suppose John could argue that that was his veto.

I've never talked to him about it. He probably would deny it – he denies *everything*! – but that's the way it was told to me, that it was John who went in and did it. I was pretty shocked that he would have been so offended. He wasn't *offended* – he was nervous or worried. It's kind of like with *Life of Brian,* we cut Otto* out. Even though it was his sketch, Eric was very keen to cut it out, and I think it was because he was living in Hollywood and worried about offending 'Jews who run Hollywood', or because he works in Hollywood and half his friends are Jewish. I don't know, I thought, 'This is crazy. We made a film to offend *everybody*! If we're going to offend the Christians, come on!' We ended up cutting it out because both Terry and I felt dramatically it could go, but I regret cutting Otto because Otto was a really funny idea, a really funny scene – its problem is it just came at the wrong point of the film.

**CLEESE:** Well, I certainly thought we couldn't use that Christ bit. I don't know how [my] cutting that would have worked, because it wasn't as though any one of us had the power of decision, you see what I mean?

**IDLE:** John was a very controlling bastard in those days – four years older than most. [Cutting a scene] is something he would be capable of,

---

* Otto was the head of a crack Semitic suicide squad. In a scene cut from the final film, he demonstrates for Brian just how eagerly his troops will kill themselves for their leader.

*Satan pays a call as Jesus is put on hold, in a cartoon cut from a second series episode.*

but sounds unlikely in this instance; more likely it's Gilliam's paranoia, which has increased with age, and the power of having people listen to him and take him seriously (see *Film Directors and Their Dementia*).

John was instrumental in cutting the 'Wee-Wee' sketch, where he did collude with the BBC because he found it distasteful.

These examples are rare.

The Python veto, which exists, is largely for business purposes, to prevent a majority vote going against individual rights, and operates like the UN (with about the same results).

❋   ❋   ❋

☞

# MONTY PYTHON AND THE HOLY GRAIL

## COME SEE THE VIOLENCE INHERENT IN THE SYSTEM

In the spring of 1974, the Pythons embarked on production of their first 'real' film, a jaunty but painstakingly realized vision of Arthurian Britain. The thin thread of story – the knights of Camelot searching for the Holy Grail – allowed for a joyfully irreverent mixture of comic riffs, mock heroics, and song in which bits and pieces of Arthurian mythology (along with the stale conventions of Hollywood period epics) were all targets for satire.

When appreciating *Holy Grail*, one might keep in mind the state of the British film industry in the mid-Seventies, particularly in the area of comedy. The days of Ealing Studios (which had produced such timeless fare as *The Lavender Hill Mob*, *Kind Hearts and Coronets*, and *The Ladykillers)* had long ended; Richard Lester's Beatles films and the few satiric standouts of the late Sixties

(*Bedazzled* with Peter Cook and Dudley Moore, *The Wrong Box* with Michael Caine) were already in the past. Even the low-budget horror flicks from Hammer and Amicus, which were usually dependable showcases for fun thrills and even artistic ingenuity, had run dry. By the Seventies, British humour (at least to movie audiences abroad) had become typified by the broad antics of the burlesque *Carry On* films, and little else.

With *Holy Grail*, the Pythons were not only able to redefine the limits of narrative structure (basically by ignoring them!), but also to take innovative and unconventional styles of filming (as had become fashionable in television advertising through such directors as Adrian Lyne and Ridley Scott) and apply them to comedy. The smokey landscapes, muddy locations, and naturalistic lighting seem to capture accurately the Middle Ages; costumes and make-up (such as poor dental work) also reflect the concept of characters trying to eke out existence in a harsh world.[*] This, plus the seriousness of Chapman's performance as King Arthur (around whom the craziness circled), made the characters totally understandable to a modern audience – which made all the silly, surreal antics (such as servants clapping coconuts replacing actual horses) all the more acceptable.

Despite the moderate success of *And Now for Something Completely Different* in the UK, it was not a given that the Pythons would be able to translate their humour to the cinema, especially in a format which would not be a transparent series of sketches strung together, like the TV shows. Their struggles for a workable script, for financing, and during filming and post-production belie the seeming effortlessness of the finished product, which is fresh, inventive, unashamedly violent (the menacing Black Knight has all

---

[*] In fact, Terry Jones points out that recent excavations on preserved skeletons from the period actually reveal very strong, healthy teeth; theoretically this is due to the absence of a processed sugar industry a thousand years ago.

his limbs severed but refuses to give up the fight), and pointedly anarchic (even God puts in an appearance, as an eye-rolling cartoon figure).

---

**MARK FORSTATER, PRODUCER:** The Pythons had made *And Now for Something Completely Different*, but they weren't very happy with it, as an experience or as a film. They wanted to make a proper film themselves. And so they showed me the script that they had and asked me if I would be interested in trying to help them put the film together. I think they weren't able to raise finance, because they wanted to make it themselves, and the industry was kind of scared at that idea.

My link goes back to Terry Gilliam in New York in the early Sixties. We met when we both went to some film courses at the City College of New York. We shared a flat for some period of time, then we both left New York and lost touch with each other. I moved to England to go to school, and when I saw his credit for one of his cartoon animations, we made contact again.

There was a point where the Pythons wanted to do some shorts, comedies sponsored by (I think) a shampoo company. Terry introduced me to the other Pythons [during] this period, and they asked me and my partner at the time, Julian Doyle, to make [the] shorts for them. These were really non-broadcast, kind of non-theatrical, corporate-sponsored films – industrials.

**JULIAN DOYLE, PRODUCTION MANAGER:** They were little five-minute internal promotional films for conferences: one was Anita Gibbs, who made toothpaste and hair products and pharmaceutical products, and the other one was Harmony Hairspray. The Pythons were trying to get away from the BBC and start up their own stuff, and the first time they tried to do these short films, they went to a company and ended up with no money. They'd budgeted the thing and gone out of budget and it wasn't any good, and they asked us to come in and cut it. And we came in, cut

*The glamour of filmmaking: Chapman on location in soggy Scotland.*

it for them, and Mark did the production side of it. Terry Jones directed.

**FORSTATER:** Their film project I think was called *Arthur King*, and it had a lot of elements that eventually got written out of the script. They had a contemporary character called Arthur King who was a kind of nebbish, a loser. I can't remember whether it was actually King Arthur or whether it was just King Arthur's relative in the present day. And so there were a lot of contemporary comic scenes with this Arthur King. But that didn't seem to go anywhere; the period scenes seemed to have much more going for them.

After I'd read the script, I met with them and talked about what was working and what wasn't, and so they started a whole new script process.

**JONES:** Originally the script went between the Middle Ages and the twentieth century, and ended with him finding the Holy Grail in Harrods. I was very much into the Middle Ages with my Chaucer stuff, and I had not been very keen on the twentieth-century stuff. Mike had come up with this horse and coconut thing at one stage, and so I suppose in a group meeting I said, 'Why don't we do it *all* Middle Ages?' And everybody seemed to agree. Maybe it was the perception that the modern material wasn't stronger, and also I said it would be more interesting, less like the TV shows, if it's all set in one period.

*The Knights of the Round Table.*

**PALIN:** Terry and I were both interested in history – Terry because he read medieval English and was very interested in Chaucer and all that, and me because I'd done three years of a history degree at Oxford. I was brim-full of all this useless information! We were looking around for the possibility of a film after we'd made *And Now for Something Completely Different*. There was this Arthurian start about swallows and the people at the battlements which caught people's eye, and from then on, yes, the idea of the knights seemed promising. A sort of hiccup from *Complete and Utter History*!

I was more keen on keeping the narrative in the Arthurian world than making jokes about Harrods. I was interested in creating this world and making the convention, the background setting, so convincing that you don't have to defuse it, you don't have to apologize for it, you don't want to *leave* it!

So when we wrote, we found that within these characters we could write material that did not need modern references necessarily but would be modern attitudes – all the stuff about the peasants discussing modern constitutions and how governmental bodies should be. Now that's a modern idea, a Sixties, Seventies concept that you could stay in costume and do it in a field; you didn't have to cut to people around a discussion table. And so once that had been sort of agreed, we were forced to invent things that could happen then and there, lovely things like Tim the Enchanter: that was fine, it didn't need Tim to be a modern character at all.

So in the end maybe those of us who believed you could keep it consistent – do it with comedy but set it in medieval times – won the day.

That use of a surreal device of somebody not really on a horse: I always felt that if you were going to have coconuts instead of horses, what one had to do was keep this conceit going throughout; there was no point in giggling about it. You had to be absolutely serious, so whenever you saw someone doing that [*pantomimes prancing-about behaviour*] they were on horseback and everybody was very serious about it. It's a *ridiculous* thing to do, but then again beautifully played by John and Graham; you absolutely believed that *they* believed that they were on horses. That was much funnier than giggling about it, saying, 'Yeah, they're not *really*.' That went throughout that joke, and it was much the stronger for it.

Again, dress people properly, shoot them against beautiful Scottish backgrounds, with smoke drifting and all that, it makes it so much funnier.

*Plus you save money on horses.*

**PALIN:** Yes, of course, plus the days you spend learning to ride, getting the horses to come back, and doing it all again. That must have been one of those very liberating decisions we had one day.

I don't think anyone else but John and Graham could have written the 'Black Knight' sequence, hacking legs off. That's very Graham-ish, because Graham's a doctor and loved all sorts of visceral ideas like the human body being ripped apart. He and Gilliam love that sort of stuff. And Terry and myself started off writing the peasants in the field – 'I'm

*Cleese as Tim the Enchanter.*

only thirty-seven' – and then John and Graham took it on and did all the stuff about 'moistened bints lying in lakes lobbing swords was no basis for a system of government'. That was theirs at their verbal best. They beefed an idea which we had, which was that people answered back to the king and it was terribly hard for him to be Arthurian!

## IN A VERY REAL AND LEGALLY BINDING SENSE

**JOHN GOLDSTONE, EXECUTIVE PRODUCER:** I had known the Pythons individually [from] about the time when their first television series was being done. When they were looking for money for *Holy Grail*, they approached me with the problem that they were not able to raise the money for the film by any normal means. They had gone to the two major sources of finance in England, Rank and EMI, and neither of them was prepared to take

*It's only a model. Shh!!*

the leap of faith they wanted to make from a television series to this film.

A lot of that was equally to do with the sorry state of the British film industry. There were very few sources of finance, and the kinds of films that were being made were not really very good. It was interesting; at the time foreign sales were not really an important part of anybody's business here. They would make a film based on what it could recoup in England alone. There was a whole slew of films from TV: *On the Buses, Rising Damp.* That was felt to be the safe way to capitalize. And a lot of them did very well – I mean, very modest budgets, it was possible to do that. But it made for very dreary films.

*Was the BBC involved in investing in theatrical versions of television series?*

**GOLDSTONE:** They tended to be ITV series, which had very big audiences. They were showing to eighteen, nineteen, twenty million people, and so the theory was if you only got 10 per cent of that into the cinemas, you could make money. In some cases it's very true, but it's not very inspiring! It was that sort of mentality that didn't want to reckon that Python could be the one that would make the leap across. They saw it as [playing to] a late-night, very alternative audience.

The terrible thing was the original budget was £150,000, and even *that* could not be raised by conventional means. So we capitalized on the fact that there was a lot of support from the music business in Python. Python was much more attuned to rock and roll than it was to British movies, so that's really where the money came from.

**FORSTATER:** Tony Stratton-Smith, who was head of Charisma (which was the Pythons' record group),* was very interested in the film business, and he had given me a number of people to approach who he thought could be interested, like Pink Floyd's management, Led Zeppelin's management, Island Records, independent younger music labels and groups. I think they were all willing to have a go; they all liked the Pythons, they could see that it would be fun to do it, and if it didn't make any money, well, at least they were backing something they enjoyed.

**GOLDSTONE:** Led Zeppelin, Pink Floyd, Jethro Tull, Island Records, Chrysalis Records, and Charisma Records each had £20,000 or £30,000 invested. And then a friend of mine, Michael White (who is a theatre impresario†), put up the rest, so that covered it.

But the overall thing was the Pythons' need to maintain absolute control over what they were doing. I was able to get that.

---

* At one time Stratton-Smith also served as manager of Neil Innes' group, then called the Bonzo Dog Band.

† One of White's earliest theatrical endeavours was bringing the 1963 Cambridge revue *A Clump of Plinths* to the West End, retitled *Cambridge Circus*. Among his film credits are *Oh! Calcutta!*, *The Rocky Horror Picture Show*, and *Nuns on the Run*.

*The 'Witch' scene (weather permitting).*

**IDLE:** John Goldstone is a sweet man, but his great virtue was saying nothing. He actually tried to get us to share bedrooms on the movie to save money! Cheeky bastard . . .

## 'WELL, WHAT DO I THINK?'
## 'I SAY LET'S BE NICE TO HIM!'

**GILLIAM:** Ian had directed *And Now for Something Completely Different*, and that was the one where I think we started [wanting] even more to be directors. Terry and I really had him surrounded on that one. So when it came, a chance – 'Here's the money to make a Python film' – we just decided we wanted to do it. We were the ambitious directors, and others went along with it.

**JONES:** No one really pretended to be a director; there was just concern to get the stuff on. We knew we had this material that had made us laugh at those meetings, that was the key thing, and it was just making sure that what was read there got *out*.

I'm not sure why it was I wanted to direct; it's just I didn't want *not* to, if you see what I mean. It just seemed natural, really, because I had always been so involved in the direction of the TV shows, taking a group responsibility for checking off on the editing and everything.

It was purely because I was the only one that was interested; the others weren't as interested in that side of it, and I think perhaps didn't feel that it was that crucial. Whereas I had this total tight feeling in my stomach, that it *was* so crucial. Everyone was saying, 'Well, you do it, Terry,' but I was feeling a bit nervous about the idea. It was I who suggested that Terry G. should co-direct; I thought since Terry's got such a good eye that it would be very good to work together. So that's how it came about.

They were all great performers, and because we cast ourselves – we all took parts that we liked – generally there wasn't much to say about performance. That was the *least* part of directing. Directing was really much more doing the creative humdrum jobs, just making sure the film gets on the screen, and to make sure we've covered ourselves and we're getting the shots right and can tell the story.

*Did you start out with a specific division of labour between you and Terry Gilliam?*

**JONES:** It's very odd, I think we sort of did it on alternate days, is what I remember, but Terry and I very much agree that we knew what we wanted, and I couldn't tell you who was responsible for what in terms of the look of the thing. I know I was very keen on making it funky and making sure everybody had dirty teeth; it was a different kind of Middle Ages, but Terry was equally keen on it.

**GOLDSTONE:** I think they trusted Terry in terms of how it would be shot because Terry Jones' attitude (as opposed to Terry Gilliam's) has been always much more about performance than visuals. He cares much more about the way a scene plays, whereas Terry Gilliam cares more about how it looks and to dazzle people with the visual of it. I remember with *Life of Brian* there was a time when having spent a lot of time and effort designing sets for it, Terry Gilliam got very upset that we weren't seeing it all on the screen; there were moments when the tension was there. But ultimately the nature of Python is more verbal than visual, and it seemed very important to make it work on a performance level and that the words were there. But it's just the way that Terry shoots things – same with *Wind in the Willows* and all the others – he'd prefer to make sure a scene was properly covered to give him the ability in the cutting room to get the performance to work than necessarily show all the visuals that your crew provides you. And again Jim [Acheson, designer of *Wind in the Willows*] was very upset from time to time, that not every inch of his set and costumes were being seen, but you have to make a decision as to what the thing is *about*, and that's Terry's strategy. That's why his films are different from Terry Gilliam's.

## I SEEK THE BRAVEST AND THE FINEST

**JONES:** There was quite a lot of debate about [who should play Arthur]. I think in the end nobody wanted to do it.

**PALIN:** No one wanted to sacrifice the chance of playing lots of silly smaller roles in order to play one big one.

**SHERLOCK:** Nobody wanted to play the lead because they thought it was hammy, it was too dry. All they wanted to do was play all the cameos, where you could then have a nice long break before doing the next cameo! But Graham realized not that his part was a star part but that it was essential to hold the rest of the film together, and I think he had a better overview. That may be simplistic, I'm sure they *all* had the overview, but they didn't want to do it, and he said, 'Okay, I'll do it.' And inadvertently stole the show.

**JONES:** Seems obvious now, doesn't it? I think I was quite keen for Graham to do it. I'm not sure, I can't even remember whether I thought Gray would be a great idea, or whether I was in favor of Eric doing it.

## FOLLOW ONLY IF YE BE MEN OF VALOUR

**JONES:** Setting up *Holy Grail* was just so problematic. We had five weeks to shoot it in. Terry and I had been all over Scotland and then all over Wales looking for locations, and we decided on Scotland. We'd picked all these wonderful castles, and then two weeks before we were due to start filming we suddenly got this letter from the Department of the Environment of Scotland saying we couldn't use any of their castles. I was in a panic. Terry and I'd been planning to go up and go through everything and make sure we knew exactly where our cameras were going to be, and instead of doing that, we found ourselves rushing around trying to find new locations for the *whole film*. It was a nightmare. We ended up with Doune Castle – that had to be *three* castles – and then we came up with Castle Stalker for the ending.

**TERRY BEDFORD, DIRECTOR OF PHOTOGRAPHY:** It was a very outside-the-industry project. We obviously all worked for very little money. And I guess because it was like that, Mark Forstater naturally came to some of the people that he'd been at film school with. By then I had made my name as a director of photography on TV commercials, working with Adrian Lyne, so I was a good contender, and Mark gave me the opportunity to be the DP. The most fascinating thing is that the clapper/loader (who's the junior in the camera department) was Roger Pratt; he was my focus puller on *Jabberwocky*, and then helped Gilliam out on the model sequence in *Life of Brian*. He's gone on to

*Interior shooting at one of the 'approved' castles.*

photograph *Brazil* and *Batman*, so he came right up through the ranks.

Anyway, we all went up to Scotland to shoot this film. It was very hippie, in my recollection of it all. It was a family affair; everybody seemed to have their children with them, if they had children. It was all very entertaining. I didn't see a great deal of the friction between them other than it was a bunch of egos trying to make one project.

It was very much a student atmosphere to me, and I wasn't long out of college, either, so as I said we were trying to do things differently from everybody else. [And] the Pythons were fairly anti-Establishment. If you were to say to Gilliam, 'This is a professional way of doing something,' it would really put his back up.

It was all very much done in a hippie fashion. Things weren't organized as well as they could have been, so it was a little ragged around the edges, a little bit amateurish to me. It was more like a circus than a film! But it all [came together] at the end of the day.

It just seemed like fun, really. Even some of those arguments to me felt like fun, because the Sixties were a time about arguing and putting your point of view and getting cross and then forgetting about it the following day. That kind of creative energy is what was expected of one – to have a strong opinion, something that's sort of frowned upon these days! If you have a strong opinion these days, you've either got to be pretty powerful, or you've got to put it in a very palatable way. You can't be confrontational in the 1990s, I find; you've got to be political about it.

**DOYLE:** They had a plan that we would shoot in Glen Coe, shoot in Killin, shoot in Doune, shoot in Stirling, shoot in this, shoot in that, it was like every four days we were going to change. Terry Jones was getting really upset with me because of what appeared to be a negative attitude if I kept saying, 'I think this is impossible.'

**BEDFORD:** On the location scout, we walked into that great hall at Doune Castle, and I distinctly remember Terry Gilliam looking up at the roof saying he liked [how] the moisture had got in on the brickwork. I was just thinking to myself, the chances are that you'll never ever *see* that, and the light would never be up there anyway. It occurred to me that, being an animator, Terry Gilliam has control over those elements [unlike] when you're making a film, especially on the budget we were talking about and the amount of light. I mean, I *had* no lights; there were one or two days when lamps were actually brought in. We had a couple of what we call red-heads and a small generator that you could stick three hundred yards away and cover with blankets to cut the noise. In fact, in the cave when they are looking at the carving, that's lit with the actual burning torches.

It's pretty threadbare stuff, you know! We just had to make do and get on with it. So in a couple of cases the exposure was quite thin, including when we photographed the sequence in the great banquet hall, there was barely enough light to get the wide shots.

**JONES:** When we actually started the first shot of *Holy Grail*, I was going to shoot this bit on the edge of this gorge, and Graham was trembling and shaking, wouldn't go anywhere near the edge. I think he said it was fear of heights, which we thought was really odd because he'd been our mountain-eering expert. I certainly didn't realize this was because he was doing cold turkey at the time, he was trying not to drink. So we couldn't do some of the shots that we wanted close to the edge. But that was all sort of slightly swallowed up by disasters such as the camera shearing its gears on the first take!

**BEDFORD:** The first day was a disaster. Again, it goes back to this sort of amateurish approach. They wanted to go to the top of Glen Coe, which is a mountaineering trip. It was a dialogue sequence, and on the budget that we were shooting we had a very old Arriflex camera, it was in like a cast-iron coffin to make it soundproof, and it was dragged up the hill along with other pieces of heavy equipment. I think it took half a day to get all the equipment up there. And I suppose in their mind they thought they'd be up there in half an hour and within a half an hour of that they would be filming. But by lunchtime the camera is only just up there, half a day's gone. That didn't help at all to get things off the ground. And then the devil got in the works because on slate one take one, the camera broke down, quite seriously; it'd stripped its gears. It wasn't something that could be fixed out on location. We had to shoot everything on the second camera, which was not a sync-dialogue camera, it was to be used for picking up inserts. So the whole opening part of the film had to be post-sunc. The 'professional' way of doing it [would have been], you'd have gone up to the top of the hill to shoot the wide shot with the wild camera – you would have been up there in half an hour – and shot the dialogue at some more accessible position lower down.

**JONES:** I remember a mistake we made, in the 'Knights Who Say "Ni!"'. We were shooting this terribly quickly, we actually shot ten minutes of cut film in one day. It goes right from the Old Man, Arthur, and Bedevere in front of the campfire to the spooky point-of-view shots going through the forest, knights appearing and disappearing, to the whole scene (which is actually in two parts), and to Robin's minstrels arriving. In one day. Mike was doing the Knights Who Say 'Ni!' When Mike read it out it was just one of the funniest moments for me, his characterization. And I remember seeing him having this beard, this moustache and everything being put on, and he had high eyebrows that were covering a whole lot of his face. And

*The Knights Who Say 'Ni!'*

then our costume lady put this helmet over him, so you couldn't see his face at all! I thought, 'Bugger me!' But they were saying, 'Oh, but it's *funny* because we've got these big antlers on his helmet.' And then we stuck him up a ladder so he couldn't move. Poor old Mike, he's acting his socks off there and you really can't *see* him. It was never as funny as when you could see his face. But we were going so fast it was one of those decisions; once you'd started filming him with this helmet, you *had* to keep it on.

I don't know whether it was because of that, but John always after that would *never* wear moustaches, and quite rightly, too!

## 'COURSE IT'S A GOOD IDEA

**BEDFORD:** I don't think there was actually a kind of decision on the [film's] style; they didn't come to me and say, 'We want this film to look medieval,' or anything like that. I think we just fell in because I wanted to make it look moody and to conjure up the atmosphere as much as possible, which is very different from anything they'd ever done before, [which was] all very much TV and in-your-face. What we were really talking about here was bringing a cinematic mood to it, but they were all very, very gung-ho for that; they loved it all, especially Terry Gilliam. I suppose one would have to say that the dark side of Gilliam was the one that was chaperoning that along. And of course Terry Jones is interested in medieval history and stuff, so it all does fit really that they would want to create this sort of atmosphere.

**HOWARD ATHERTON, CAMERA OPERATOR:** There was a great atmosphere on the film – a lot of humour obviously on-camera as well as off. I can remember at times it being very, very difficult to keep the camera steady because everyone behind the camera was laughing their heads off during these antics. They were quite serious when they're doing comedy, they're very intellectual about the whole process, but for us they were just the Pythons. Particularly the rabbit sequence: one of the things about it was the special effects were so crude, so makeshift that they were part of the comedy. I think on any other film they would have been laughed off the screen, but because it was Python they're accepted as part of the humour; in fact you can see the cables this rabbit was sliding along, bouncing up and down, [and] it was even *more* humourous.

Terry Gilliam and Terry Jones, both lovely guys, Terry Gilliam some-times would tell me the set-up he wanted, and I would set it up and get things organized, and then Terry Jones would come across and look through it and say, 'No, this is not what I want,' and I'd have to move it. And Terry Gilliam might come back and have it moved back again! There was never any animosity between them, but they would go off and have a little, you know, 'I wanted it this way' sort of thing, very gentlemanly. And they'd sort it out and they might do it one person's way one time and the other way another time. Even though Terry Gilliam is more famous for his visuals, I don't think in particular he was more demanding on the visual side of the set-up because Terry Jones also had his ideas about what he wanted.

Terry Bedford would be struggling to get the light right, and I would be struggling to get the camera move right or a composition right. John Cleese was very impatient quite often. He would say, 'How many laughs in that?' In other words, you're wasting time on the wrong thing. He thought the only thing you should spend time on was getting the humour right, whereas Terry Jones and Terry Gilliam especially wanted it to look like a film and not like television. So there was always that battle going on between the Pythons and between us as well, because we were always trying to make it look as good as we could as a film. I think even John Cleese wanted it to look good, but he just didn't want to waste the time (if there was going to be any time wasted) spending that extra couple of minutes getting an extra lamp in or a reflector or adjusting the camera. I can see it from his

*Cleese flexes his muscles.*

[side], he's very, very serious when he's going about his thing, and he more than any of the others dominated his sketches. When he had written a sketch he was very much, 'No, no, this is the way I want it.'

I remember feeling very sorry for the wardrobe department because every single night they would work very late trying to clean off the wardrobe. The actors were *always* in mud; if there wasn't mud on the set they used to import it! That was the whole theme of the period: mud, dirt, excreta.

I remember them having to eat excreta at one time, and they'd made up various concoctions of chocolate and all sorts of other things, and they were testing which was the most edible of the concoctions. Which looked the worst and tasted all right?

**JONES:** I remember Mike getting really ratty when we were doing the 'Plague Village'. His job was being a peasant who had to crawl through the mud and go to one spot where there was some chocolate in the mud and he had to start eating this chocolate. He'd spent the whole morning doing this, then he realized that he wasn't on camera all the time. He did get a bit ratty about it, quite rightly!

**CAROL CLEVELAND:** Graham's drinking problem was pretty severe on *Holy Grail*; it sort of reached its peak there, really. At that stage the fellas were getting quite concerned about it. The day I arrived I remember him sitting there in a terrible state, he had the shakes something awful. And though this occurred on the television series, because we didn't have very long in the studio we always managed to get over it there. There had been retakes because of Graham, but I don't think the television audience was ever aware of that because it was all done in little bits. But when it came to the film, it obviously was a great worry, and I think John (being Graham's best mate) was particularly concerned.

There was still a lot of lunacy certainly with the two Terrys, who have always been the two loonies of the group – their directing it together caused a lot of problems! I wasn't around it that much but even the scene that I was involved in, 'Castle Anthrax', what would happen is they would sort of designate different scenes to each other and that particular one was quite a long sequence. I can't remember which came first but I think Terry G. was going to do the first part of it anyway, he was there in the morning setting it all up, the lights, camera, da da da, and got everything going, and then later on Terry Jones came along to take over and didn't like at all what Terry G. had set up and so changed it all: the whole set-up, the lighting, everything was changed. Now this apparently was happening all the time, because they just couldn't agree on what they were doing. And so the crew were tearing their hair out, literally; they were apparently often near rebellion by the time I arrived to do that scene because to them it all seemed so unprofessional, so disorganized.

Every time one or the other Terry came on and said, 'Well, no, we won't have that,' you can see them all throw their eyes up to the heavens going, 'Oh, *God!*'

## I DIDN'T EXPECT A KIND OF SPANISH INQUISITION

**JONES:** The directing wasn't really regarded like someone taking control, it was the director basically having to do a lot of legwork and a lot of graft that nobody else wanted to do, really. [The anger] was mainly focused on Terry G., because he was so focused on the look of the thing and on what he was shooting that he could sometimes forget that people were being [made] uncomfortable.

There was a little bit of bad feeling that went on between Terry and John and Graham. I think John didn't feel Terry was paying him enough [attention]. There had always been a little friction between them in a way, because John is always making fun of Terry being American, and I think Terry wasn't tactful enough with John in asking him to do things, and John would find himself in very uncomfortable situations where Terry is getting the thing to look right. Whereas I had always been a bit more careful with the *artistes*, I suppose.

**GILLIAM:** When we actually got around to making *Holy Grail*, it was like, 'Oh, now we've got to do all the things we claimed we could do that Ian *couldn't* do,' and I think we did. But I think it was the end of the first week of shooting, where everyone got pissed one night, Terry and I were just shattered because everybody was going, *'Wrong!'* A lot of shit had been dumped on us and a lot of things had happened and we were actually managing to survive and keep things going. And Graham got really pissed one night and said what a complete disaster we were making – this was a time we were feeling very, very vulnerable! – and how Ian should be in there, and what egomaniacs, megalomaniacs, useless pieces of shit we are. Oh, that's *great*. 'Fuck you, Graham! Get your lines right!'

I just thought, 'This is horrible,' but the one sad thing is, deep down I think we both felt they may be *right* – we might *not* be able to do this.

### Did you actually think you could function as co-directors?

**GILLIAM:** Yeah, we did. Terry and I tended to agree on most things, until we actually started working together and then we discovered we didn't agree *quite* as totally! The real difference came in that I've got a better eye than Terry, is what it's about. I'm better at those things, and he's better at other things. Ultimately that's how we ended up working it; I ended up being at the camera, and he worked with the guys, because having been in my little garret all those years, my social skills were not as highly developed as they are *now*! The idea of going out there, slogging your guts out and trying to get *them* to do what was needed for the sake of [the shot]? Again, John and Graham didn't particularly like all this cumbersome stuff. Eric was all right. I mean, they just want to go out and do the funny lines; that's a *bit* extreme, but it was kind of like that.

**CLEESE:** Filming is an appallingly technical process, doing the same business over and over and over again from different angles, and on the whole directors forget – I'm not talking about our directors, because they're good on it – but most directors simply do not understand the process that actors need. And when I'm working, I will sometimes say, 'All right, we've got the technical stuff settled, now it's the *actors'* turn. Let's do four or five takes back-to-back.' Because what happens is you get warmed up. What *normally* happens is you do the first take and then it all *stops* while somebody adjusts this bulb, this light, somebody adjusts the position of a lamp, somebody else comes and takes some fluff off your jacket, somebody else is worried about the fact that there's a bit of glow on your nose. By the time you're ready to shoot again, you're *cold* again.

In movies everybody concentrates on the fucking technical aspects! And they *don't matter* when you're making comedy; what matters is whether it's *funny!* A take can vary tremendously from being dreadfully, embarrassingly unfunny to being hilarious. And it all depends on whether you go into that particular take with the right energy and the right degree of focus. It's great if you work with directors from television; you don't get this problem because they understand what the actor needs. But in filmmaking you can find yourself being made completely subsidiary to all the technical requirements; and then when they've got a take that everyone else is happy with because it's in focus and the sound was all right, they want to move on. It's absolutely putting the cart before the horse.

It is something as you can tell that I feel strongly about. And that's why I think actors become difficult and self-protective, because if they *don't* get difficult, their performances are going to suffer because they're not going to be given the circumstances they need to produce their best stuff.

I thought Jonesy had a great, nice atmosphere on the set; I remember very few disagreements with Jonesy, partly because by the time we'd got on the floor the disagreements had already been heard at the writing stage, so we all walked on the floor knowing exactly what the material was about. I thought he was very good, and I always felt it was right within the Python group that he would direct because that was more in tune with his talents than with Terry G.'s talents, which are to produce the most extraordinary visuals but not so much to make a funny two- or three-man sketch.

There was one occasion when I exploded at Terry G. when we were doing a shot where the composition was very crucial, and we were kneeling while wearing full armour and it was very, very uncomfortable. And I remember that Terry G. was lighting a shot with *infinite* care, which meant that we were kneeling there for ages, and he was moving the camera a couple of inches this way, then he'd move it *back* again. I remember complaining after a time, saying, 'Do you realize this is really uncomfortable?' And I certainly realized that he'd been doing all this kind of thing for years in the animation, without the bits of paper complaining to him, and I think it was hard for him at that stage to think of the actors as *people*. At some point I just got up and said, 'Well, fuck this' – or whatever rude remark I used at the time – 'I'm not kneeling there any more because I am now *in pain*.'

But what happens is that people are always interested in negative emotions, and so for all the twenty sessions you have when things go down quite well, people are really interested in the twenty-first session, when there was a big argument. And there are famous moments when people got angry, and so those are the things that everybody remembers. What they don't actually remember is the *context* of it, which was that most of the time we got on pretty well.

**GILLIAM:** The one scene where it blew up was the scene where all the animals were being thrown over the battlements, and to do the shot I had to get their heads below the parapets so I could do a matte to put the animals in the [shot]. That meant digging a hole in the ground and sticking the camera in the hole and they had to be on their knees, so everybody was the right height. John just was like screaming and shouting.

I finally said, 'I don't want to sit here and have to beg you guys to do this so that *your* sketch that *you've* written works! I don't want to have to sit there and have to tell you *how* all this stuff and *why*, I'm doing it because I need your heads *below* the battlements.'

'This is really uncomfortable, Terry –'

'I *know* it's uncomfortable, but if your head goes above that line I can't do the matte, blah blah blah.'

'We can't act like this –'

'Well, I need another five minutes, we're not quite set up.'

'These things are killing me –'

'*Shut up!* This is *your* fucking sketch; *you* wrote this fucking thing, I don't need this!' And I walked off; the dam finally cracked and I went off in a huff and lay there in the grass: 'I'm not going to do

*Co-director Gilliam making sure there is enough light.*

this shit.' It was *appalling* behaviour! I left Terry to take them on.

It was really difficult for me, having only had to deal with pieces of paper, things like that. To actually be able to convince *people* to do things (which you have to do as a director) – my skills were not at all there. I was pathetic!

Terry and I disagreeing – it wasn't big things, but purely practical things: 'The camera should go here because that's that.'

Terry goes, 'Why don't I go over here?'

'Well, I think it should be there.'

'Well, I want it *there!*'

'Terry, the shot's better *here!*'

'*Eeeauuuewwwl...*'[!]

But what was happening on *Grail*, these enthusiasms [of Terry's] I knew weren't right. Now this may sound wrong, but I just know when it came to where the camera should go and certain technical things – that's what I'm good at. And I find trying this other way – '*Eeeauuuewwwl*, it *might* work!' – is wasting time we don't have; the light's going down, we're going to lose that and the shot will fall apart. And so that's really where we divided in a sense, and because I couldn't stand talking to the fucking group to try to convince them to do anything *my* way, Terry and I split – and it worked out very well. We ploughed on.

I think they always deeply suspected me of being more interested in the image than the comedy, that was the basic thing. John in particular just thought everything I was doing was getting in the way, because for him it had to be comfortable and easy and then the comedy would flow, and I was always trying to stick a helmet on him and then stand him in a ditch and that was getting in the way. I mean, they're pretending that you don't have to do all these things, and I think you *do*.

I want it to be both great looking *and* funny. I think most of the stuff we pulled off in *Grail* worked really well. I was just looking at a little clip this morning, 'Bring out your dead'. It's gorgeous. Shit has never looked so beautiful! And because of that, it's *funnier* because it feels so much of a serious movie, a *real* movie, with *real* people groveling in the mud, and then: 'I'm not *quite* dead, I'm feeling much better!' It's funnier that way.

**JONES:** Terry hated working with me, I don't know quite why. He didn't really like the experience. Because Terry's a real perfectionist, you see, and I'm not. I want to make sure the thing gets on the screen as well as possible, but I'm not really a perfectionist to the extent Terry is. There was one day, when we were doing 'Constitutional Peasants', I think it was. The location wasn't very good, actually, I'd been rushing around trying to find this location, we finally got this field and it wasn't great, and Terry was trying to make it look better than it was really. He had started off, and I was late being made up or something, and I kind of took over because nothing had actually been shot because of some problem. Maybe I was a bit untactful in that situation, and I think Terry felt a bit ruffled about that.

**IDLE:** You don't 'direct' comedy; you just avoid trying to get in the way of people being funny!

You must understand that the rest of us have a healthy contempt for directors. This was the least-wanted job; obviously the two who wanted it got it. Since they are both control freaks (as are all directors), it drove them *both* mad. But Terry G. won; he drove Terry J. *more* mad! Terry J. would be cutting by day and Terry G. would undo it and be recutting by night. In the end, the balance works great. Terry J. is good with the acting, Terry G. is good with the location feel, the sinister boat, the visual elements.

**PALIN:** Gilliam's early experience with Python was to come from the ranks of being an animator who worked in his own little loft producing inspired stuff but on his own, and doing occasional performances, which he did and they are much treasured! He appeared in a suit of armour hitting someone with a chicken; that was the great Terry Gilliam in there! But it was quite something for him to then mix with the group in the same way as all the rest of us had been mixing. Because during the television series certainly Terry worked very much on his own; he didn't come to group meetings, not nearly as often as the rest of us. So when it came to the first bit of directing, which was *Holy Grail*, Terry had to interrelate with the rest of them.

We were making our first movie for a small amount of money. There were tensions; for instance, we were doing a scene where we all have to kneel down, rather uncomfortably, while a rabbit is dropped on us or something like that. And then it works, and then Terry Gilliam says he would like another shot because the sun is now at a lovely angle, just glinting off the top of John's helmet. And I remember John saying, 'Fuck the helmet, you know, *fuck* the sun! It's late, it's quarter to seven, it's time to go, I'm extremely uncomfortable, that's it!' So, that's what Terry had to put up with there. I think he had to learn ways of dealing with that. The Pythons were not an easy group to work with!

I think Terry was almost too deferential to actors, too respectful, and didn't really know quite how you got the best performances out of actors.

You get the light streaming in the right place, you get the look of the scene fresh and different and unusual and not like anything you've seen before, and then he would expect the actors to come in, do their lines, and go. Which is, you know, quite permissible; that's the way a lot of directors direct, and they do it very well. But I think probably as Terry moved on to dealing with the bigger stars – I'm thinking really post-*Brazil*, when he was doing *The Fisher King* and *12 Monkeys* – he had to find a way of working with people who needed him a lot, needed a director to spend a lot of time with them. When he was working in England, the English actors just got on with it, really; on *Jabberwocky*, I can't remember anybody going up to Terry, saying, 'Terry, how should I do this, am I right, do I look good, is this the way my public should see me?' There was none of that – you just got on with it, and I think Terry was happier with that. But I think that he has certainly learned how to deal with actors more now; he's got a great deal more confidence, and rather deftly handles a lot of good actors and thus produces some great performances.

*Did the fact that two of their own were now in charge*
*change the dynamics of Python?*

**PALIN:** Yes, it did change things – quite considerably, really. [It may be] all very democratic where we all discuss how things are going to be done, nevertheless you know it's power which the others don't necessarily have. Terry Jones became not just a writer and actor but also the director, Gilliam as well. It gave the directors more to do and more of a stake in the way the film was going to look like. As long as that was effective it was fine, but if it was cause for doubt – people thought this is *not* how something should be done, or a feeling that Terry Jones is taking this over, or Terry Gilliam's taking this over – then there were tensions which had not really been there before on the television series when we had an outside director.

What was most difficult was the combination of the two directors. And there was a sort of merciless divided-room attitude of John's – if he didn't like something that Terry Jones was doing, he'd praise Gilliam extravagantly and say, 'I wish he were here'; if he didn't like something Terry Gilliam would make him do, he'd say, 'Well, Jones is the only one who *really* understands how to do comedy!' So I think that was pretty intolerable, and never repeated. It was very hard for the two of them to co-direct like that. You had to have *one* person who was responsible.

**SHERLOCK:** They were all so new to it, the only people who knew about how a film should really go were some of the producers. Graham's version as I remember it is [that] Terry Jones was so keen to get as much in the can as possible that they were working overtime something like four hours a day, they'd been working for over a week, they were exhausted, the crew hadn't been paid, and were doing all this overtime because Terry was so *keen*. And the two Terrys were alternating, so there was all of that going on; they were actually getting behind the camera in costume and then walking back around to do [the part], so it took so much longer, so they *needed* to do overtime in a way. I mean, it's this real power struggle to 'Oh no, I don't like that shot.' 'Well, in that case we'll have to do it *two* ways!' And all shacked up in this terrible hotel in Stirling. Nobody was enjoying it.

They'd saved all the rushes – there was no point doing anything but the first week all at once – and everyone was terrified wondering what we were going to get. Most of the crew thought, 'Oh my God, we're with this tin-pot company [who] know nothing about making movies, it's all caving in, we've got a disaster on our hands, and we've all said we'll take a half-cut in everything!' So the tension was incredible. Graham went straight to the bar because he knew psychologically what to do: he got them all drunk. He opened his own pocket and said to the barman, 'Drinks are on me for the evening.' The whole crew were immediately happy! He then went to have a word with Eric Idle; Eric got on his guitar, someone else probably got on the piano, they had a sing-song, and this broke the tension before they went in to see the first rushes.

When they saw the rushes, the crew were so amazed at the standard visually that was coming out that they said there and then, 'We don't care when we get paid, we're going to work on this.' Well, that's a real sort of show-biz backstage story, because from then on they really had them eating out of their hand, to slog through that mud, the terrible, wet, hideous conditions in Scotland.

And they were joking, saying already, 'Well, of course the next movie's got to be somewhere *hot!*'

## WE MUST EXAMINE YOU

**ATHERTON:** Coming from a film background, I can remember the rushes have always been a secret. I worked as a loader for a particular cameraman for a couple of years, and he was very protective of his rushes in that he wouldn't let anyone else see them. And being brought up in that school, I thought the rushes should be a very private thing as well. But the Pythons had it set up in one of the main rooms of this local hotel, and of course all the locals heard about it – it wasn't a very big town we were shooting in, and half of them were *in* the film – so they always used to come along and watch the dailies as well. The first couple of days I tried to stop them. I protested to Mark Forstater: 'We can't allow them in, people watching our dailies.'

But as it turned out, it was a blessing in disguise because they used to sit in the back and laugh their heads off! It was good feedback to the Pythons as to whether they got their humour right. And it was a good cover for us if ever we made any mistakes. Because as everyone was laughing, no one was worried about looking for our technical errors. Everyone goes to watch the rushes for their particular angle; wardrobe are in there to see whether they might have got the wrong tunics on that day; the camera boys are in there watching for our side of things. So having the local audience actually lightened the whole thing and made it quite a fun affair, something we all looked forward to.

**JONES:** I think once we'd started seeing the rushes we felt pretty good; we had good material in there, we liked the look of it because Terry Bedford's camerawork was just superb, so yeah, I think the rushes were the thing that kept us going, really, because everybody laughed, everybody had a good time. You'd come out of rushes feeling a charge of adrenaline, thinking, 'Wow, this is really good, this is really worth doing.' Otherwise you might have given up!

**BEDFORD:** There was a lot of material not shot during the actual main production. When we wrapped, the 'Black Knight' sequence in the forest had not been tackled and that was shot as a pickup in Epping Forest in East London. And a lot of inserts were done by Julian Doyle. Julian is another ex–film school guy who was a little bit of a jack-of-all-trades. I suppose because we'd been through film school we knew everybody else's job in a way. Julian, I think, was good for the Pythons because he got a lot done for them, and if anything he was the one who represented the 'amateurish' way of approaching it that satisfied that aspect of it. So when the pressure was on about getting a close-up of something or other, he'd say, 'Oh, don't worry, I can pick that up later.' Things like the bodies going over the cliff at the Bridge of Death, which was at Glen Coe, we never shot any of that; it was shot down in London by throwing dummies out of a tall window in someone's backyard with a bit of fire and a clever camera angle.

**SHERLOCK:** I was occasionally working for the costume department on *Grail*, mainly because Hazel Pethig, who had designed the costumes for all the TV shows, was still contracted from the BBC (as were quite a few – they moonlighted), and so suddenly they went over schedule and had to find people to fill in because she was actually doing a TV show at the time.

I helped the special effects man on the 'Black Knight' sequence. Cleese's stand-in was a man with one leg, that's how that sequence was done. When the first leg came off he'd already got his arms behind his

*Terry Gilliam and John Cleese practising medieval therapy as the warring Red and Black Knights.*

back, but he could balance because he was used to it, whereas anyone with a leg tied up behind him, it would be much more difficult. Plus you'd have to film him from certain angles to look more real. And of course for the second leg coming off it was in fact [a dummy] suspended totally by wires.

They dug a hole for this guy when he's just the stump: 'You cowards!' The poor guy with one leg was getting pins and needles from being stuck in this hole for about four or five hours while they had every angle.

*Were there specific lessons learned from the experience of* Holy Grail?

**IDLE:** Always have sufficient budget. Try and stay out of soggy woollen armour.

**DOYLE:** You had to be stubborn about what you feel is funny because over a long process, especially a difficult film like that, you lose a sense of what's funny and what isn't. And especially the artists lose the sense of it. *Especially* Eric. Eric worries about his stuff; he's for cutting it out all the time – as soon as it's shot he's bored with it, and so somebody [like] Eric will cut his own stuff out almost immediately. He's seen it once, he'd done it in rehearsal, and then it's boring by the time he's shot it. So when I actually cut some of their films, I had be careful and be stubborn about trying to remember what was funny.

The first thing was this rumour that the Black Knight was killing the film: it wasn't funny, it was too bloody, and they made us take it out. I thought, Christ, I'm *sure* that's funny! And then things were in and out, in and out, we had one viewing and I managed to get the Black Knight back in. And John Cleese was always saying, 'It should be somebody else's voice, mine isn't right.' He didn't think it was deep enough. I finally got him to voice it, and why *shouldn't* it be his voice?

The one thing that didn't work was Robin with the three-headed knight; I think the dialogue for that was funny, but the actual execution wasn't thought through, and when we got to shoot it it didn't work. That was out [for a time], but it seemed to be thin without it there, and when Robin reappeared you hadn't seen him because he hadn't done his thing with the three-headed knight – so we felt we *had* to have it whether you wanted it or not.

## BRING OUT YOUR DEAD

**GOLDSTONE:** *Holy Grail* was very risky. There was no completion guaranty, it was just *hoping* it could be done, it really was. The budget really was ridiculous and somehow at the end of shooting they were on budget. It wasn't until the post-production and first cut that anything seemed to be awry, but suddenly the moment of truth came that we didn't have a film that was particularly saleable and showable; they were worried!

We had this disastrous investors' screening when the film was supposedly finished. What had happened was, Terry Gilliam and Terry Jones decided to make it as *real* as possible, to have a soundtrack that was *very* real, bone-crunching and everything. They were very medieval in terms of the sounds of it, but also the music as well. It was all as authentic as they could possibly get. Neil Innes did the music, it was a sort of semi-religious chant that in fact was kind of *too* real. And so at this screening we had it wasn't getting the response from the audience that we'd expected.

**JONES:** Terry G. had done the dub, and you know what it's like when you're making a film: you've got two or three sound editors working away for months and months building up wonderful, incredibly thick soundtracks. We had a screening for our investors – Led Zeppelin and Pink Floyd and anybody who'd put money into the thing – and it started off everybody laughing at the beginning and then after a while just *nothing*; the whole film went through [with] no laughter at all. And it was awful, I was sitting there saying, 'It just can't be *unfunny*.'

**DOYLE:** This viewing with the investors was in a place where the projection box was upstairs and you had to go out of the place, round the back, up some stairs to get to the projectionist. Anyway, we started running it and we hadn't masked the film, so the guy had the rack wrong – you were seeing the boom in shot; it wasn't even a small boom, it was a *big* thing coming in from out of frame. Shit, the investors won't understand that's not actually *in* the film. I rush out of the cinema, go up to the top, 'The rack's wrong!' The third reel he's got it out of rack again!

The boom in the shot made us look like a bunch of amateurs and the investors were worrying about what they'd financed. They probably didn't worry that much, but the Pythons probably worried *more*. It's all too tense, like you're all sitting there listening for *somebody else* to laugh.

**FORSTATER:** Every screening has a certain mood that you can sense, and the mood at the end of that screening was certainly pretty grim. People weren't responding, they weren't laughing the way they should have been. I mean, they were laughing at individual scenes, but there wasn't a build-up, it didn't have a rhythm of following through on a film. My memory is that the music was the problem, that the music – how do you describe [the] music? I can't remember what it was like, but I remember the feeling was that it was too loud, there was too much of it, and that it was the wrong quality. There were too many effects and the effects were too prominent, so that the sound was overwhelming the film. Because the comedy is quite slight, the jokes need to have a context in which they work, and if you overwhelm them with sound, they will just get drowned, which I think is what was happening.

*How did the Pythons themselves react?*

**PALIN:** No walk-outs, but some long faces!

**FORSTATER:** I don't remember in detail who responded and how, [but] there was a certain feeling of, 'Yeah, you fucked it up,' or 'This is a mess, what have we let ourselves in for?' I think there were people who probably felt there was disaster looming. And it's very easy, when you're in a position like this, to panic.

*Being inexperienced filmmakers, they didn't understand that rough cuts are part of the process and are not necessarily a finished product?*

**FORSTATER:** Yeah. After all, this was the first time that either of the two Terrys had ever done this kind of mixing, so it's very easy to try something which doesn't work, and at that point it can all be thrown away, can all be redone. But to someone who doesn't know the technical side, you might think looking at it, 'God, this is it, and we've got to live with what we're currently seeing,' which of course is not the case. So I think probably a certain amount of inexperience may have led people to think it was a disaster which couldn't be repaired.

**JONES:** I remembered the lesson of the 'Dirty Fork' sketch and I thought maybe the same thing's happened with the soundtrack, this wonderful soundtrack with bird songs at the beginning when they're shouting up the castle walls and this wind and ravens and all sorts of things going on in the background. So I went and redubbed it and as soon as anybody started talking I just took all the sound effects out, all the atmosphere, everything. I went through the entire film doing that, and that seemed to help, it was something about the soundtrack filling in all the pauses.

**DOYLE:** Terry Jones swears that it's all the noise that went on in the film, that they were losing the dialogue, and Terry Gilliam sort of half-believes that. I think the dialogue was perfectly clear; I think what happens is when you do a dub, the first viewing after a dub is *always* a rotten viewing because you always hear the *new* things, so you're listening to the birds and the wind in the background and you think, 'Jesus Christ, did I put them on *that* loud?' Two viewings later, you don't even *hear* the birds, you only listen to the *new* things, the *new* footsteps. And of course you *know* the dialogue, so you don't listen to it, you're listening to every other bloody noise. It's a real bugger; I like to get that viewing over with and try to listen to the dialogue again.

**GOLDSTONE:** We'd already spent all the money by then and couldn't quite go back to them and say, 'Can you put up some *more* because we'd like to refinish it?' So we had to go to a bank and borrow money against personal guarantees to make up the difference. The decision was clearly [that] the soundtrack was too real and that the music track would work better if it were more mock-heroic, so we went to a music library and bought the music for it, and it worked.

**JONES:** Neil Innes' music sounded quaint, it didn't have an epic feel to it. And we'd run out of money by that time, so I went along to De Wolfe Music Library in London and just took out piles and piles of disks and just sat here at home trying out music to it, trying to get something to work. Some of the 'Castle Anthrax' scene, I seem to remember there was about three different records playing at one point, trying to get some sort of atmosphere going.

So it felt like what you needed was really corny, heroic music.

**FORSTATER:** Once we had remixed it, we knew the film was very good, it was very funny, it was working well. The next screening was very positive. I think everyone was very happy with it. So it was night and day. And I think a lot of credit has to go to Michael White that he didn't panic. He could see that there was a good film there; he could see that if we went back to the cutting room and remixed it, we'd have a funny film. And that proved to be correct.

**IDLE:** We had thirteen previews, ranging from bloody awful to finally hilarious. That's what good comedy editing does, shifts it from a theory to tailored to the audience's response. It helps when you have four new brains (who are also the writers and the stars) coming in and suggesting what should be cut and what could be moved elsewhere!

## OUR QUEST IS AT AN END

**GOLDSTONE:** I found myself a lot more involved in post-production, and then consequently I was totally involved in selling it and going out with them on the road to promote it. I think that was why they came back and asked me to do *Life of Brian*, because they could see I was very committed to their cause and was able in distribution deals for *Holy Grail* to keep certain controls and integrity in terms of what happened. That was very important to them – and continues to be.

It was quite nerve-wracking because we didn't have any distribution for it, and I was in charge of arranging distribution throughout the world; no one else would get into it! And we made the decision to take it to Filmex, which was the Los Angeles Film Festival. This was about February 1975, and so very much in trepidation because we had no idea how an American audience would react to it, I'd invited a number of distributors. It was playing at the ABC Complex at Century City. And the Pythons were at the end of a North American tour doing some live dates and also promoting the PBS broadcasts, and [they] happened to arrive in Los Angeles just about the time of Filmex, so most of them were there for that.

It was extraordinary. We'd got to the ABC Complex and there's this huge queue of people outside and we thought they were queuing for some other film, and it wasn't [the case] – they were queuing for *our* movie! That kind of underground thing had happened, it was partly to do with the record albums being available and some kind of recognition of *Python* as a television series, and they were there, and it worked.

I actually wasn't able to get anyone to pick it up in Los Angeles. I took a print to New York and had two or three distributors set up to see it there. One in particular, Don Rugoff of Cinema 5, I just called up out of the blue. He took my call and said he'd like to see it. He arranged a screening with all his people. I'd also arranged a screening for a guy at United Artists to see it, and they both started within an hour of each other, and I couldn't change it. So I had to run from one cinema to another with reels, to get to the Rugoff screening in time for it to start. When I got there, just towards the end of the Rugoff screening, I crept in and all of his people were there and there's this man sitting in the front row snoring away! And this was Rugoff. *Obviously* he was not going to buy this!

And the film finished, and then he came to life, stood up, turned to everybody and said, 'What do *you* think? What do *you* think?' They all loved it. He said, 'Okay, I'll buy it.' So he took me back to the office and we worked out a deal and opened it about eight weeks later, in late April 1975.

**This could be yours**

because 1000 coconuts will be given to the first
1000 customers at the Plaza theatre on Wednesday,
June 11. Come, meet a Python, get a coconut, and see
MONTY PYTHON AND THE HOLY GRAIL.

It turned out Rugoff suffered from narcolepsy, just fell asleep at very odd moments, so it was nothing to do with the movie at all!

He kind of got it. I think he used 'Sets the Cinema Back 900 Years' [for the ads]. I'm sure that was a Python line. 'Makes *Ben Hur* Look Like an Epic' was one we used a lot. He had great style; he gave out coconuts on the first day to everybody who would turn up, the first one thousand people. It just took a grip, queues around the block for days.

We opened in London subsequent to that, in May. EMI, [who] had turned it down, were happy to distribute it, just on a straight distribution basis; it actually worked out to be a very good deal because it meant that most of the net revenues came back to us.

# WHY DO YOU THINK I HAVE THIS OUTRAGEOUS ACCENT?

**GOLDSTONE:** I then had to address what would happen to the rest of the world. I took it to Cannes and we had a very good screening there as it turned out; it was encouraging. It helped that the film had opened in America, because they all read *Variety* and saw that it crossed over enormously. And we began to pick up various territories.

France was kind of interesting. I sold it to a French producer, Gilbert de Goldschmidt, who'd done things like *Umbrellas of Cherbourg*, and he had a partner, Yves Robert, who was a very well-known French director-writer-actor who had done classic comedies (*The Tall Blond Man with One Black Shoe*). They together took it on to do the French version (albeit subtitled), and it's played ever since, because it really did capture it. It needed that in any foreign language for it to work. Italy picked it up very quickly, but they never got a good translation of it. It was difficult to get the sense of that kind of comedy, so we saw there might be limitations.

**GILLIAM:** John Goldstone only says positive things! I remember when it was subtitled in French, they got it all wrong, because [in the witch scene] when they start talking about things that float on water, and we have words like 'church', 'stone', *heavy* things that in no way can float on water, they translated [it as], I think church became 'a cricket'. So they actually translated things that *did* float on water! They clearly missed the point of the joke and assumed that the text they were given was wrong, and they had to translate the objects into floatable things.

**GOLDSTONE:** The reactions in America to sequences were completely different than the way they were [in the UK]. They just laughed at different things and were picking up on different things, but I suppose that's kind of understandable. People have asked how or why Python travelled in the way it has, because we sell to some strange places, like the Far East. One would be constantly surprised at how many countries have picked it up and made it work where often British comedies haven't. One of our very early deals was to Thailand, and it worked. So, as I say, one finds different things happening in different countries; it hits different nerves in local humour.

I think [because] it's actually about themes; they take rather big themes that are probably more universal than most British films.

**PALIN:** I still think that's one of the best designed and directed films about the medieval period that I've seen, it really is superb – the buildings we used, and the costumes, the look of the people, the army at the end, and all that stuff. This wonderful idea of the anti-Hollywood medieval film was very important to us, where people didn't all have even teeth, blond hair, horses!

❄ ❄ ❄

# THE US INVASION BEGINS

## CABBAGE CRATES COMING OVER THE BRINY

Prior to the first US broadcasts of *Monty Python's Flying Circus* on public television in 1974, awareness of the group in the States had grown steadily among a sort of humour cognoscenti, as well as among college students returning from abroad with Python albums and books in tow; a few early press reports about the BBC series seemed to whet an appetite. And although this cultural invasion was slow compared to Beatlemania of the early Sixties, when it *did* finally arrive, it was greeted with a passion that surprised even the group's most ardent supporters.

Nancy Lewis, a promoter in the music industry, was the first to actively push Python in America, eventually serving as their US publicist and, ultimately, their personal manager, a relationship which perhaps continues in spirit if not in practice. And to her amazement, she even meets people who still have their coconuts.

---

**NANCY LEWIS:** I had been living in England back when *Flying Circus* was first on the air. I remember I saw it listed in the paper and deliberately didn't watch it because I thought it was a circus, you know, with *clowns?* I'm an American! What do I know from a circus? And then I started hearing talk about it, and I watched it a few times. I wasn't one of those who just thought it was *great* – I enjoyed it, it did make me laugh.

Anyway, I worked in the music business in England, I was back and forth a bit, and then I was based in New York doing publicity for Buddah Records. Tony Stratton-Smith had a label called Charisma in England. I had worked with Strat on some other projects over there, and [in 1972] he called me up and said he wanted to get a distribution deal for his label in America; he had this band Genesis that he really wanted to launch over here. So I set up a meeting with Neil Bogart, the head of Buddah. Strat came over and he brought a stack of his product to Neil and at the very bottom of this stack were these two Python albums which I had not heard, and I went, 'Ooh, Monty Python!' We started talking, and Strat said of the series, 'I can't imagine it will ever come over here.' So Tony and I decided we should really try to get it organized; there was a whole series sitting there, and we found out it was sitting at Time-Life Television, who had all the BBC rights.

*Was there interest on the part of Time-Life to sell it here?*

**LEWIS:** No, none whatsoever. They said, 'Oh, its humour is too English, it's never going to work in America.' I had the most discouraging meetings with them – would just come out pulling my hair out. And in those days it did cost a lot to convert from PAL to NTSC standard. It was an expensive procedure and they were not willing – at all – to put money in. They had shown some of the episodes and a few PBS stations were

*Michael Palin as Gumby, on the NBC late-night variety series,*
The Midnight Special *(1973).*

quite keen on it, but not enough, and they said, 'There's no market here to justify the cost of converting it.' I had to beg them, I had to take people over to the Time-Life Building to screen episodes.

Buddah put the first album out (*Another Monty Python Record*), and it was amazing, we started getting response from FM radio stations, from people who had never, ever seen the visual side of Python. It was pretty staggering. So we thought, if it works *without* the visual side, it can't be too British to work *with* the visual side. There's *got* to be a market here!

The albums never sold in enormous numbers, but they provided a wonderful base. There was an FM radio station, I think in Boston, that made public service spots saying, 'Put Monty Python on television!' We really promoted the Pythons more as a rock band in a funny way, going through radio channels, because that was their audience, rather than going straight to a TV audience. That was my background, too; I suppose it lent itself more to that.

There was a movie, *And Now for Something Completely Different*, which had been made specifically for the American market as an introductory element of Python. But then one of those ironies: they had decided just to put it out in England, not bother here. Columbia Pictures had it sitting on the back shelf and didn't know what to do with it. Neil Bogart was very good friends with the head of Columbia Pictures in New York, so Neil talked to him, and we got them to release *And Now for Something Completely Different* and Buddah would do the promotion for it here. It was a mini-campaign, it wasn't an *Armageddon*-type thing, but we did a silly promotional thing on that.

It initially opened in August 1972 at the 68th Street Playhouse. I remember we hired a lot of street performance people, trying to have an atmosphere of craziness there in the street. It was so bizarre. We had five guys in 'Charley's Aunt' drag paraded with sheepish menace under a black banner calling themselves 'Hell's Grannies'; there was a girl in a Girl Scout outfit with painted freckles hopping around on a pogo stick; a street gymnast; and an organ grinder with his monkey. We bought vast quantities of some type of popcorn snack called 'Screaming Yellow

Zonkers' and gave them out. We hired a Grauman's Chinese–type spotlight. Sha Na Na did *not* arrive in a sanitation truck – I don't know what happened to them, they were part of the Buddah Group, which is probably why we had them, and probably why they didn't turn up! Alice Cooper and company did arrive, but they were not in their make up and costumes.

It sounds quite grim looking back!

We started shipping the print of the film all over the country to various FM radio stations. I think they just gave away tickets: *Come and see this film.* Columbia didn't keep it out very long, they withdrew it. It just wasn't out there; people read reviews [but] it wasn't anywhere to be found.

I must have seen *And Now for Something Completely Different* about a hundred times; I knew it backwards and forwards. I thought it was a very effective, very funny movie, because they'd really picked the cream, the most accessible sketches.

I used to send out these memos to all of the Pythons individually. I have to say in those days Eric was the most responsible about getting back and giving me answers. I would send all these memos with questions and things trying to get answers, and we didn't have email and faxes; a telex machine I had. I have more letters from him with actual answers to questions on how we could do this or that. I think Eric has a more business-approach mind; he's more single-minded at focusing in on things and going for them. He wasn't always eager to do things in America at that stage – not considering how he is nowadays – but Eric was by far the most responsive.

Eric is strangely more ambitious than John. I think John agonizes and analyses, he's very into analysis. He's married to a psychiatrist now; what could be better?*

Python did one promotional thing before the series was on the air,

---

* *Was* married to a psychiatrist, which, in this particular case, Cleese might be the first to tell you *is* what's better.

because they did a stage show tour of Canada, which was the first time I actually met them. (I had been talking on the phone with their manager at that time, a man by the name of John Gledhill in the early days.) I flew up to Toronto, where they greeted me with the news that they were never going to work together again after this tour. That was my greeting! Here I've been knocking myself out trying to get them on the air . . . oh, wonderful! *That's* good news!

So after the end of the Canadian tour in 1973, everyone except John came down to San Francisco and to LA to do some general promotion, more for the albums at that stage, and Annie Leibovitz did a photo session of them for *Rolling Stone* in San Francisco in a hotel car park.

And they did an appearance on *The Tonight Show*, which was one of the grimmest things. Joey Bishop was hosting it. He came out and gave the killer introduction of all time: 'This is a comedy group from England and I hear they're supposed to be funny.' Just about in that tone of enthusiasm. I think they used the Pepperpots and some rather obscure things that were not immediately accessible. And you know the sort of audience you have at *The Tonight Show*; they sat there wondering what was going on. I mean, had they done 'Dead Parrot', for example, I'm sure they would have got that. But John Cleese was not there.

I do remember standing at the back of the audience, there was just a *deadness*. It was terrible. I was ready to slash my wrists! *What have we done?* It was not an auspicious beginning! I often wonder how different it would have been had Johnny Carson introduced them.

*How did the Pythons themselves respond?*
*'America isn't ready for us'?*

**LEWIS:** I don't know, they were sort of defiant about it – 'Hey, well, who cares?' They also did a show called *The Midnight Special*; they taped some inserts for that which were good, and were used for years, as long as the show was on.

In the beginning they weren't terribly interested in doing things specifically for mass-market America. Group-wise, that was never one of their ambitions. John, of course, with *Fawlty Towers,* was immediately offered vast amounts of money by NBC to do the series over here. He pointed out to them instead of making twenty-however-many episodes a year, it had taken him a year to write six half-hour shows. So he quite wisely has resold the format rights – *several times* – and made a lot of money without having to do any work.

**IDLE:** We were convinced Python wouldn't go in America. We were so convinced that when they asked to buy the format (!!) for US TV, we turned them down, just to piss them off!

**LEWIS:** I was trying to talk the Pythons into doing a TV special; a lot of people were approaching us with the idea of doing a special just for America, to sort of test the waters. This was before the series [got] on the air. I think people would have loved them to do something like they did for *And Now for Something Completely Different,* specifically aimed for American TV and allowing for lots of commercial breaks! I think they would have been delighted to [get] that. Don Mischer, who directed *The Great American Dream Machine* series and a lot of late-night specials for ABC, various rock things, wanted to do that late-night Friday night spot where they had *In Concert.* George Schlatter wanted to do a special for NBC, but then he wanted them to go on *The Cher Show;* they did *not.* Cat Stevens wanted to do a TV special with them in the US.

We kept trying to revive *And Now for Something Completely Different,* get it out. They did do a rerelease. It got very good reviews, actually, but it was not a mass-market thing at all. It's depressing, but I'm sure Columbia didn't make two beans from it.

At one stage we were invited to this party during one of the promotional visits to LA, I think it was before *Holy Grail,* and they were at George Schlatter's house. Jerry Weintraub, who managed John Denver originally back then, said, 'I'm prepared to offer these guys a *million dollars* just to do whatever they want!' He was trying to sell this to me. I said,

'Fine, why don't you just run it past them? They're playing badminton in the backyard.' And he went out, and it was I think Eric and Terry G., maybe Michael, they never broke stride with their game, they just said, 'No, no, not interested.' And in those days a million was a lot of money! And he came back and said, 'They're *really* not interested!?' Oh, were you surprised? In Hollywood they couldn't believe that they weren't just sort of lapping up to everyone and trying to get these deals; they really were not interested in that. It was wonderful – a more Gilliamesque attitude prevailed among the group in those days!

*Was it because they were already focusing on their solo work and didn't want to commit to a group project?*

**LEWIS:** I don't think [so] at that stage. I think it was more the principle of the thing, to do things only on their own terms. They were happy with what they were creating out of England; they made material to make themselves laugh, for that's how their material was judged. They didn't want to come and take over American prime-time television. I think they wanted very much to keep it on their level and keep it a homegrown product; I don't think it was yet a disassociation with Python. That came later! Although they were all thinking about other projects they were going to do, in separate directions, I think they were all content to work under the Python umbrella at that time. Except John; some elements of working with the group drove him crazy.

There was also a devoted following. Carl Reiner was a great fan. Apparently Julie Andrews had come back from England at one time and given out copies of Python books as Christmas gifts to a lot of people in LA before they were here at all. I think Carl Reiner was perhaps one of the people who got them from her. People really did get into it very quickly and fervently. On one of those visits, Carl invited us over to his house for Chinese food, Eric and Michael I think were the only two there, and we just sat around talking. His son and then-daughter-in-law Rob Reiner and Penny Marshall came over, too, just to meet the Python

*At a Los Angeles press reception, c. 1974, with Neil Innes (seated).*

guys. Carl always wanted to do something to help. Nothing actually ever developed, but there were some very nice people who were fans, trying to get involved, just to help in those days. And from some unlikely directions, too. I mean, Julie Andrews seems like an unlikely direction to me; I don't know her, but Mary Poppins you don't associate with being a Monty Python fan!

Eventually a deal was done with Greg Garrison, a producer who had done all the old Dean Martin television shows. He was doing a summer replacement series called *Dean Martin's Comedy World,* which was to feature odd comedy bits from all over the world. He wanted to use Monty Python material. The thing is, he paid Time-Life enough to use the thing, to pay for the conversion [of the entire series] to NTSC. The Pythons were sort of against having segments taken out of the show, and I thought it was definitely worth it. I said, 'It's summer, who cares? *And* it will pay for [the conversion].' And that's what happened.

The group of PBS stations who couldn't have done it financially [before the conversion], part of the Eastern Educational Network, now could. And it finally launched in the fall of 1974 on TV over here, in Dallas; New York; Buffalo; Scranton; Providence; Pittsburgh; Erie; Washington, DC; Watertown, New York; and Chicago.

**CLEESE:** When Ron Devillier put it out finally in Dallas – and it always amused us that it started in *Dallas* of all places – all his pals were ringing him up saying, 'Have they burned the station down last night?' or 'Did they stone you on your way to work?' And the moment Rob said it was fine, they *all* started putting it out.

**LEWIS:** Originally there was a man at PBS, who was the head of local WNET in New York, who'd sworn he'd have Python only over his dead body, he really hated them. Then – somehow – they bought the package as part of the group, it went on and it got good ratings. For the first couple of weeks they outdid *Masterpiece Theatre*. And the station got 509 calls after the second show, pledging. And then he was *so charming* when we had a reception, it was wonderful!

*TV Guide* gave it one of the worst reviews ever. I think it was one done by Cleveland Amory, he really hated it, he didn't get Python at all. It was nice; I like extreme reactions. I think that was the nice thing, that it invited that; either you loved it or you just thought, 'This is the biggest load of rubbish I've ever seen in my life!' Nice to have those.

It was very exciting in those early days because we *knew* it was saleable over here; it was just crazy that it hadn't been. When they were being written up in *Time* magazine, all these things, then suddenly Wynn Nathan, the man at Time-Life who is unfortunately no longer with us, went on saying, 'We always knew it would work, we finally succeeded in getting them on the air!' And you just go, 'Wait a minute –' But in a way I didn't mind who wanted to rewrite history right then, because you think: 'It's *on*, and it's working, and it's opening doors.' And since then there is so much British comedy that followed Python that worked just wonderfully. *Some* of it.

When the show was airing, PBS brought the Pythons over. They did a mini-promotional tour, I think to five or six cities.

They were quite amazed by the fervour of it. I think American fans have always been more devoted – 'fanatical' is a good word. Starting with the FM radio listening audience, you got people who were really listening carefully to everything. People who discovered Python felt they had made a *major* discovery.

In England the series had just played once, then was repeated, and that was it. Here they've never really been off the air for any length of time, the shows did keep appearing. Plus you had everything available: you had the records, and we did the deal for the first books, *Monty Python's Big Red Book* and *The Brand New Monty Python Bok*. People would memorize sketches; I'd get people coming up to me quoting bits of sketches all the time.

A friend of ours who happened to be staying in our apartment several years ago who was English got off the plane and got a taxi into New York City. This young guy who was the driver, the minute he heard his English accent, he goes, 'Hey, you're from England? I really like those Monty Python guys!' The whole trip into New York he did nothing but quote Monty Python sketches. John said had he known he was coming to an apartment that had some vague connection with Monty Python, he never would have got out of the taxi.

I spoke to a screenwriter by the name of Ed Naha; he wrote *Honey, I Shrunk the Kids*. Ed used to be a journalist, he was a real early Python journalistic convert. We were catching up, he'd since been married, and he said his whole relationship with his wife was based on the fact that she 'got' Python. They couldn't have gotten together had it not been for that!

The Pythons were always pretty impressed with the devotion from American fans, a small but select group to begin with. They were very responsive to that right away, [and] quite encouraged by that; I think that's probably why they did that last series, which was a surprise to everyone, including them, I think. They had seen this wonderful support for Python which they hadn't felt to that extent in England. I think England enjoyed and got into it, it was a sort of cult thing over there, but that was it.

**JONES:** When *Holy Grail* came out, we came over and did some publicity for that, and it was a very different sort of feeling. We sort of felt, yes, our audience had found us, totally different from the Joey Bishop/Johnny Carson audience. And of course in the States it's a big enough audience to make a difference.

I'm not sure whether 'fanatical' is the word, but it was a much more enthusiastic response. I think much more generosity. I mean, in England people were always wanting to qualify things, saying, 'Oh yeah, really love it, didn't like *that* bit, though!' They can always find bits they didn't like. Whereas in America if they didn't find something funny, I always got the feeling that American audiences made allowances and thought it was because *they* didn't understand it rather than that it wasn't *funny*.

*Did the passion of fans surprise you at all?*

**CLEESE:** I kind of understood it because when I was young I had a similar passion for *The Goon Show*. I've come to the conclusion that what it's really about is that younger people looking at the adult world that they're about to enter can't quite believe that it is to be taken *seriously* – as least as seriously as the people in the middle of the adult world take it! And I think over and above the fact it makes people laugh (and you always feel great affection for anyone who makes you laugh, even if they do so with an appalling persona, like W. C. Fields or Basil Fawlty), I think the emotional connection is something saying, 'You know, there are people out there who are simply telling us not to take it all seriously.' And I think that strikes an unbelievably loud chord, and *that* is what people respond to.

And I think the fact that it has been successful in countries that I hadn't even *heard* of when I wrote *Python* was that we somehow seem to come across archetypes that occur in all the different cultures. De-spite the enormous number of specifically British mentions (like Reggie Maudling and Dawn Palethorpe and Brian London), and the fact that Graham and I would sometimes spend ten minutes on which of two or three words to use because of the connotations, it travels so well, which is very heartwarming and very pleasing.

**GILLIAM:** It was fantastic; we were like rock stars. What's so weird about it, it was at a time when becoming a rock star was the dream – *everybody* wanted to be a rock star. And we kind of did it in a different way. It wasn't like we set out to do it; but we ended up on those American tours, and it was like that. Having the Hollywood Bowl with fifteen thousand people sitting out there doing the lines with you, it was good fun. But the other good thing was, it ultimately wasn't that thing that one needed desperately; one could do it and walk away from it, as opposed to a lot of people who just have to get *more* of that feeling.

But there were really some silly times. Graham often was the centre of it, Graham and his outrageous behaviour. It always became a weird kind of catalyst for the rest of us. We were silly, but we wouldn't actually go out into the world and *behave* in this bizarre and dangerous way. *He* did. Like when we were doing the German shows, every morning there'd be another tale of some outrage the night before, some awful, 'What, you did *what* with *who?*' So we'd wake up in the morning curious to see what state Graham was going to be in.

*Or in America, which state Graham would be in.*

**GILLIAM:** Yes, exactly! And the stage shows, the Canadian tour was very strange. It must have been in the late Fifties, early Sixties, when they built all these new theatres around Canada, but they were all built to the same plan; it's like they had one architectural drawing that they moved from province to province. And we were doing these tours, we'd travel for a thousand miles, and end up with the *same* dressing rooms! It was the most weird, déjà vu-ish experience.

PBS was great. PBS was really important, finally getting on the air in America. I mean, if it hadn't been for PBS, we wouldn't be sitting here. What I've always liked about putting it on PBS is we didn't make any

☞

*Graham Chapman and Terry Gilliam at KERA in Dallas, Texas, doing weird things with a stuffed armadillo in a blatant attempt to raise pledges for public television.*

money. People *thought* we were making a lot of money because we were on television. You *don't* get any money from PBS, but we were being seen and building an audience, which paid off for the movies. And it was the one place where they would show it without commercial breaks, the way we wanted it.

**LEWIS:** In those days they refused any kind of marketing or merchandising. They've changed their mind very recently!

As a group they refused to do commercials, always. And just two weeks ago I had a phone call, because I was working with Michael and he was in town, from a woman saying she had a HUGE offer from a soft drink company – she wasn't prepared to tell me who – who wanted to do a massive TV commercial with the Pythons, at least three of them, and John and Eric had agreed, and she said, 'Can you ask Michael?' Terry Jones had already turned her down, and Terry Gilliam doesn't do that sort of thing, so Michael was her last hope. Michael said 'good luck' to Eric and John if they wanted to do it, but he wouldn't consider it. He said, 'We do not do Python commercials.' It was a vast amount of money, apparently; I was never told but they'd said money was no object, that sort of thing. Michael always loves to hear about commercial offers, he's always being offered commercials; he's always refused them, but he wants to hear about them.

It's very funny, he once accepted to do some TV commercials for an FM radio station in Chicago, which was mind-blowing. Of all the ones he's been offered, that was the least likely. It just sort of appealed to him in a perverse way, a little local FM radio station. It wasn't much money, and it wasn't a product endorsement as such. I think he actually didn't enjoy it and wish he hadn't done it, [but] it was no big deal.

*What's one of your oddest stories from those days?*

**LEWIS:** There was a sleazy club in downtown Manhattan that called itself 'Monty Python's Flying Circus'. We couldn't believe it. Then they went out of business, and *we* started getting odd bills, things they hadn't paid!

❉  ❉  ❉

# THE FOURTH (AND FINAL) SORTIE

## I DON'T THINK WE HAD ENOUGH OF THE REALLY GROSS AWFULNESS THAT WE'RE LOOKING FOR

Following the filming of *Holy Grail*, Chapman, Gilliam, Idle, Jones, and Palin agreed to another series for the BBC, which was recorded in the fall of 1974. Although Cleese begged off participating, some material which he had co-written with Chapman (including some Harrods material originally earmarked for *Arthur King*) ended up in the shows, hence his writing credit.

The series of six episodes is generally viewed as uneven by fans (and by the Pythons themselves), but it contains some stellar material, including the 'Light Entertainment War' (in which the military bemoans that 'the enemy are not only fighting this war on the cheap, but they're also not taking it seriously', armed as they are with fairy wands); 'Mr Neutron', in which a supposed alien agent of world domination must put up with tiresome suburban housewives; and 'The Most Awful Family in Britain 1974 Competition'. The level of surrealism was also quite high, as in a bit in which a post office official, dedicating a new mailbox, delivers a long speech, which he then repeats in French, then German.

A marked difference from the earlier series was the length of sketches; 'Mr Neutron', 'The Golden Age of Ballooning', and 'Michael Ellis' (in which a distraught department store customer tries to return a defective ant) nearly consumed the full running times of their respective shows. Even though none stuck to telling a story *per se*, it was evidence that the Pythons were more interested in examining the possibilities of character development and less in a stream-of-consciousness flow of disparate material.

---

**CLEVELAND:** Everyone started getting rather serious then and concerned, because everyone really wanted to continue with Python, and it was a period when John had decided that he really didn't want to go any further. The friction was noticeable and he was not an easy person to be with. The most difficult period I remember was when we were touring the stage show in Canada, and he was just so unfriendly to everyone. I hadn't realized quite what was going on with him until we got there and I was taking it personally at first – I thought, 'Oh, no, he doesn't like me anymore, what have I done?' And they were, 'No, Carol, he's going through one of his questioning periods in his life,' like what's life all about, and of course he was going through his divorce with Connie.

I remember one evening he wouldn't socialize with any of us, we would all go and have a meal after the show and John didn't want to talk with anyone after the show – he just would go off and do his own thing. I can remember one evening when the rest of us all went off to a restaurant and at the end of the meal we were just getting ready to pay our bill when we noticed over in the corner there was John, he had been there all the time, and he was just getting up and leaving. So we quickly paid up our

*Cleveland and Jones stopping traffic on Westminster Bridge, under MacNaughton's watchful eye.*

bill and went after him, about five or six of us. I remember going down this road, down a hill, and he's sort of striding along as he did and we were sort of tiptoeing, having had a few drinks we were all giggling: 'Oh, let's all pounce on John!' We were tiptoeing up behind him and he'd suddenly hear something and he'd stop, and we'd all jump into a doorway and hide and then quickly tiptoe up behind him. He'd stop, we'd stop in another doorway. He was obviously aware by now that we were coming, and we got about four feet from him and he turned on us and pulled himself up to his greatest height and looked out and – I have never seen such an evil look! He just screamed and abused us and we're all shaking in pure terror, thinking, 'We better not do *that* again!'

No, it was not an amusing time for him, he was not amused by anything. And I was very glad when he'd got through all that.

### How did the rest of the Pythons feel about continuing the series without John?

**JONES:** I guess we announced to him that we were going ahead with a new series even if he didn't want to get involved. But John proffered some material he and Graham had written. There was no bitterness.

**MACNAUGHTON:** We obviously missed John on the first episode of the fourth series; I think *any* show that had John in it would miss John when he goes, because he's an enormous personality. But when you're working together solidly and constantly, well, that disappeared and we didn't miss John anymore; we just went on our own way.

Eric Idle picked up quite a lot of the slack there, in terms of the writing, and also he played a lot more characters; naturally, they all had to increase their output a little bit. Terry Gilliam – I would put it this way: even Terry Gilliam *appeared* more often! Acting is not really Terry's top thing. But he's always great fun and that's the point. As the man eating beans, sitting slobbering on that sofa with that huge thing of Heinz beans, farting – ah yes, he was splendid at that! Funny enough, always a slightly childish thing comes into some of the humour. And I think that's great.

**GILLIAM:** They had given me some parts, and it was really disastrous. For 'Mr Neutron' I had to be an American voice coach and say, 'No, no, no: O-*kay*! O-*kay*!' And I couldn't do an American accent! It was just bizarre.

I don't know, the fourth series was funny because, for all the screaming and shouting [with] John, the balance wasn't there in the same way [with him gone]. Graham was a sort of ballast in there, he was somebody we would complain about – he was always late, he didn't know his lines – so that was *great*! I think it's absolutely vital that there's a scapegoat that we could *all* agree isn't pulling his part of the whole thing.

### Why was the fourth series only six episodes?

**MACNAUGHTON:** I think it was the choice of the Pythons, basically, and I think they were absolutely right. Because you know when these series go on and on and on, they don't often get better. You take any series; the only one I know of that I think kept an absolute top standard all the way through was Johnny Speight's *Till Death Us Do Part*, which became *All in the Family* in America.

[After Python ended,] I found it very difficult to go back to doing normal sitcoms and supposed comedy shows with other supposed comic actors, because I found the others not as funny. You see, I used to laugh a lot while the Pythons were in rehearsal; it was of course serious but never,

*Oh God, I've got to do this job.* Never. It was always far too much enjoyment, far too much fun. I think we were lucky there.

## OUR RATINGS GAVE US 97,300,912, AND ITV NOUGHT

**GILLIAM:** When you turned on *Python* it was kind of a dangerous experience – you didn't know what would happen. The element of surprise is essential to what *Python*'s about, this refreshing, original, outrageous thing. [But] we reached a point when we weren't being outrageous, we became predictable – people could guess where we were going most of the time. So you have to wake people up from the predictability that *Python* had become, and it was that I kept wanting to do.

I had this theory about starting a new series and doing the dullest, most *awful* shows ever written – boring, not funny, just *bad*. And the first one goes out, 'What's happened to Python?' And you need to run about two or three before people would all *stop* watching them. You run show after show and, 'Oh, fuck, it's *awful*!' So by the time there's only maybe ten people left in England who are watching, you then do the *best show you've ever done*. And they run and tell their friends, and everybody won't believe it! I thought that's what we should be doing: you just lower the expectations *so low,* then you suddenly build them up again. It *would* require a bit of self-sacrifice! But nobody else went along with that.

I was always pushing, I suppose more than the others, to shock; I really wanted to keep shocking people, waking people up and not just be funny all the time – even at the *expense* of being funny.

One of the kinds of shit I was thinking about was to do a sketch, and as it's going on we actually lower the volume of the sound – you've got to do it slowly so people are leaning forward having trouble hearing, give them time to get up and turn their volume up a bit and then they go back to their chair and slowly the volume starts dropping again. And they get up, turn up the volume again. And you keep doing that till they've got it full blast. And then of course you'd make **THE LOUDEST NOISE YOU CAN,** and blow out all the television sets in England!

That's where *my* mind was!

It was just trying to break through complacency and all of that. Television I just think has a soporific effect, it's a deadening medium if you allow it to be (and most people do). I find the minute I switch on the television, I can just be there for hours once it starts. There's always something to watch and it's easier than going out and *doing* things. And so maybe it's just me that I'm fighting against, my ease of seduction, the ease with which TV seduces me.

## IT SAYS SOMETHING ABOUT FILLING MY MOUTH IN WITH CEMENT

As *Monty Python's Flying Circus* entered its second year on PBS, ABC sought to bring the show's humour to its late-night umbrella of music and variety specials, *Wide World of Entertainment*. Since the fourth series of *Python* had not been sold to public television, ABC purchased the rights for the six half-hours, intending to use them to fill two ninety-minute time slots in the autumn of 1975.

Unfortunately for them, the Pythons did not have total control over the sale of the shows to commercial television and (as it turned out) had even less control over how they were edited, for ninety minutes of original Python material had to accommodate nearly twenty-four minutes of commercial advertising *and* the red pencils of the network's Standards and Practices Department.

Censorship on American network television had been thrown in flux in the early- to mid-Seventies, as groundbreaking sitcoms like *All in the Family* and *Maude* stretched the boundaries of language and subject matter that a network would be willing to broadcast. But as the Pythons learned, such leniency was not assured even to a hit group being presented long after children had gone to bed.

The length of deleted passages ranged from a few seconds to entire scenes. Even taking into account breaks in the shows for advertising, the cuts severely disrupted the flow of the material and created odd continuity problems. Punchlines would be cut out, thus making the jokes themselves pointless – and the editing process sometimes allowed the original audience laughter to remain. In a most bizarre instance, deleting the shots in which Chapman becomes aroused over 'woody-sounding' words only to be doused with a bucket of water meant that viewers would suddenly see a bone-dry actor get up from his chair drenched to the skin.

While some of the cuts were understandable (it's hard to imagine a commercial network at that time running 'He used to ram things up their –'), the cuts were pretty scathing and in many cases ludicrous. Some of the excisions mandated for the ABC special included:

- 'Entrance of man in wheelchair with sword in head, deleted to eliminate offensive references to handicapped individuals.'
- 'Remove two *damns* from *Croquet hoops look damn pretty* and *Croquet hoops look frightfully damn pretty.*'
- 'Animated sequence of grumpy man trying to sleep. 9 seconds deleted to remove lines *God!* and two *hells* from *What in hell's going on?*'
- 'Removed navy officer dressed as woman and naked man playing piano.'
- 'Cartoon sequence of boy flying balloon; shot of naked woman eliminated, plus exploding woman.'
- 'In ant-buying sequence, :02 deleted to eliminate word *bitch* from *King George bitch.*'
- 'In first scene between Michael Ellis and his mother, :14 cut to eliminate reference to tiger: *He used to go through four Jehovah's Witnesses a day.*'
- 'Delete mother's line *His droppings are enormous* in reference to polar bear invading neighbour's garden.'

The winner for most ludicrous deletion was in an animated seg-
ment of 'The Golden Age of Ballooning', showing the Montgolfier brothers engaged in a boxing match while taking a bath. The
original narration went: 'Starting on his face and arms, Joseph
Michael Montgolfier went on to scrub his torso, his legs, and his
naughty bits'. ABC severed the words 'naughty bits'.

**LEWIS:** In those days I was a friend of Bob Shanks at ABC. Bob had
approached me about the group doing some specials for late night, with
their usual response.

ABC bought the last series for *Wide World of Entertainment*. Time-
Life had sold them the rights; they just said, 'Go ahead, here's ninety
minutes, do with it what you want.' And I talked to Bob about it; he said,
'Maybe the Pythons would like to be involved in editing?' And we said,
'Yeah!' Suddenly he went quiet, and then [some time later] said, 'Oh,
don't worry, we've already put it together.'

I got very nervous because I thought, you know, ninety minutes of
programming really means how much cut out per hour, how much are
you going to *lose*? It couldn't be as-is. And it was announced, it was a done
deal. I had not seen this last TV series; I taped the first special that aired
and quickly sent this show over to England and said, 'What's wrong with
this, why isn't it *funny*?' And they were all horrified. Because ABC'd just
gone through it with a hatchet, literally.

They gave us a list of cuts ABC had made, and John and Graham just
rolled on the floor when they read it; the list of cuts was the funniest docu-
ment written. One of the things they did was bleep the words 'naughty bits';
that was a classic! So we immediately tried to get an injunction to stop them
airing the second one, and that's where the court case came about.

**GILLIAM:** What was absurd, what I loved, was they could not understand
us, because [they thought] they were doing it for our benefit, they were
providing us with a larger audience. This guy, Bob Shanks, couldn't un-

derstand why we didn't *want* this larger audience. They thought they were doing the best for us and we were just these ungrateful children. It was really, really bizarre, that blindness.

The BBC sold it, and we had this clause in our contract that Terry Jones was really responsible for, that they couldn't cut the stuff without our approval – it had to go out as we made it. Now nobody would *ever* allow a clause in a contract like that these days, and I don't know how we managed to get that in there, but I remember Terry was the one that really pressured for that. And it just sort of sat quietly down there, and the years went past and nobody noticed. So when they came to sell it, that was basically the thing we were dealing with: the BBC was selling rights they didn't have.

**JONES:** It was something I'd thought up, actually. I said, 'Well, we're working so hard on these things and I hate it when they muck around with our stuff, let's put in a line saying that they can't re-edit the shows once they'd been broadcast.' That went into the first contract and then we all forgot about it! So five years later when we had this court case with ABC, our New York lawyer, very smart chap, went through our original contracts and found it. It must have been such a wonderful moment, suddenly to find this clause which had just been repeated and totally forgotten about. I don't know how it got in in the first place, it's just when we negotiated the contract in the first place, we said, 'Oh, we wanted that clause in,' and I think the BBC didn't really mind.

In those days the BBC charter was to make programmes for Britain. I remember when I was on a course there, this was in 1968, '69, I said, 'Well, why don't we go into co-funding, do co-productions?' And the answer was, 'No, we can't do that because then we'd start making shows for American audiences. We're funded by the British taxpayer and our charter is to make shows for the British audience.' And so in 1969 it wouldn't mean anything to have a clause like that – they never expected to sell the shows to the States at all!

Last-minute negotiations between the two parties did not get any-where. Consequently, on December 19, 1975, at the United States Court House in Foley Square in New York, Judge Morris Lasker presided over the suit for injunctive relief brought by the Pythons against ABC Television on the basis of copyright infringement and unfair competition against their own work. Representing the group, Gilliam and Palin claimed that the edited programmes did not con-stitute 'Monty Python'; therefore, broadcasting them would dam-age the group in the eyes of its audience and potentially alienate a larger audience presently unfamiliar with their work, thus jeopar-dizing the future sale of Python books, records, and films.

Because the broadcast of the second Python compilation was scheduled for the following Friday evening, ABC argued that to have the injunction granted would damage the network in the eyes of the public and its affiliates. They also asserted that it would cost upwards of half a million dollars to substitute a programme at the last minute. Besides their forebodings of damage to their reputa-tion by cancelling the broadcast, the network still stood by the cuts, saying they did not distort the original material.

Eventually the judge and all parties sat in the jury box and watched a screening of two versions of the 'Light Entertainment War': first as originally run on the BBC, and then as it would ap-pear on ABC as part of the special. Nearly eight minutes had been cut from the half hour.

**GILLIAM:** I loved it because they were in the same courtroom that John Mitchell had been arraigned in! And then their lawyer was so bad be-cause he thought we were doing this all to publicize the stage show,* which had *nothing* to do with that.

---

* The group was to appear at City Center in New York in the spring of 1976.

I think their biggest mistake was letting us show our version [at the trial] before they showed their version. That's so *stupid*; ours comes out, we get all the laughs. Then they show their version and there's no laughs. Not only has it been chopped up badly, but it's *old* material, it's not as funny as it was the first time. That's just *dumb*! If they'd shown theirs first, maybe they would have got the laughs so when they showed our stuff maybe ours would have looked long-winded. [The feeling could have been,] maybe ABC did the right thing – they weren't trying to ruin it, the stuff *deserved* trimming.

**LEWIS:** I had to testify. I was terrified. I was so annoyed, I take things too personally – I was ready to punch the ABC people out! And then at the end it was ruled that the show would air the way ABC had edited it, but it had to have a disclaimer on it, and [so] the ABC people came over and said, 'Would you guys like to do a *humourous* disclaimer for us?' I can't believe it: they don't *get* it, do they? They don't get that people really care about what they've created and having it chopped this way. It was astonishing. So they put a disclaimer of some sort, but the shows were not very good. I imagine for some people it could have been their first introduction [to Python], it would have been pretty disappointing.

And although the judge ruled against the Pythons in that initial court thing because he said it was too late – it would cause damage to ABC to change it – the judge worded it so that it really allowed a turnaround, and it gave the Pythons ownership of the series in the end. Amazing. It turned out to be a landmark case, really an important one, because it gives people *some* control over their material.

---

Judge Lasker favoured ABC in his decision partly because of the network's claims of damages which would be incurred, and partly because of questions about copyright: the Pythons held copyright over their scripts, but the BBC owned the copyright of the *tapes of* those same scripts. There was also an unresolved question about Time-Life's responsibility in their sale of the shows. Allowing for a disclaimer which would in some way indicate the Pythons' disassociation from the programme, the judge turned down the Pythons' request for a preliminary injunction, but did leave open their lawsuit (which demanded $1,000,000 in damages).

By the time the case reached the US Court of Appeals in the spring – long after the second compilation had aired – ABC could no longer argue that an injunction would be financially crippling to them. Therefore, the appeal judges concentrated on matters of copyright, finding that the Pythons could conceivably win a full hearing as creators of the (now-mutilated) work. The suggestion that ABC's naming of their show *Monty Python* was a mislabeling of inferior goods, illegal under the Lanham Act, was also given credence.

Cognizant of the rising court costs, Python decided to make a deal with Time-Life and the BBC (who might have been responsible for ABC's legal fees if the network lost) to settle the case. For dropping their suit, the Pythons received full rights to all forty-five episodes of *Monty Python's Flying Circus*.

In a small way, *Monty Python v. ABC Television* proved to be a landmark case on the subject of moral rights, a part of copyright law not as fully appreciated in the United States as it is in some other countries. Because US law recognizes the rights of owners of material and not necessarily its creators, this case demonstrated how writers and artists could further protect their work from unacceptable changes.

Having won ownership of all their programmes, the Pythons ultimately sold the six episodes of the fourth series to PBS, and have made them part of the regularly syndicated package which has also aired on cable. The tapes preserve the material that had been deleted by ABC – including the dreaded reference to 'naughty bits' – but curiously (and with no explanation for it by Terry Jones), the shows are actually missing some material that *did* air on ABC. Most of it is inconsequential – extended exchanges which are condensed, or repeated gags not repeated – but the 'Mr Neutron' episode did contain this charming aside with Idle as the prime minister talking to his secretary on the intercom, with shades of Rose Mary Woods and Watergate:

---

### VOICE ON INTERCOM (CAROL):

The Secretary of State to see you, Prime Minister.

### PRIME MINISTER (ERIC):

Very well, show him in.

### VOICE:

I beg your pardon?

### PRIME MINISTER:

Show him in!

### VOICE:

Ah, that's what I thought you said.

### PRIME MINISTER:

Good.

### VOICE:

Sorry, I didn't quite catch the last bit.

**PRIME MINISTER:**

Show him in!

**VOICE:**

No, no, the bit after that.

**PRIME MINISTER:**

I didn't say anything after that.

**VOICE:**

I'm sure you did.

**PRIME MINISTER:**

No, I didn't!

**VOICE:**

You did! It was just one word.

**PRIME MINISTER:**

Well, it doesn't matter anyway.

**VOICE:**

Oh, it does! You told me to write *everything* down.

**PRIME MINISTER:**

All right, I'll have a listen. *(He shuts off a tape recorder and rewinds it.)*

☞

**VOICE:**

What?

**PRIME MINISTER:**

I'm just going to listen to what I said. *(He turns on the tape and it plays back the previous conversation.)*

**VOICE:** *(on tape)*

'The Secretary of State to see you, Prime Minister.'

**PRIME MINISTER:** *(on tape)*

'Very well, show him in.'

**VOICE:** *(on tape)*

'I beg your pardon?'

**PRIME MINISTER:** *(on tape)*

'Show him in!'

**VOICE:**

I'm sorry?

**PRIME MINISTER:**

I'm, I'm just listening to what I said.

**VOICE:**

Oh, sorry.

## PRIME MINISTER:

Oh, damn, now I've missed it! *(He shuts off machine and rewinds it again, but a bit too far.)*

## PRIME MINISTER: *(on tape)*

'I *am* the Prime Minister. *I* am the Prime Minister. I am the *Prime Minister . . .'* *(He embarrassedly turns off the machine.)*

# CAUGHT IN PYTHON'S ORBIT

A veteran of Cambridge University's Footlights Revue, a story editor for *Doctor Who*, and author of the classic radio serial and books comprising *The Hitchhiker's Guide to the Galaxy*, **Douglas Adams** has sometimes walked parallel to the Pythons, and for a time walked in step with Graham Chapman, with whom he collaborated on a number of projects when the Pythons' TV series ended in 1974. While his actual Pythonic output is tiny, he was a friend, colleague, and fan of the group, and he asked both Terry Jones and John Cleese to participate in his multimedia game venture *Starship Titanic*.

**DOUGLAS ADAMS:** It's astonishing, actually, particularly in perspective now in that there's so much comedy, *everybody* is a comedian, every weathercaster, and you just wish somebody could say something that wasn't tongue-in-cheek; I hate that dreadful expression! I wish somebody could be straight and not try to be a comedian. Going back, to the beginnings of Python, it was very, very different.

The interesting thing about when it happened was, in those days comedy was not thought of as being something that somebody terribly intelligent or highly educated would necessarily go and do. So the idea of seeing comedy being done by such incredibly clever people was really quite astonishing. The real freshness and originality of it still shines through as being something that was unique then and remains unique. Some of it now is terrible, some of it's absolutely dreadful, but the best of it is just incandescent.

*Cambridge and Oxford seemed to be producing a lot of comedy writers and performers in the Sixties.*

**ADAMS:** Yes, it suddenly became a new way of expressing yourself, presumably. That's going to sound terribly pretentious, but it was.

If you look at Python, its roots very, very clearly came from two different directions: one would be Peter Cook's stuff and the other is Spike Milligan. Everybody develops from what their predecessors did, and absolutely *Hitchhiker* took many cues from Python.

I felt what happens in Python is you have some aspect of the world [that's] twisted and you follow the logic of that twist and see where it leads; either it leads somewhere very funny, or gives you a few good laughs and then you veer off into something else. Which is the license that Python always gave itself: to spend just exactly as much time on a sketch as it's worth, and then if you haven't got to a resolution you can jump onto something else, which was great.

Growing up in the Sixties two things had a huge impact on my imagination: one was the Beatles and the other was *Python*. *Python* started when I was seventeen. Right from the word 'go' it had just a huge impact on me. I was at boarding school, so those of us who wanted to watch *Python* would congregate in the television room, just to make sure everybody agreed that we were going to watch *Python*. And I remember one day there was a football match or something like that, and it gradually became clear that the rest of the room was not going to watch *Python*, it was going to watch the football, and there was a bunch of about four of us who suddenly went into a full panic at that point because we were going to miss *Python*! It so happened my grandmother lived in the same town, about two miles away, so we just leapt out of school, broke out and ran, covered the distance to my grandmother's house in record-breaking time, burst in upon the poor frightened grandmother, and said, 'Excuse me, we're going to watch *Python*.' And I can remember what happened was, we turned on what I thought was the right channel and it was a pirate movie, so I go, 'Shit, which one is it? It isn't that channel, it isn't that channel, it *must* be on, but it's a pirate movie!' So we went around again, and the fourth time we came back to the pirate movie there was John sitting at his desk!

It's funny how the things that were on television in those days were fantastically important to you. I don't know if it's the fact that television has changed or one's just got older, but I can remember the enormous lengths we'd go to watch something on television. I can't imagine anything [today] that would remotely command that kind of [passion].

I was at university, one day I was at the Round House going to see some show, and I was at the bar at the interval and the person standing next to me was John Cleese. So seizing the moment, I said, 'Excuse me, can I interview you for *Varsity*?' which was the Cambridge University magazine. He very graciously said, 'Yes, all right,' and gave me his number and I went off to interview him a few weeks later. A curious thing came out of that long conversation I had with him: he was explaining in great detail how he just had this to do and that to do and the other thing to do, and then he was really going to take a lot of time off and maybe see if he could retire. He was about thirty-two. I thought, 'How interesting that he'd got his life that well worked out.' But subsequently I discovered that every single conversation I've had with him since then, another twenty-five years, has been explaining how he's just got this to do and that to do and the other to do and *then* he can retire!

Then there was a show that I had written a lot of material for in my last year at Footlights – I wasn't actually in it, I'd just written for it – and it went on briefly in London and a lot of old Footlights people came along to see it, including Graham Chapman. And so I sort of milled around afterwards and got to chat with Graham, and it turned out that he particularly liked one or two of the sketches that I had written. So he said, could I pop around and have a drink sometime, have a chat? So I did – dropped in to see him at his house in Highgate.

Graham was at a bit of a loose end at the time because it was around the time the Pythons were writing that last half-series, the one without John, and I think Graham probably found that particularly hard to adjust to. Graham had been either having to write stuff by himself (which I think he didn't particularly enjoy doing), or was writing bits with other Pythons. It hadn't been the easiest thing for him, having to adjust.

It's easy to underestimate Graham's great role in Python, because he was in many ways the least distinctive in a lot of people's minds. He found himself a real role in the films, first as Arthur and then as Brian – I think that Graham found a kind of realness in that character that had eluded him in a lot of the parts he would more normally play in Python. [But] he was the one who was least at ease in front of the camera; there was the least identity there. But his role was I think very, very important and it was [to be] essentially extremely subversive. Now given that the whole bunch of them were subversive, being the subversive one of this subversive bunch was a particularly complicated role!

The others would all tell stories of how they'd all be suggesting this and arguing about that, and Graham would sit there puffing on his pipe and quietly, in his tweedy way, think very, very naughty thoughts, and then every now and then would just interject something completely off the wall that would catch everybody by surprise, and then substantially turn something around. There's a much-repeated story I certainly heard from Graham, which was a sketch that John had written by himself. It was based on something that made him very, very cross, which is often where a good sketch would come from, because he'd been sold a faulty toaster and he was going to complain about it. He wrote this whole sketch about his faulty toaster, and it was a beautifully written, beautifully crafted sketch, good sort of pear shape to it, and Graham must have listened to it or read it. As the story goes John was feeling a bit cross that he'd done all this work and Graham was merely sitting there, and Graham's only remark was, 'Yes, it's boring, why not make it a parrot instead?' Whereupon it suddenly transforms into one of the most famous sketches they ever did.

So Graham's the one who could just turn something and flip it, would rely in a sense on somebody else having done all the spade work, in order for him to find the nugget that was buried there. I think Graham really was the most anarchic one of them (I mean Terry Jones is a bit of an anarchist, but he's a *nice* anarchist!). Whereas with Graham there was always that kind of edge, danger; his life was a dangerous life, he did live out on the edge in a peculiar kind of way. It's odd because in one way his demeanor was so much the sort of quiet, tweedy pipe-smoking Englishman, but there were demons there, demons which obviously he spent a lot of time sousing in drink, which was very sad. I remember when they'd had the whole cellar of their house in Highgate remodelled so he got a wine cellar, but he had filled his cellar completely with bottles of gin. A gin cellar!

Anyway, the thing about Graham was he was a dangerous person. I mean he always courted that sense of danger, sense of outrage, sense of how can you really twist the knife? It was that in many ways that gave Python its real edge, because otherwise I think it could have been a much safer show than it was. I think it's not in John's instinct to be that way at all. But it took somebody like Graham to see there was that wildness in John to get at; if he could just push that button, he could dig it out.

## HELP ME? YEAH, I'LL SAY YOU CAN HELP ME

**ADAMS:** Now Graham invited me – it wasn't a sort of formal collaboration – and said, 'Well, since you've come over, there's a sketch I meant to be sorting out for this script, do you want to give me a hand with it after lunch?' So I said, 'All right.' I can't even remember what it was, actually, something to do with a doctor, and a man stabbed in the doctor's waiting room. Really my contribution such as it was would have been probably, literally two lines or something. But nevertheless, a source of immense pride and self-importance to me! But it's rather like being a passing taxi driver who's asked to be the tambourine on a Beatles record.

There was one other thing I contributed that actually had to do with Python. They were doing the record album of *Holy Grail* and the Pythons had decided in their sort of Pythony way that they really didn't want to put much of the actual movie on the record, so they wanted to record a lot of other stuff. There was a sketch of mine that Graham had seen that he quite liked, about a film director announcing he was making a new movie with Marilyn Monroe, which meant digging her up. I think it was one I'd already written and rewritten for one or two other people, and then I rewrote it with Graham, and then I think Mike and Terry rewrote it *again*, by which time it was a shadow of its former self. So that was one other contribution to Python.

### *How unusual was it that the Pythons would collaborate with others at that time?*

**ADAMS:** I think there had been odd things here and there, not so much that somebody'd been brought in but one of the members of the team happened to be writing something with somebody else and it ended up being in a Python sketch. Ian Davidson's name you'll see from time to time, and every now and then he played a little part, so it wasn't completely unheard of, but it was pretty unusual.

One of the things I do want to make absolutely clear is how absolutely minimal is my connection with Python as such. It became a bit of a problem for me at one point, because when *Hitchhiker* started, there was nothing for journalists to write about me at all because I hadn't *done* anything. The fact that there was even this faint connection with Python was always made a big thing of, which was extremely embarrassing to me, and I suspect probably annoyed one or two of the Pythons. I kept saying, 'I'm sorry, it's not me.' It would get to the point where I would say to journalists, 'Look, I just want to say before I say anything that I have nothing to do with Python.' In fact, what made it bad was that I *had* written about half a dozen lines that appeared here and there in Python, but I would say I didn't write for Python.

They'd say, 'What, you mean *Monty* Python?'

'Yes, I didn't write for them.'

And they'd say, 'What was *that* like?'

I'd then read the account of the interview: 'Douglas Adams, one of the major writers on Monty Python . . .' And I kept on saying to the Pythons, 'I'm sorry, I did not say this.' It wears a bit thin!

### *How did your relationship with Graham continue beyond Python?*

**ADAMS:** Graham was quite pleased with the couple of hours' work, whatever it was we'd done. He wanted to create his own sketch show. There were one or two other people he regularly worked with. One was Barry Cryer. I think Barry's a really old-school professional comedy writer, and Graham's slightly more anarchic feel could work together [with that] quite well. Then John and Graham had pioneered the *Doctor in the House* series on television; John and Graham had written a number of those, and Graham had written one or two others with a man called Bernard McKenna,[*] who was a belligerent Scotsman who had also come to write a lot of the *Doctor*s by himself. So Graham was groping: maybe Barry, and maybe me as well, to see how that would go, very much the sort of fresh-faced new boy inexperienced unknown quantity. On the other hand, I was extremely available. So we worked on that for a while. It became *Out of the Trees*. I think only one ever got made, but we did two or maybe three scripts and it was mostly me and

---

[*]    McKenna also appeared as various guards and centurions in *Life of Brian*.

Graham. I wasn't performing at all. It had some good bits, but it wasn't really that good.

*How similar was it in style to Python?*

**ADAMS:** I would say too similar, to be honest.

Graham and I ended up doing a couple of jobs for Ringo Starr. An American television channel was interested in Ringo doing a one-hour special, so he got us – well, when I say he got me and Graham, he got *Graham*, and me because I was part of the package at the time.

Ringo had just done a record album called *Goodnight Vienna*, and the record sleeve was a pastiche of a scene from *The Day the Earth Stood Still*, he as Michael Rennie, and then there's the big robot next to him. And Ringo wanted us to write this script to somehow take off from the sleeve cover. So Graham and I wrote this show in which this giant robot came to Earth to find Ringo, who (in some strange case of mistaken identity) was working as a very menial office worker somewhere, and take him off to join his ancestral race in the stars. I had a couple of things I'd done, a show opening at Cambridge, that had science fiction elements in the comedy, and doing this just fitted very, very neatly with my particular bent. It didn't get made, but it kind of stuck with me.

The other thing was something that only a rock star would ask you to do. He and Harry Nilsson had made a movie called *Son of Dracula* for which Harry Nilsson played the son of Dracula and Ringo played the Van Helsing character, and Harry had done some songs for it. It had been released very briefly and I think not unsuccessfully, but then they had pulled it back in again because they weren't happy with it. It sat on the shelves at Apple for a year or two gathering dust, and they thought, 'We better do something with it – we need to make it *funny!*' So they set up in Graham's house one of those big Steenbeck things, gave us the film, and said, 'Okay, go through the film and write new dialogue for it.'

'What, you mean *over* what the characters were saying?'

'Yeah, different dialogue to go with what their lips were doing.'

We said it's not necessary because the movie is not bad, actually, it's actually quite good, and this is the way to really destroy the movie – this is an exercise that can't possibly work. They said, 'Well, never mind, here's some money, do it.' So we did it, and it didn't work very well, so they said, 'Thank you very much', and put it back on the shelves. That's what you get for working with rock stars!

### How did you witness the effects of Graham's alcoholism?

**ADAMS:** I guess most of the year working with him, he was basically drinking a couple of quarts of gin a day. So it wasn't the best possible atmosphere for doing the best possible work. You basically entered Graham's house at ten o'clock in the morning and everybody drank all day, so by the end of the day everybody was completely pissed, or Graham was pretty pissed. I was basically too young and inexperienced; I didn't know how barmy this all was, or to know what to do about it being that barmy. I mean the Pythons all had a long history with him, I'm sure they loved him dearly, but I also think the others had got to the point of finding Graham to be terribly hard to deal with. I don't want to paint too negative a picture because he's an extraordinary man, obviously an enormous talent in writing, even if he became a bit undisciplined or self-indulgent. He was somebody who commanded an enormous amount of real affection and loyalty, from a very wide and eclectic bunch of people who just thought he was wonderful, strange – and exasperating.

He basically took up residence in the bar, the Angel up in Highgate. He would quite often end up really behaving quite abominably. The landlord was obviously of two minds: on the one hand, Graham was a terrific customer, and brought a lot of people and created quite a lot of atmosphere in the pub, and it became quite well known for that; but on the other hand there were times when it really got seriously out of order.

When he wasn't drinking there would usually be a period of DTs, so he'd be very wobbly. When that happened, I always got the feeling not that one's gone somewhere safer, but that you are somewhere *really* unsafe now. I don't know what it was, and who can *tell* what it is, that devours people.

It was a terrible waste of a person. I mean, you are what you are, you do what you do, but it must have been to the other Pythons kind of difficult and strange that this person who they knew so well and had worked with so much, shared so much with, had descended into this sort of drink hell. Of course Graham would say it wasn't a drink hell, it was tremendous fun! Up to a point.

*When he was drinking, did he ever think he was being funny when – to the outside world – he clearly wasn't, he was just being drunk?*

**ADAMS:** He would never *try* to be funny as such. It's more that he would amuse himself by being outrageous and belligerent, so it would amuse *him*, but it wasn't actually intended to amuse other people.

*So he was trying to push other people's buttons to get a response?*

**ADAMS:** Yeah. And there's also that drunk thing of 'the rest of the world just not being up to understanding this'. It's interesting because he was capable of random acts of great kindness, almost a touchstone of his personality, but he was also capable of extreme unpleasantness as well. He also got it handed back to him in a very, very unpleasant thing that Keith Moon once did to him. Because Graham was kind of living hand-to-mouth, he always imagined there was more money around than there actually was. He was a celebrated person, a successful person, but the movies – they were successful, but they were not exactly *Jurassic Park*! And remember it's all being divided six ways. I don't know how much money the movies made. We knew when any money had come in because suddenly there'd be lots of chauffeur-driven Mercedes around for a bit, but he was often quite hard up.

I remember being told about one night he and Keith Moon were out at the pub, and Keith Moon was not the kind of friend that somebody who's already drunk necessarily needs. Apparently on the way back from the pub, they passed some really filthy full dustbin, and Keith pulled out of his pocket some money – I don't know how much, couple of thousand pounds – he said, 'Here, Graham, it's yours,' and stuffed it right into the bottom of the dustbin, and Graham had to then dig it all out.

### How did Graham change when he stopped drinking?

**ADAMS:** Well, that was quite a long time after he and I had stopped [collaborating]. When we went our separate ways we had a row, I can't quite remember even what it was about, but we were definitely on bad terms for a few weeks or months or something. Though we repaired relations after that, we were never that close again.

Once he stopped drinking, he lost a lot of weight and was trying to get himself fit, and at the same time I don't feel this really marked a major re-engagement with reality, I have to say. Whenever you saw him, he always had lots of projects that were terribly exciting, but none ever seemed to come to anything. And then he fell in with these people from the Dangerous Sports Club* who were complete lunatics, I mean dangerously mad people, in my estimation. One of them used to come around here every now and then to try to sell us on involvement in one mad scheme or another.

### They never got you to slide down a mountain on a grand piano?

**ADAMS:** No, no. My wife has enough difficulty trying to get me to slide down a mountain on a pair of *skis*!

---

* An association of daredevils whose exploits include hang-gliding over active volcanoes, skiing downhill while playing a grand piano, and catapulting themselves into the air via bungee cords.

*Was Graham subversive because he needed something to react to,*
*and would only be comfortable in that role?*

**ADAMS:** He'd started actually before Python as a young, keen diligent writer, had been very proactive, and then had found himself a position in Python where he was able to be *reactive*, and that oddly enough had brought him his greatest success and renown. His life had really changed because it had been *easier* for him as part of the group, [and] becoming proactive again was more difficult for him. He was happy to throw in his moments of really great inspiration and expect that somehow somebody else would make it work out; in this case it would have been me, and I really didn't have the experience or discipline or self-knowledge to be able to do that.

*What qualities did he bring to a writing*
*relationship outside of the Pythons?*

**ADAMS:** Well, I think our writing relationship certainly had the seeds of some pretty good stuff in it. Again very much in our work he was the subversive one, but instead of subverting a group of his peers, he was a lot of time giving me a hard time, as the sort of wet-behind-the-ears guy who didn't know anything.

*So he was being a mentor and a tormentor?*

**ADAMS:** Yes, that's quite true. Glib, but true! I think if I had had more experience at that time and was better able to stand up to him, or to know for sure what to stand up to him *about* – in other words, if I had had more grip on my own craft at that point – then I think I could have fared better and *we* could have fared better. But in the end it was a marriage not of equals. He was a big, celebrated, successful star, a member of Monty Python and so on, but kind of in danger of losing it with the drink problems and so on; and I was young, naive, inexperienced, wet behind the ears, but terribly excited to have this wonderful opportunity to write with one of the Pythons. There was a lot wrong with that model, really.

He was a very, very funny man. Very, very perceptive, extremely perceptive. And it was that perceptiveness that enabled him both to be capable of gigantic acts of random kindness and gigantic acts of massive unpleasantness. He knew when to stroke and also when to stick in the knife. Very, very complicated man.

*What were your impressions of the other Pythons,*
*and their roles within the group?*

**ADAMS:** [Although] I already knew his voice from radio, *I'm Sorry, I'll Read That Again*, I can remember the first time I ever saw John on television, which would have been *The Frost Report*. I just thought, 'That's it, that's what I want to do, I can do that – I'm as tall as *he* is.' Well, the job had already been taken!

No, it's curious what a powerful effect that whole sort of tightly constrained inner turmoil, the way that resonates with me very, very strongly. John was really an iconic figure for me in all kinds of ways. I've got to know all the Pythons, [yet] I've always found it hardest to relate to John as an actual ordinary human being, because he was always that iconic figure to me. There was something about his performance that I found so mesmeric and extraordinary, that it just made it harder to see the actual human being.

John and Terry Jones were kind of at opposite ends of the spectrum. It's not a coincidence that one's from Weston-super-Mare and the other is from North Wales, because that's a border which people famously despise each other over. Terry being all sort of Celtic and volatile and full of romantic ideals and ideas. And John being rather meticulous, methodical, and cerebral; Terry was sort of emotional and not always best at explaining himself clearly and simply at exactly the right moment. That was the most difficult relationship. But they're like all relationships, [where you would] suddenly become very close.

The member of the Pythons that I know by far the best is Terry Jones. And I think he always found Graham a bit of a mystery, I'm not sure how much real connection there was between them at all. I mean they got on perfectly well, he worked well with him; Terry tends to get on with most people, he's a very friendly, warm, giggly person. But I never really got a sense of what the relationship between Terry and Graham had been.

I first met Terry, actually, when I was on that *Python* shoot in Exeter. And he and I just sort of idly drifted [together] and grew into really quite good friends.

All the Pythons have their own love/hate relationship with the group. The story would always go that there were fights between each of the Pythons *except* for Michael; Mike was always the one that at any given moment *all* of the others liked.

*I understand you very nearly killed them all?*

**ADAMS:** When they went off to do the filming for that fourth series, Graham said, 'Look, if you want to come on down and see how it's filmed, then do.' So I got in my mother's batty old camper-van and drove down to Exeter, where they were doing it, and I went along for the days they were filming. It was very, very extraordinary to be out with the Pythons filming. I think they got me to do a couple of walk-on things; you can probably count the number of frames I actually appeared in on the fingers of two hands, but nevertheless a big thrill.

One evening we thought we'd all go out to dinner, and since I had this big van we'd all go in the van, so we drove off to this quite nice restaurant, had a very nice dinner, and on the way back it was a bit foggy. The strip road seemed to go on a bit, and after a while Eric said, 'Uhm, where are we exactly?' I said, 'We're on the strip road of the motorway.' He said, 'I don't think we are, and the reason I mention this is because if we're not on the strip road of the motorway then we're actually *on* the motorway – and if we're on the motorway, then I've a feeling we're going the *wrong way*.' I said, 'No, no, we're on the strip road, we're not on the motorway.' So a bit of a discussion ensues and after a while the consensus of opinion in the van is that we *are* going the wrong way on the motorway, and at that moment we get overtaken by a car on the other side of the central divide going the *same* way we are. It means we're in the fast lane going the wrong way! So I hurriedly do a U-turn, and just literally a few seconds later a car went past that otherwise would have hit us head-on.

# LIFE OF BRIAN

## NOWADAYS PEOPLE WANT SOMETHING WITTIER

During a promotional tour for *Holy Grail*, when asked what the group's next film would be, Idle responded, *'Jesus Christ: Lust for Glory'*. Apart from the ridiculous juxtaposition of the Son of God with George S. Patton (or, given the general's ego, perhaps not so ridiculous), the title suggested a brazen new direction for the group, involving a much more controversial subject matter than their previous film.

*Brian* tells the story of a young contemporary of Christ's who through happenstance suddenly finds himself to be an adored holy figure. Though first an initiate into a revolutionary group trying to free Judea from the Roman occupation, Brian stumbles into the role of spiritual leader when he is mistaken for the promised Messiah. Burdened with the celebrity of his new position, and now a target of the ruling elite, Brian tries to rid himself of his followers by professing that they do not need leaders for their faith. Imprisoned and sentenced to crucifixion, Brian watches from the cross as in his coming death he becomes an object of admiration, parental scorn, and inspiration for a parting song.

The film marked a maturation of the group, for while *Brian* lacks the breezy innocence that *Grail* exuded (and is much less self-conscious that it is a movie), it is a complex, thoughtful, and ultimately moving portrait of a character and his period. It is adorned with some surreal passages and filled with wildly eccentric characters: the Virgin Mandy, Brian's mother, to whom Three Wise Men come mistaking her hovel for the manger next door; Stan, a revolutionary who wants to be known as Loretta; Ben, an ultra-right-wing prisoner who loves his captors with a vengeance; and Pontius Pilate, whose speech defect completely negates his authority among the masses.

*Brian* also featured humourous asides to the Gospel, such as the difficulties posed for those standing too far away from Jesus at the Sermon on the Mount ('I think He said, *Blessed are the cheesemakers'*). No matter that Christ was an obvious outside figure to the proceedings; many churchgoers took the Pythons to task for what they called a blatantly disrespectful and blasphemous take on the Son of God. The controversy that met with the film's release in 1979, however, merely confirmed that a central idea in *Life of Brian* – that religion or spirituality should not be left in the hands of a powerful few – was sharp enough to sting even when wrapped in the guise of a knockabout farce.

A coy reminder of the film industry's initial lack of enthusiasm for backing the Pythons was the brief spurt of other religion-themed comedies (*Wholly Moses, In God We Trust*) inspired by the success of *Brian*.

**IDLE:** After the initial quip in New York at the opening of *Grail*, Gilliam and I got drunk in Amsterdam and began to make bad-taste carpenter jokes, about J.C. (Jack Christ, not Jesus Cleese), and him being nailed inadequately to a cross by a poor workman, and trying to give the carpenters advice since they were so bad. [And] the cross kept falling over and he went slap face-first into the mud – those sort of sophomoric gags which are *hilarious* when you are in a nice warm bar in Amsterdam with several bottles of Dutch beer inside you.

When we got back to London people were taking the idea seriously, and what attracted us was the freshness of the subject – nobody had made a biblical comedy film. So we rented a lot of Hollywood biblical films, and watched Charlton Heston's breasts and the sheer seriousness with which they treated everything, and this gave us a fresh look. Of course it became clear early on that we couldn't make fun of the Christ since what he says is very fine (and Buddhist), but the people around him were hilarious, and still are!

So it really is an attack on churches and pontificators and self-righteous assholes who claim to speak for God, of whom there are too many still on the planet.

**PALIN:** I remember Eric coming up with *Jesus Christ: Lust for Glory*. What a wonderful, wonderful title. How do you put a film to that?

We knew we needed to work in an area which would stimulate us and which would be different from anything we'd done before, and would be in a sense quite abrasive. And religion was something I think we all had very similar views about: we had all been spoon-fed it in large, regular doses when we were young and yet none of us were religious now, so what was going on? What were the mistakes? So the idea of doing a film about religion was really intriguing. But how you do it, how do you make it *funny*, so it's not just amazingly *dull*?

We realized that the key thing – the way we'd done *Holy Grail* – was to create the biblical period so convincingly that if you put modern characters and modern attitudes in it, it would still convince as being part of that period. Once we'd come up with that, then in our reading up about Jesus' life (which we all did), there were certain things which were absolutely so modern and so absolutely spot-on that we wanted to talk about. For instance, the Messiah fever: at that time there were signs and portents that the Messiah would be coming. Suddenly it seemed a terribly clear idea: everybody's thinking about the Messiah, maybe it's the man next door who's the Messiah; no, it's *him*! You've got Brian there. You've also got the Roman occupation, so you've got the whole of British imperialism, which was something which we were all brought up on. You can have the modern resistance groups, all with their obscure acronyms which they can never remember (the PFL – no, the PLJ) and their conflicting agendas.

I remember getting to the crucifixion period, thinking, 'How on earth do we do this?' And I said, 'Let's apply the same rule: let's just look at the historical background.' The historical background is that Jesus's crucifixion was not a unique event, it was part of a regular entertainment that was put on by the Romans to both impress their power and authority and to entertain people – you know, people would be crucified and there would also be fairs: bread and circuses and crucifixions. Once you accept that it wasn't a unique event, then you can begin to introduce characters who would have been around then, like the terribly decent man who offers to take the cross and the guy just runs off.

If we said we're going to have somebody doing a song on the cross, we started [off thinking], 'We just *can't* do that, it would offend so many people.' Once we had a *reason* for doing that, then it suddenly became like the 'Undertaker' sketch – it had a truth to it. You can quite easily argue that, at that time, there must have been some people who just dealt with this in a not-reverent way. I mean, the stained-glass windows is what has been imposed later on all these events, it's all been very selective, and a few people throughout history (or rather, a *large* number of people) have said, 'This is what we must learn from this, this is what we're going to let you know about it.' And suddenly it all came together.

*Jones on the set in Tunisia.*

So our target, what made the film valid, was not 'Jesus didn't exist' or 'Jesus was a fraud' or that 'Jesus was wrong', but that we rely on interpretation, and interpretation is a *political* thing, and it's been used by people throughout the ages to condone all sorts of excesses. And yet these are just people who will take this story, the story of this man, and use it in any way they want – usually to extract money from poor, gullible people and all that. That's exactly something we could say.

*'History is written by the winners.'*

**PALIN:** Yes. I've always been more interested in the more ordinary people – not in the heroes, but in people who get in the way of heroes *being* heroes.

# AND I SHOULD KNOW, I'VE FOLLOWED A FEW

**JONES:** Terry Gilliam had done *Jabberwocky* in the meantime, so he'd directed his own film. He hadn't really enjoyed shared direction, and then I think there was a feeling among some of the group that it would be better to have one director. And I was quite keen to do it, too. It was by default, really!

I'd always liked history anyway, and the thing I do like about films is creating a world. I'm not particularly interested in films about what's here and now, a world that you can just see as you go out of your door. I do like fantasy and I like entering into the world of the film. On the other hand, I wasn't particularly keen on doing a biblical film because I always thought they had such boring costumes! But Hazel Pethig did a really good job on the costumes, it was a relief to find it wasn't all long robes.

*Why was Terry Jones the ideal director for the group – and why the sole director this time?*

**GILLIAM:** I think Terry instinctively understands the material, he understands what's right and wrong, what's needed and what isn't in that sense. And he works really hard, and he badgers and he just goes on. After *Holy Grail,* I said, 'The director's job is a dogsbody job,' because we were running around doing all the work – for *them,* the other half of the group. It actually started to create a kind of split in the group, because there was Terry and me over here and [they were] there.

When we did the first dub of *Holy Grail,* we showed it [to them]. Eric just hated seeing what we had done to ruin the film; he stormed out. I can't remember if Graham did. It's like, *Jesus!* Terry and I were getting the blame for fucking up the film, and that wasn't a good time. It all got sorted out, but that was a worry. Maybe in a way with just Terry directing, it became so uneven you couldn't blame *just* Terry for it – everyone had to be involved in it more. But with Terry and I together it was like this little unit moving around.

Terry's got so much energy; he's got more energy than I do. He wakes up in the morning, claps his hands, 'Let's get to work!' – this smile, he can't wait to get going. And I'm just like, 'Oh, fuck, another day,' have to drag myself into it. And again with performances, that sense of 'Let's do it!' is very good, where I am going to take longer setting up a shot, to get the smoke and all the elements right. Because I'm *always* adding elements to the thing – I'll be going through six levels of stuff – whereas Terry will deal with two or three levels, and that's much better for Python, to work at that pace.

So Terry's the right director for Python. In a sense I think it was more about me learning that I *wasn't* than anything else, because I don't have the energy to fight the group as a director. For me being the designer [on *Brian*], what I actually do is try to work for the film, but that may not be the same thing as working *with* the director. But the way it's worked out is the right way. And everybody's happy, because again Terry's got more patience than I do with them.

*Is Terry's enthusiasm to direct the group a kind of competition, or test, with the other members of Python, in that he can be seen to be the one to keep them all in line?*

**GILLIAM:** I don't think so; I've never quite felt that. I've always felt there's more of a competition between Terry and me. It's just that he's so passionate, so enthusiastic about it. I don't know if he feels he's competing with the others. I mean, he still obviously has that sense of *he's right*, but then I have the same thing, John has it, we *all* have it. Most of us – Mike is more malleable, and Graham didn't seem to care as much. That's what's so extraordinary: you've got six egos that are all pretty strong and all yet working together, which astonishes me, it still gets me. And it always came down to that fact that we all thought each of the others was brilliant – you may have *hated* them, but it was, really.

## SPARE A TALENT FOR AN OLD EX-LEPER

**JOHN GOLDSTONE:** It was kind of lucky the way certain things happened. They had gone off to Barbados to write the final draft of *Life of Brian* in the end of 1977. The script that came back was wonderful, you could just see it was going to work. And word had got through to EMI, which had become a very different kind of company [post-*Grail*]. It was run by Barry Spikings and Michael Deeley, who were much more into doing 'real' movies by then.* Barry had heard about it because he was in Barbados at the same time they were writing the screenplay. He called me up and said, 'I've got to see this, I just want to do this.' So we sent him the script because they were still one of the few financing bodies in England. He read it immediately, [and] said it was the funniest thing he'd ever read, and he had to have this film. That weekend we shook hands on a deal. I'd established in that deal that we would have complete artistic control over every aspect, we would have final cut, and they accepted that – he wanted it so much, he agreed to those terms.

Despite the fact that we'd agreed [to] it, that deal didn't go through. Lord Bernard Delfont (who was the chairman of EMI) had been told by a member of his board, Sir James Carreras (who had made his fortune with the Hammer horror films, but was a Catholic), that this was a blasphemous film and EMI should not put their name to it. So Bernie told Barry Spikings to find a way out.

We came to a settlement, but it left us without funding. We were already preparing to go out to Tunisia and shoot in April of 1978, and suddenly the money wasn't there. And there was a cutoff point by which we'd have to start shooting or else it was too hot to shoot in Tunisia. There was no way we were going to get the money together in time, so we said, 'Okay, big deep breath, let's say we'll do it in September and it'll

---

* Among their joint credits were Nicolas Roeg's *The Man Who Fell to Earth* and Michael Cimino's *The Deer Hunter*, which won the Academy Award for Best Picture of 1978.

give us a bit more time to get it together.' So I went off to America to raise the money.

I went to Mike Medavoy, who was then head of production at United Artists, who in fact I'd shown *Holy Grail* to in Los Angeles. He'd sent me off to their New York distribution head (who'd turned *Grail* down), but he'd seen that they should have picked it up because it had done very well. So he was very keen to give me an American pickup deal for *Brian*, but it was only for 50 per cent of the costs – the budget for this was now four million dollars, quite a leap forward from *Grail*. So although I had a pledge from him for half the money, it didn't really give me the confidence that I could come back to Europe and raise the rest here, because in those days the places you could go to raise that sort of money didn't exist.

It just so happened at that time that Eric Idle was in Los Angeles and we were looking at options, and he said we should try George Harrison. He's always been a huge Python fan, he'd never invested in movies, but he's got a lot of money and he was a good friend of Eric's. And so we went up to see him at his house. He said, 'Oh yes, I want to do this.' He was clearly serious about it but this was, like, too good to be true. And he said, 'Talk to my business manager, Denis O'Brien [who was back in Europe], and he'll sort it all out.' So I accepted that because I didn't see any real alternative at that point.

Denis was this rather smart ex-banker who had initially taken on Peter Sellers to manage his [affairs] and done very well with Peter, had sorted him out, and Sellers recommended him to Harrison because [when] the whole Apple thing collapsed it all got very messy. Denis had already done a lot to sort out George's affairs [when] I went to see him, and he said, 'Yeah, George wants to do this, but we've never done films, and I don't really know very much about film contracts or anything; you're really going to have to help me through this.' So I presented him with the draft contract EMI had prepared that gave us final cut and artistic control, and he said, 'Fine, we'll use this as the basis of [our] contract.'

So we entered into an agreement [with] one of Denis' companies, a limited partnership, which was the origin of Handmade Films, a company just set up to make *Life of Brian,* of which George was a general partner. Because of that structure, Python kept the copyright in its name, kept final cut, kept artistic control, and Handmade were just licensed to exploit the rights. Interestingly, because they weren't familiar with the film business, we had a provision where we would have consultation on distribution and advertising, and they were not allowed to cut anything without our knowledge and us doing it. And if they defaulted on these points, the [licensing] rights would revert back to us.

(As it turns out twenty years later, the company that they then sold the Handmade library on to, Paragon Pictures, ultimately defaulted on those issues, which was why the Paragon court case went in our favour and the rights [to *Brian*] have been given back to Python.)

But it was all done in good faith and the relationship with George and Denis was very good; they let us go off and make the film and do it the way we wanted to, and they didn't really interfere at all.

What happened with Mike Medavoy was, not long after I'd met with him, he left for Orion; and Orion picked up the rights to *Life of Brian* for America. And he picked up *Erik the Viking* for America when he was at Orion, and didn't interfere, really. He was always very supportive.

## AS MUCH GOLD AS THEY COULD EAT

**GOLDSTONE:** Well, we've never, ever had enough to spend, it's always been having to be quite creative in terms of how it could be done. *Holy Grail* had been such a difficult one to do because the budget was really limited and it needed an enormous amount of invention; I mean the very thing about not being able to afford horses and having to use coconuts was inspired. The *Life of Brian* budget – which we maintained – worked because we found this set in Tunisia built for *Jesus of Nazareth*[*] that was still

---

[*]    Produced, coincidentally, by Lord Delfont's brother, Lew Grade.

standing, which we then added on to and elaborated on, and in fact used some of their costumes from a Rome costume house. We were really able to give it a look and a scale without having to spend the kind of money it might have cost. But in those situations, they all rose to the occasion.

There weren't any huge difficulties with *Life of Brian*. Once we'd sorted out the finances, we actually had time to prepare, and I've always found that preparation is crucial to making these things work.

The other important thing is the screenplays don't really vary that much. A certain amount of work happens in rehearsals, but essentially they keep to what's on the page; it's not as if they're improvising or doing anything unpredictable. It's all been worked out before, and that does make a big difference to being able to run a film effectively. There are no enormous surprises. The only things you might run into is weather.

## I'M BRIAN, AND SO IS MY WIFE

**JONES:** I think John was quite keen to play Brian, actually, and I think others of us didn't want him to do it, partly because we thought Graham was such a good straight man, and partly because there were so many other parts, like the revolutionaries' leader, that we really wanted John to do – he wouldn't [have been] able to do them at the same time. The Centurion *had* to be John, so we felt quite strongly that Graham ought to do [the lead].

**CLEESE:** Yes, it was the one exception to the rule about people not fighting about casting. I wanted to do Brian for a very simple reason: We made *Brian* in 1978, and at that point I had reached the ripe old age of thirty-eight and had never had the experience of playing a role the whole way through a film. And I was fascinated by the idea of doing it. I didn't know what it would be like, I didn't know how difficult or easy it would be to do scenes out of order, it was so different from just turning up and being a centurion. And I really wanted to have this new experience; I wanted to learn, because if I'm learning I'm happy. And the others resisted, and I have to say they were absolutely right, and I was disappointed for about forty-eight hours when they basically said, 'Well, Graham *has* to be Brian.' And they were right because I was funnier in the other roles than Graham would have been, and Graham was very, very good as Brian.

**DAVID SHERLOCK:** By the time of *Life of Brian*, Graham had stopped drinking. Well, he was given less than a year to live if he didn't; he saw a guy who had also been at St Bart's who said, 'If you continue as you are, I reckon you could be dead within a year; do you want to live or do you want to die?' Graham said, 'Well, I'd rather live.' And he survived for another ten years. But the damage that he'd done to his liver was colossal. From then on he became, not a *total* health freak, but pretty much. I think the thing that protected him up until then was the fact that we were both very keen amateur cooks and thoroughly enjoyed preparing food – because he ate well, which is very unusual for someone who drinks hard, it wasn't really until the year before he collapsed and having tried to dry himself out that it was really noticeable that things were going wrong.

*You played some of the more colourful characters in* **Brian**. *Can you explain the mix?*

**PALIN:** Well, Ben was someone who's got nothing going for him at all; he's in great pain, great discomfort, but he's still incredibly aggressive. It's like the Black Knight with no legs: 'Come back, you bastard, I'll kill you,' or whatever he says. Ben was a bit like that, someone you just think, 'Shut up, don't say *anything*!' But no, he's going to have a go. He's *always* going to have a go. He's very chirpy: he loves the Romans, the way they deal with all these things. That takes a situation where a character behaves completely the opposite to how you would expect him to behave; I suppose that's where the comedy is.

*Do you approach the creation of characters
from a psychological standpoint?*

**PALIN:** Well, I think they are very instinctive. Certainly it's the way I write. I just write something which comes into my head, or a situation, and it comes out like that, and then probably at the end you can make a connection: 'Ah, yes, I can see where this comes from.' But at the time it feels very intuitive.

Unlike Ben, who was created from nowhere, Pontius Pilate was a legitimate historical character, part of the Bible story, [therefore] he had to be dealt with. How do we deal with this man? I must have felt: ruling class, British ruling class, very often distinguished through some aristocratic inbreeding by vowel difficulties of some kind, or vocal distinctions. I think it might have just come from there.

Pilate never acknowledges that he has a problem at all. This is the wonderful thing; again I think this must have come in my mind from listening to Violet Bonham Carter or people like that, the English aristocracy. They have vewy stwange ways of tawking, and they doughn't think eet's vewy extwawdinawy at awl! And I had an aunt who said *parafeen*, she always referred to paraffin as *parafeen*. This is something they're not aware of, so I felt that I had to play Pilate as somebody who, if he was aware of the way he spoke he wouldn't have chosen the words that he did.

*Ben, the incorrigible prisoner.*

So one had a character who

is exercising power, that's what Pilate is doing; he is the top man there, he can go up to people and be sort of, 'Why, you know, you haven't got your hair cut! You call *that* a uniform?' or something like that. It's going up to someone and saying, 'I am more powerful than you, and I'm going to show you what my powers are.' It just so happens that in this case, you have a man of great power in the region [who] has something about him which is *impossible* to take seriously, namely 'Wisable Bwian' and all that sort of stuff. People are aware of this, but as long as he's got soldiers around then that's fine – nobody dares laugh. Hence the scene with Biggus Dickus, where he gets very angry at the soldiers just trying desperately *not* to laugh.

I suppose it's the sort of paper-thin division between being powerful or being ridiculous. Ceaușescu, for instance, was this amazingly powerful man in palaces; overnight, he's suddenly just a frightened man who ends up lying on a yard with a bullet through him.

*Well, having power and having authority are slightly different things.*

**PALIN:** Yes, yes. Well, once we'd got the idea of Pilate, the pronunciation problem, then one had to up the stakes to really exploit it, so it can't just be a few guards wanting to laugh; what happens when you've got a *whole crowd* of people corpsing somebody? We built the great temple, there's all this wonderful imperial toga and all that sort of stuff, and he goes out to the people, and that was just an extraordinary scene to play. Because when you find six hundred people all rolling over and laughing at you, it's just as strong as people screaming abuse at you. It has the same effect: you suddenly feel your power is completely negated.

I suddenly realized, 'God, ridicule is such a strong weapon in the hands of a really determined crowd.' I think much more [so] than hatred. You know, hatred sort of breeds hatred; comedy just breeds more comedy! It's all about people's fear about comedy. That's why people in positions of power don't like comedy, because it's essentially subversive, and that was a subversive use of laughter in the Pilate scene for all to see. We all know (long before he does) that he's been made to look a complete idiot; but he carries on, and so does Biggus Dickus.

The name Biggus Dickus, there's nothing subtle about it at all, it's obviously a silly name to have. Again, brilliant, absolute brilliant playing by Graham, looks magnificent, and if Graham had just done one sort of little giggle or looked to one side and been *aware* of it, it just wouldn't have worked. It had to be played absolutely superbly, which is always one of the things which gave me the most tremendous pleasure in Python; it all boiled down to how people performed, how clever they were at getting really what the humour was *about*. You know, sometimes missing a short-term gag for the long-term benefit by playing it straight.

And so, in people's minds now, Biggus Dickus is a man of no humour at all, Pontius Pilate is a man of no humour at all – both of whom take part in one of the funniest, most humorous sketches of Python!

### *Was it a precursor of the stutterer you played in* A Fish Called Wanda?

**PALIN:** 'Michael Palin. Speciality: speech defects.' I used to spend so much time at school mercilessly dissecting any verbal anomaly in any of the teachers because you heard them all the time talking at you; the great teachers you just don't hear it, but there are a lot of others who are extremely boring and the fact that they spoke in a certain way just lodged in my mind. I remember that patterns of speech became terribly, terribly important; certainly when I was at school my first attempts at humour were always being able to mimic how people could speak, because I listened to them day in and day out, droning on in Latin, so maybe I have a particular ear for speech patterns. I didn't actually dislike bad teachers. Sometimes I liked them, I felt very sad for the ones that just couldn't teach very well, but I liked them as people. So there's a certain amount of odd affection for Pontius Pilate in a way; you couldn't *hate* him!

# MY HOVERCRAFT IS FULL OF EELS

**JONES:** Until we actually started, I felt, 'Oh my God, what's this going to be like, so far away, filming on location in Tunisia?' Once we'd started doing it, it was great, but for example we didn't know how we were going to organize the crowds to do anything, because we couldn't communicate directly with them.

One day we had a crowd of five hundred people in the square, and we had to get them all laughing. We hired a Tunisian comedian to tell jokes and we filmed the crowd listening to him, but that didn't really work very well. And I wanted everybody to lie on their backs and kick their legs in the air. So we got our assistant director (a Tunisian) to tell them what we wanted, and there were a lot of blank stares. Finally I said to him, 'I'll tell you what: tell them the director's going to show you what he wants you to do.' So I fell on my back and kicked my legs in the air and started laughing hysterically, and then he said, 'Now we want *you* to do that.' And of course they *all* went down on their backs absolutely hysterical with laughter, it was the most wonderful sight, and the dust rose and these Tunisians were just so abandoned, lying on their backs, kicking their legs in the air. And of course we weren't turning over [the camera], because we were just *telling* them what to do! That was heartbreaking. Of course then they had to do it again, they did it quite well, but it was never quite as funny as that first moment when they all went over.

The other thing was, a crowd had to shout back in English, when Brian is in the window with the Virgin Mandy. We had about two hundred and fifty there, I think, they were all Tunisians; if any of them spoke a foreign language, they spoke a bit of French. I'd always assumed we'd have to dub it. So we had about eighteen English speakers, we put them all up at the front, and then I just said, 'Okay, say these words after me,' and I just shouted out the lines, and they shouted them back. And then I'd shout [more] and they'd shout them again. It was perfect, it was just unbelievable. It sounded pretty good, and in fact that's what we used in the end.

*Jones demonstrating proper laughing techniques to his extras.*

**GILLIAM:** In a way, with *Brian,* we kept trying to do really dramatic things which I don't know if it ever works with comedy. I mean, *Brian* is just a more clever version of disguising the fact that they're a bunch of sketches than the others have been, because at least there's a tale that flows through the thing. But when we start setting up a thing like the chase and people are running, I don't think the audience ever gets *really* caught up and excited. It's jolly, it's fun, [and] you're always slightly back from it; it's not like being in a real thriller where your guts are in your mouth. And yet I think Terry and I always wanted to be able to do that to an audience. We always had a tendency to turn them into dramatic pieces with tension and suspense. But I don't think we've done it with Python; it's much better we go off and play with those elements in our own films.

## WHERE IS THE NEW LEADER? I WISH TO HAIL HIM

**GILLIAM:** It was *Jabberwocky* that spoiled me. I got through *Holy Grail* and then [had] done my own thing, it was just, I don't want to do it, I don't want to get into arguments with Terry about 'We should be doing it this way, we should be doing it that way.' I thought, 'Let me just design the thing.' It was like going back to being at the camera. Because on *Holy Grail* that's what I did anyway as well, I mean the whole look of the thing was just stuff I really concentrated on.

And so I did the same thing with *Life of Brian*, but unlike *Grail*, where as a co-director I was in control of where the camera was, as a de-signer I *wasn't*, and so I became the 'resigner' at that point! I mean, you can have all this stuff, but if you don't put the camera there you don't *see* it. I don't *mind* if you don't want to put the camera there, but if we built all that stuff and spent all that money, *put the camera there!* And I got a little bit crazed about it as well. I think working with the group was mak-ing me fraught, because it's one thing to be crazed on your own project where you've really got control over it, but the group thing was just for me becoming more and more difficult.

It's like the writing on the wall: *Romani ite domum*. Now all that's set up to be shot as day-for-night – it was supposed to be night – and to do day-for-night you've got to point the camera in one direction as opposed to the other direction so that [it can] be front-lit, so that you can crank everything down; the sky goes dark, and you still have light on the faces. And John didn't want to do it that way, he wanted to hold his sword in the other hand, and so he couldn't do it left-to-right, he could only do it right-to-left – whichever, it doesn't matter – and so Terry sticks the camera there. So basically to get the scene looking like night, you've got to drop it *so* down you're missing a lot of stuff in the eyes; but it doesn't look like night, either, because they couldn't bring the sky down enough! I go crazy with things like that, and I'm *glad* I wasn't directing, because I would have just exploded at that point; but Terry – 'It'll be fine, put the camera here' – didn't have the problem that I would have had.

It's like the scene where Ben is hanging in his cell. Roger Christian designed this set, it was a really good set; there's a long wall and then Ben is hanging way up there under a sewage outlet so sewage is dripping on his head the whole time. He's way up there and Brian's down there, so it's not like they're level. Roger had done this thing, and I said, 'This is great.' Then Roger took Terry to the set, and Terry says, 'Well, he's going to be too high.' And so Roger chopped the whole thing down and lowered Ben. So of course when Terry gets in there with the camera and tries to see the angle, he can't do it, so now he's got to dig a hole in the ground to get the camera where it belonged!

There's a weird, I suppose, competition between Terry and me, and that's what's funny. It's always there, and maybe it shouldn't be, and I think it is because in a sense we seem to see things in the same way, but how we get there is different. I can't do a patch on what he can do, [yet] I'm much more technically adept at getting the idea, the image of that idea, on the screen more so than Terry is, and yet I feel he's still trying to compete at that level rather than just accepting that's what I do better than he does.

Like the crucifixion: Roger Christian and I went out to Matmata. Terry is so excited and he's convinced the crucifixion scene is going to be out here. Rather than waste time we split up, we'll go in two separate areas. He goes roaring off that way, Roger and I go this way. We find this spot that's fucking great; it's got everything you want – not only this beautiful ridge, but there's a range of mountains behind it, the sun will be at the right angles, and on the front part there's this huge opening with an acropolis there – 'Golgothic' is what it should be. So you've got all that working for you, and the sun and the mountains, everything would be perfect! And so we come back, and Terry I can see has not found what he's wanted, he's disappointed, and we decided we've got to be really careful how we present this.

So I go, 'Okay, we found something that *might* work, we're not sure.' We were walking on eggshells! We go out to this thing and say, 'Well, what do you think?'

Terry said, 'Hhmmm, yeah . . . Oh! Look at that *over there*!' And it's in *the wrong place*! So Roger and I go, 'Oh, fuck!' And that's where we shot the fucking thing – we shot the crucifixion in the wrong fucking place.

*Cleese flagrantly flouting some Islamic law or another.*

He would just not accept (and he didn't want to) when we said, 'The light will do this . . . ,' because *Terry had to find it.* It was this competition. At that time, *he* had to get it. And he found the place, and it's *fine*, the film goes on, all that's fine, but there's a *better* place, it would be such a spectacular end to the film. [*laughs*]

That's why I just can't get involved directing the group. This stuff is too important to me to just take it easy. And Terry's more lax in a strange way, it's less important to him.

There's one bit that I did go down and shoot, that was the opening scene with the Wise Men coming into Bethlehem; they come in, then we go to the set inside, and that's Terry, and then we come outside [and] see the Holy Family, that's me, and they're really beautiful shots! [*laughs*] And it's just that difference; that's what I am trying to do, and I know the rest of the group is not interested in working at that level. And for me to do that takes this, that, and the other thing; it takes longer. So it's better that I just step back from it.

*Gilliam under mud.*

*Do the other Pythons appreciate that after the fact?*
*Do they look at the finished film and say, 'Yes, it's better and*
*funnier for having held out for that visual quality'?*

**GILLIAM:** I don't know, nobody's ever said anything! Not that I ever sat down and really talked to John. I mean, Eric understands it, and I think Mike understands it. That's what's so funny about us as a group: we've never sat down and discussed things like that. We don't spend a lot of time congratulating each other and patting each other on the back, which is the *good* thing. I think we're very critical, so *that's* good. I just always felt there was sort of a shared respect, that was the main thing, which was unstated but it was there. And that's when the group worked best.

I love *Life of Brian*, I think it's great even though it doesn't have visually as much beauty – not just beauty, but things of interest – in there. That's one of the reasons, when I was being the jailer and some of these other characters, I cover myself with mud; it was a way of adding texture to the movie!

But it's not that vital because ultimately what we were *saying*, these ideas, was what was important. Such funny ideas, such really intelligent, outrageous, and strong and smart ideas.

## I'VE GOT BETTER THINGS TO DO
## THAN COME DOWN TO THE DAIRY

**GILLIAM:** I honestly don't remember whether it was my idea or not, the idea of the spaceship for getting Brian from the top of the tower to the ground safely. Does anybody else claim credit for that? Because if they don't, I will! It might have been Graham, for all I know, but the reason I think it might have been me was because I was very much impressed with a lot of what was going on in *Star Wars* at the time, the scale of that; all I wanted to do was play around with that. So once we decided on the spaceship, then I was on my own and just did my spaceship sequence, invented my little creatures.

I think it was my desperate bid to escape from being the animator, escape from that role. It was my first chance to play around with model shooting. We'd done some very basic stuff on *Holy Grail*, like using little cows from train sets thrown in the air, but this is me and my interest in special effects moving forward. I wanted to show we could do a *Star Wars* sequence for five quid! It was really the first step towards *The Crimson Permanent Assurance*. I got my own little film group, a good crew, and we did all that in a room about twenty-five feet by twenty-five feet, got Graham to come in and look frightened for a bit, and that was it!

I need to be just a step away from [the group] to get where I really feel confident enough and comfortable enough to do what I do without feeling I have to explain it, justify it, any of that stuff – I just *did* it. I think it's been like that even now when I go to Hollywood; I have to talk about a script that I did very, very hesitantly. 'I know what I'm doing, I don't have to sit and tell you people what I'm trying to do.' 'You *have* to, because *we* have the money, that's why you do it.' But I've learned in Hollywood that what I do is just make a lot of noise and flap my hands and get re-

*Biblical alien.*

ally excited: 'AND THEN THIS THING COMES IN, AND, AND THEN, *WOW!!* AND THEN . . .'

I'm sure they haven't a fucking clue what I just said, but it *sounds* exciting! The medium becomes the message.

*I like how the spaceship's engine shifts gears.*

**GILLIAM:** Well, if you're going to do a chase, it's like *Bullitt* with gears changing. What we actually used were motorcycle gear changes. *Brrrrmm VVVRRRrrrmmm!* That still makes me laugh!

**JONES:** The filming of [*Life of Brian*] was great fun, actually; it was really enjoyable. You just felt you were on a roll, you just knew it was working. But the editing wasn't very fun. I always felt with the films I'd be *left* out there, especially by *Life of Brian* – everybody else would go off and do other things and I was there six, seven months later still toiling away, trying to do the dubbing and this and that.

I didn't enjoy the editing, and that was partly because Terry G. and Julian [Doyle] had just set up a company together in Neal's Yard and they were working very closely. And Julian was editing it, and I felt slightly excluded in the editing which felt like a bit of, 'I have to get in.' Terry G. was a bit fed up with me at that point; we'd been on location and I'd said something rather sharp to him and he was feeling a bit put-out about it, so there was some odd thing going on.

**DOYLE:** I learned then what had gone wrong with the editing on *Holy Grail*. In *Brian* there was a scene of Brian and a salesman haggling over a beard. Now they played that out, rehearsed it, and shot it, then we'd see the rushes. And there was this two-shot at the beginning, the wide shot of the two haggling, and the audience was in stitches it's so funny, and then there were some close-ups of Brian and the beard salesman, and *nobody laughs*; of course they're close-ups, they're only half the performance, and you've *seen* the performance in the wide shot. So I had Eric come to me, and he said, 'Don't cut the two-shot, it's brilliant, the close-ups don't work.' And the same with Graham, he came to me: 'Don't cut the two-shot! The two-shot works brilliantly.'

This is a thing: comedians will tell you two-shots work, because you get the timing right. Somebody can cut in close-ups and ruin somebody's performance by changing their pauses, and that's why I think comedians are [keen] about the two-shot – at least nobody'll *ruin* it.

I'd done a rough cut of *Brian*. When we ran the film back in London, they said, 'Oh, it's working great except the haggling doesn't work.' And Eric was, of course, 'Well, we'll have to cut out the haggling.' And I said, 'Let me have a go at it.'

What it was, the haggling was too slow in the two-shot. It works fine when you play it on its own, [but] when you put it in the film, where Brian's being chased by Romans, the performances are too slow. I can speed them up if I go to the close-ups and put shots of the Romans getting closer; there's more panic on him. I cut the two-shot with close-ups and stuck it in the film. Cleese came around and I ran it: 'Well, that seems to work.'

# NO ONE IS TO STONE ANYONE UNTIL
# I BLOW THIS WHISTLE

**JONES:** Oh yes, I remember when we were writing it sort of thinking some loony might take potshots at us, something like that. I thought it would be controversial. Having said that, the controversy surrounding it usually came from people who hadn't seen the film, people who just didn't like the idea of it. As I say, the film is heretical; it's not blasphemous!

*Some might not understand the difference; they both sound bad!*

**JONES:** Well, it's not blasphemous because it accepts the Christian story; in fact, the film doesn't make sense unless you take the Christian story, but it's heretical in terms of [being] very critical of the Church, and I think that's what the joke of it is, really: to say, here is Christ saying all these wonderful things about people living together in peace and love, and then for the next two thousand years people are putting each other to death in His name because they can't agree about *how* He said it, or in what order He said it. The whole thing about 'The sandal!' 'It's a *shoe*!' is like a history of the Church in three minutes.

**CLEESE:** Terry always says it's a heresy, and I've never understood this because a heresy is a teaching which is at variance with the Church's teaching, and I don't know in what way we're a heresy. What we are is quite clearly making fun of the way people follow religion but not of religion itself, and the whole purpose of having that lovely scene at the start when the Three Wise Men go into the wrong stable is to say Brian is not Christ, he just gets taken for a Messiah. And that's a very important point.

I would defend *Life of Brian* as being a perfectly *religious* film.

*Did the controversy divert a potential audience by
making them think the film was something it wasn't,
an attack on a revered figure?*

**JONES:** Might have done. But usually our audience is very intelligent. I mean, we've never had a mass audience. Python's always been [accepted by] sort of an intelligent, articulate minority, so our audiences would soon cop onto what the film was, really. I don't think it distracted people in terms of appreciating the film.

**PALIN:** Yes, I was just totally indignant at the level of the debate. I think I'd expected there to be argument, I'd expected there to be opposition, but the level of it was so depressing. It was just, 'They're comedy writers, therefore nothing they say is to be taken seriously. They have no serious point to make.' I mean, John and I went on television [with] a bishop and a prominent religious writer, and they were pathetic – they were just sort of sneering at us [for] attempting to deal with this subject. And the rest of it was just laughable because people were saying it was Python's send-up of Jesus.

'No, he isn't Jesus, he's *this* character.'

'Oh, we all *know* what you mean.'

'We have Jesus in the film *and* we have Brian in the film; Brian is *not* Jesus. We make that quite clear.'

'Oh, yes he is.'

You can't deal with people who have that level of resistance, just head-in-sand attitudes. The opposition was of a very, very poor quality, just exactly what you'd expect: knee-jerk. There was no real attempt to argue with us and say, 'Well, perhaps you'd got it historically wrong here,' or that sort of thing; it was, 'Python, they're irreverent. They made a Bible story with no respect for Jesus. We all know they hate everybody and they have no respect for anybody. Therefore our case is, we rest our case.'

So consequently I remember being tremendously rewarded by the attitude of some churchmen I knew and heard about who said, 'This is exactly what you *should* be saying, this is terrific that you've done a film like this. I want to show it to my congregation.' Members of a church at St John's Wood, the guy said, 'We showed it to them, we had a discussion, we raised these points, we loved it, terrific.'

**CLEESE:** The offence is what a friend of mine called 'public offence'. He said when you really offend people they tend to come up to you privately and express their offence quite gently – you feel uncomfortable afterwards because you really do feel you've upset someone. There's also what they call 'institutional offence', and he had a lot of this running a department of the BBC, which is people complaining because they're the heads of organizations and they feel that their members will complain to them if *they* don't complain.

One of the themes in the film is, 'Do make up your own mind about things and don't do what people tell you.' And I find it slightly funny that there are now religious organizations saying, 'Do not go and see this film that tells you *not* to do what you are told.'

I think originally the movie might have gone into two hundred movie houses, and once the protests started it was soon decided to put it into six hundred. So it is wonderful when people embark on a course of action that they can really achieve something so totally counterproductive. One can only think that either they are profoundly stupid – and these people are obviously not – or they have become so enraged that they are incapable of thinking. Because obviously if you don't want people to see a movie, the thing to do is to just let it quietly die away, get a tiny little review on the movie page, and nobody knows about it. But if you do want to make a success of a movie, get people cross and angry and protesting. It's extraordinary!

They have actually made me rich! I feel we should send them a crate of champagne or something.

**IDLE:** The film has appealed to many seriously religious people, including the Dalai Lama and some Jesuits. It [also] plays better in Catholic countries – go figure! But it was wonderful – anger is the hallmark of the closed mind, and we certainly flushed out some raving bigots, and that was part of the joy of it.

**PALIN:** It was quite bracing at the time; also it had a delightfully Pythonic effect, in that in this country the film was passed by the British Board of Film Censors, but local councils could ban it under a rather obscure law governing hygiene in cinemas! For some reason under this law, they could if they wanted to decide not to show a certain film, and a number of councils decided not to show *Life of Brian*.

> *There were two towns in Surrey without cinemas that banned it anyway!*

**PALIN:** Really? Well, my favourite story is that Swansea, a large town in Wales, had banned it. And this little cinema, a flea-pit up the coast in Porthcawl just sort of going out of business, put it on, and busloads of people used to come up from Swansea from the university and places like that to see it. So this cinema suddenly enjoyed a complete new lease on life – rejuvenated by *Life of Brian*!

**NANCY LEWIS:** I was coordinating with whoever was doing publicity for *Life of Brian* at Warners.[*] I know we had originally planned this wonderful launching party for it. The Pythons had come up with the idea of having these cardboard cut-outs of famous people around, dotted all over the party. Terry sent over a prototype I have still in our storage container in New Jersey: a life-sized black-and-white photo of Frank Sinatra. Of course the party was cancelled because Warners thought it would just invite controversy.

They were all very nervous and twitching at it. Strom Thurmond

---

[*] At the time Warners was handling distribution of Orion product.

*Otto's crack suicide squad, in a demonstration cut from the final film.*

and his wife* and all the people who hadn't seen it came out and said it shouldn't be seen, it should be banned, but it was not as controversial. Everyone was told to tread carefully, and as a result they did very little publicity for it, they low-keyed it.

**GOLDSTONE:** I suppose we went into it blindly. I mean, you can't really consider the consequences, otherwise you don't do your best work. You can almost take the view that if the public can't take the joke, tough! It's that thing of hitting a nerve; and the resistance to it was from groups just reacting to the *idea* that anyone should lampoon a piece of sacred history. And that wasn't what it was about at all. I think when people saw it and enjoyed it, that kind of took over from all the controversy. And everywhere it was banned ultimately played the film, it was only a matter of time – some decades! Certainly the same thing happened in America; in the Bible Belt it was viewed with a lot of suspicion, but where it did play it played very well.

**CLEESE:** Many years later I stood in a queue to see the Marty Scorsese film *The Last Temptation of Christ,* and I was standing there with all these nice, thoughtful, quiet, well-behaved students who were reading books or talking quietly to each other, and opposite were all the people protesting against the film who were as batty and unpleasant a bunch of ravers as I've ever seen! It was something terribly funny about these weirdos protesting at these very normal, quiet, well-behaved people.

Let's face it: about 20 per cent of the population is quite disturbed, in *any* country. Some of them only slightly, but by the time you get to

---

* At the behest of a Presbyterian minister in Irmo, South Carolina, who had spoken with the senator's wife, Nancy, Strom Thurmond called an attorney for the General Cinema Corporation to say that there was 'overwhelming sentiment against the showing of the movie in South Carolina' and suggested that [they] suspend showing it in the state. GCC subsequently cancelled its engagements there. Other reports of opposition led to the film's cancellation in a few other cities, including Baton Rouge, Louisiana, and Charlotte, North Carolina.

the bottom 7 or 8 per cent, I mean *really* getting quite disturbed. And of course they tend to latch on to religion or things like that for comfort, rather than extrapolating theories as to how the eye works or something.

**PALIN:** In the end, we'd been through all the possible dangers of people dismissing it and I think we'd come out with something intellectually defensible, so I quite enjoyed the reaction. Because in many ways it made us exactly what Python is about, really, the reaction from the sort of people who were inspiration for Python: the little petty local officials who close cinemas for hygiene because they don't like the comedy film about the Bible story.

In a way, comedy doesn't want to change the world, and it never does, but occasionally you need to have your own prejudices reinforced! These people *still exist,* so there's a reason to be doing Python!

> *Didn't Hugh Greene, a former head of the BBC, say that there were some people who **deserved** to be offended?*

**PALIN:** Yes, probably all of us!

## ALWAYS LOOK ON THE BRIGHT SIDE OF LIFE

Perhaps the most curious side note to *Life of Brian* came during the Falklands/Maldives War. On May 4, 1982, the destroyer HMS *Sheffield* was struck by an Exocet missile. As the ship was sinking, its crew – waiting on deck to be rescued – struck up a rendition of 'Always Look on the Bright Side of Life'.

**IDLE:** I was pleased, since the entire fleet was steaming away from them, as they had been hit by an Exocet missile and they may have had nukes aboard. I felt very proud and moved [that they sang that song]. The RAF pilots in the Gulf War would also sing it before going out on their incredible low-flying sorties. The success of this song has brought me great joy and it seems now to be a classic.

**PALIN:** Well, I was really moved in a sense that they sang that rather than 'Abide with Me' or 'Rule, Britannia.' Part of me felt glad that there's a song there that can rally people in times like that. The reasons I think Eric wrote it, the spirit of the song, is it's a very British thing – no matter what goes wrong, keep smiling, we're all cheery. All those aspects of Britishness that we've seen in wartime films and on stage, the chirpy Brit coping with life through terrible adverse situations. Eric's caught the spirit, and these people are just confirming that a song like that actually expresses something which is British which is something they wanted to say. Not, you know, 'Praise the Lord, we are at war' or any nationalistic thing like that. And also I think an element of 'we've fucked up again, we shouldn't be here in the Falklands'. Maybe it's just an acceptance of the new face of warfare: 'Is this really necessary? Did we really need to come here and be torpedoed for these islands? By a missile invented by one of our close European allies? You know, it's all very confusing!' I think when all the jingoism is sort of taken away, a lot of those people who went to the Falklands (including some professional soldiers) [had] a deep mistrust of the whole venture.

Anyway, hearing that they'd sung that song confirmed what a good song it is, in a way. Also, it's very interesting that Python thrives in closed communities; I'm constantly hearing of soldiers in barracks, or people who do dangerous work – fighter pilots or mountain climbers, whatever – [who] all seem to know the Python films very well. It seems to [relate to] some aspect of coping with adversity, because humour *is* important.

**JONES:** Yes, it was odd, really, that song. I was not particularly keen on the song when Eric came up with it. He wrote it when we were out there in Tunisia. We didn't really have the end sewn up, and Eric came up with the song and played it. I thought, 'This isn't really *that* wonderful,' but then it really worked on the film, so it shows you shouldn't listen to me when it comes to songs!

# FLYING SOLO

## 'COS THINGS 'BREAK', DON'T THEY?

The strains that were evident in the group during the shooting of *Holy Grail*, and the absence of Cleese from the fourth series, reflected the push-pull that each of the Pythons felt when it came to pursuing their own solo careers away from the group (which for some was difficult), and away from public identification as a Python (which was even harder). Indeed, the sobriquet 'Python' was not to be shaken off lightly, for many of the group's solo endeavours revelled in the crazed madness (*Fawlty Towers*), stream-of-consciousness narrative (*Time Bandits*), blithe surrealism (*Ripping Yarns*), or anarchy (*The Rutles*) that were hallmarks of the series. Such comparisons could not be avoided or ignored.

Though working separately, the Pythons still collaborated in their criticism of each other's work by reviewing scripts, and formed Prominent Features in the late Eighties to produce their own solo projects (e.g., *A Fish Called Wanda*).

---

*How hard do you think each of the Pythons was working to evoke an individual style, or was it hard for them to* avoid *a Python style?*

**GOLDSTONE:** When the group were very much together and operating as such, any use of the Python name [outside the group] was always a bit sensitive. They were very protective, obviously, because it represented a very definite combination of those six people, and that chemistry produced something unique – it wasn't something that any individual member of Python ever could replicate in that way.

It was clear in those earlier films, before the individuals really found their own styles, that one could understand there was a certain confusion because there was still something in there that was trying to be Python as well, or could not *avoid* being Python.

*Jabberwocky*, which I worked on, was something that happened in between two Python films, *Holy Grail* and *Life of Brian*. It did have strong Python influences and of course Michael Palin playing the lead confused people enough to make them think it was *Monty Python's Jabberwocky*, which we obviously got rather upset about. Terry Gilliam wrote it with Charles Alverson. It seemed quite a lot of the jokes were sort of sub-Python in a way; you can see the influence without it being total, and yet it had its own character as well, which was very much to do with Terry's visuals. But he kept resorting to moments, scenes that have a kind of Python nonsensibility, that *kind* of worked but didn't as well as their originals.

But I would guess that, far greater than anybody else's, Gilliam's career is the one that's really developed away from that style into something that is unique. Whatever he puts his hand to (albeit with other writers) has got a great original flair about it.

*Yellowbeard*, of course, has got Graham and John; there was always the Python connection. But it's not good at all; it was a very hit-and-miss piece. It's kind of representative of Graham in many ways, a rather hit-and-miss kind of career, and person. I mean, sweet and lovely, but he needed very much the support of everybody else (particularly John) in creating what he did. He individually was inspired with some of the ideas that he had, but it needed to be contained.

But even with Terry Jones – I mean, there are moments in all his films that use a certain style of comedy. I remember there were moments in *Erik the Viking* that still [contained] an element of Python, and *Wind in the Willows* a lot less – a lot, lot less.

**PALIN:** I think we were all very sensitive during the period of post-Python of things being called Python that weren't Python. We'd get very angry, and there'd be late-night phone calls – Graham especially, they always came late at night – so they'd say, 'Bloody John's *Golden Skits of Muriel Volestrangler,** it says it's from Python, I mean, this is *shocking*, isn't it?'

'Oh yes, yes, we're all *very* shocked.'

But in the end I think everything has in an odd way helped everything else.

*The Wind in the Willows* is an interesting case in point where the producer wanted to get all the Pythons into it, to put all their names on it. And we all played because we love Terry, but what I worry about is Python fans going and seeing John's only in one scene and I just play the Sun, and there's no Terry Gilliam animation. There's a superb performance by Eric and a very boisterous performance by Terry, so it's got that much, but I was worried at that time that they were trying to sell it as the next Python film. But I think we've always been more worried about it, more concerned about it, than the audience.

It was something which was in our minds much more than in the people's minds. But nowadays everything merges a little bit, and it's very hard to say to die-hard fans, 'Well, you shouldn't really be lumping this

---

* A collection of Cleese's sketches, many of which predate Python, published in 1984.

with Python.' It's not for us to be pedantic about how they should approach it.

*How are reactions when you venture into a different medium,
such as your novel* Hemingway's Chair?

**PALIN:** I've not really found it a great problem. I think people are quite generous. Especially in the States, people have taken this quite seriously. And I think the fact that it is something which is quite different from Python – I'm not trying to write a 'Python novel'. One of the few reviews that didn't like it was the *Cleveland Plain Dealer*; the heading was 'Not Many Laughs Here for Python Fans'. Which was I suppose a bit of a lumber, but that's very rare. I mean, all the others gently reminded you the author's a Python but that [the book is] something rather different. And once you've done that, then I think the *next* one will be slightly easier. Because when people write about you they talk about the last thing you've done rather than the next thing.

*Working on your own, away from the group, do you have a
preference between writing and acting?*

**IDLE:** I am sick to death of being in movies and avoid them usually. They are boring and by and large overrated. I like to stay home and create – writing, songs, musicals, books. Filming as an actor is 98 per cent drudgery, followed by 2 per cent flattery. I am too old to be interested in sixteen-hour days stuck in a trailer park. I do enjoy acting, but I detest waiting.

---

While Cleese's partnership in Video Arts (which produced entertaining training films for businessmen) proved a financial boon, Cleese's greatest public success – and likely the greatest solo success of any Python – came via *Fawlty Towers*, a brilliant exercise in barely contained anger masquerading as situation comedy, first broadcast in 1975 and 1979. Inspired by a notoriously bad hotel experience in Torquay during location shooting for *Python*, Cleese and his then-wife Connie Booth (an American actress who also appeared in bit parts in Python, such as the 'witch' in *Holy Grail*) wrote twelve half hours of sharp, inventive comedy following the travails of hotel manager Basil Fawlty and his long-suffering staff. Cleese's ability to fill such an overpowering role made Fawlty an indelible character, though Basil's penchant for invective (and a rather opportune silly walk) harked back to some of the actor's Python roles.

In fact, the series made such an impression that for many it was difficult to see some of Cleese's later performances (in *Clockwise* or *Privates on Parade*) as anything other than variations on Basil Fawlty. It wasn't until his own *A Fish Called Wanda* (1988), in which he portrayed a barrister breaking free from his stifled existence by having an affair with a mobster's moll, that Cleese's ability at playing a softer, romantic comedic character was recognized.

---

**CLEESE:** I never had any doubts in my own mind that I had a reasonably wide range both as a writer and as a performer. And I was always a bit surprised that people seemed to have an assumption that there was *one* thing that I did (which always was what I was currently doing). My own tastes in humour are catholic; it doesn't matter whether it's farce or high comedy or satire or vaudeville, or quite subtle writing like James Thurber or S. J. Perelman – provided it's good, it makes me laugh.

So with this very catholic taste with what I enjoy, I always felt that I had a similar kind of range; it's just that certain circumstances have given me a chance to work in one area rather than another.

*You were the first to really pull away from Python.*
*Do you think that was inevitable?*

**CLEESE:** I think as the series began to get acknowledged as being very good and funny and original, what happened is that some of the huddling together for warmth became unnecessary when the sun came out. I think this sometimes happens with groups; when they become more successful, ironically, people begin to feel more independent, a little more confident, and so that's the moment when you begin to see more individualistic ways of thinking taking over in the group. With pop groups it's often after they become very successful when people begin to pull outwards, to pull against each other more. And I would say that happened with us.

My point of view, by the way, is that on the first series we got on very, very well. And we were still getting on very well at the beginning of the second series. By the time we got to the third series, it really wasn't very much fun – I thought we were very derivative, *and* I had the Graham problem. I suspect the others also didn't enjoy the third series as much as the first two, but it wasn't as bad for them because they didn't have a 'Graham problem'.

**Fawlty Towers** *was the polar opposite of Python, in that it was in a situation comedy format and was character-driven. Was it a conscious decision of yours to make your first solo project entirely unlike what Python had been doing?*

**CLEESE:** The interesting thing is there's an assumption in your question that I was in some way thinking of this new project in terms of Python. And I don't think I was. The only thing I assumed was that it would not be as successful as Python; I always thought that if we got half the Python audience I would be perfectly happy. But when Connie and I sat down to write *Fawlty Towers*, we didn't start saying, 'Well, what do we do that would be different from Python?'

I was wondering whether we should be trying to do that man–woman stuff that Mike Nichols and Elaine May had done, and John Bird and John Fortune and Eleanor Bron had been doing in England, and after five minutes we simply decided that was not what we should be aiming at. And then I said, 'What about something in that hotel?' Connie had stayed in the hotel, too – she was filming with Python on that occasion – so she'd experienced the hotel with me, which was a great help. And we simply thought about that for ten minutes and said, 'Let's do that.' But we were never consciously distancing ourselves from Python.

*You made a pointed public exploration of psychotherapy in your books co-written with your therapist, Robin Skynner (*Families and How to Survive Them *and* Life and How to Survive It*). Did your therapy (and the break from Python which developed somewhat parallel to that) represent a need to move from a group identity to a need to establish a solo career?*

**CLEESE:** Well, I still would say that *A Fish Called Wanda,* that group – Jamie Lee Curtis, Kevin Kline, Michael, and myself – was a kind of a group, and I used them in the writing stage far more than writers usually use actors; they were helping me to write their own parts.

I believe that most people for most of their lives are on automatic, that habit is for us so strong that we underestimate how it's running our lives. Now sometimes that habit is acquired because of unconscious forces, and to the extent we're not aware of what forces are running us in the first place we're even *less* aware of how the habits can be broken. And I think that the effect of my therapy was to break an enormous number of emotional and behavioural habits. Once I'd done that, I confronted the fact that on most days I would rather read a book and go to an art gallery and have lunch with a friend than I would sit and work. That's the way I am.

I still find it very difficult because an awful lot of people need me to make things happen. Next week I'm doing an interview with the BBC for a programme about sitcoms. The last thing in the world I want to do is to sit down and talk about *Fawlty Towers*; I've talked about it all my life – well, for the last twenty years – but they're doing a series on British sitcoms and it would look very strange if I'm not there to talk about it. So my life gets filled up with an enormous amount of that stuff, and I'm still not able to find the time to do what I really want to do. But work in itself hardly attracts me at all. I had a cup of coffee with Steve Martin yesterday; he and I agreed that it's only people, the thought of working with someone, that draws us towards working.

I don't get much out of work now, but I went to a conference two weeks ago on *The Confessions of St Augustine* and I got an *enormous* amount out of that. So I'm not terribly interested in *work*.

Also, I feel very out of tune with the audience. I go and see something like *Pulp Fiction* and, frankly, it appalls me. Most of it is dialogue tricks which had been explored by Harold Pinter thirty-five years ago; the structure did not strike me as being as clever as it did everyone else; and the content seemed to me (and to an awful lot of my generation) as the product of a sick mind. And I don't understand the kind of humour where quoting from other movies is considered important. It seems to me exactly the opposite of what the point of a movie is, which is to involve people; all that business about quoting has an alienating effect. So an awful lot of what people do in the movies now, I am completely out of touch with. So from the point of view of content, yes, I could imagine a movie would come along that would interest me, but being funny for its own sake now is never enough to get me out of my house to do those extremely long hours, which are very tiring and often under uncomfortable circumstances, to produce something which the odds are heavily stacked against it working in the first place.

The thing about movies is, it's 240 years out of your life if nothing goes wrong. It takes you over completely, there are so many decisions to be made. I was talking to a very old friend of mine who's produced a number of movies, and I asked her, 'Did you enjoy the last one?' And she said, 'You know, I've come to the conclusion you don't really *enjoy* producing. It's so demanding.' Terry Gilliam wants to make movies more than anything else, and I think if you said to Terry, 'Do you *enjoy* making movies?' I think he'd laugh in your face. I got a note from him when he was in the editing stage of *Fear and Loathing in Las Vegas,* saying, 'I am living in hell.' Sometimes it all goes right, probably about one time in ten. And on *Wanda,* it all went right.

*Did professional jealousy ever enter into the group, and was that an impetus for any of the Pythons to move on?*

**CLEESE:** I came to the conclusion that there was a lot of competition between us, and the way that we handled it was never to talk about it. There was an unspoken convention, a funny kind of tradition, by which we would never ask about each other's projects or talk about them. It was as though once we were together as the Python group, we would only talk about Python business. And I didn't think it was terribly healthy. I remember that I quite deliberately started to ask people about things they were doing outside the group. And given a straight question people would respond, and I think that people got a little more comfortable after a time talking about things outside of the group, and I know that at one point I did that quite deliberately, but there was real sibling rivalry – we were just like siblings. And it wasn't particularly unpleasant, but it was there. And the way it was handled was not to talk about whatever people were doing.

*Is that similar to stereotypical English behaviour of not revealing emotions?*

**CLEESE:** Yes, the 'British thing'. Because we keep our relationships more at a distance than I think some Americans do, people are often really depressed because they don't want to make emotional contact when they meet; and also in the English culture, anger is not easily expressed, so that of course is a problem.

*Much of your work in Python is about the
expression of anger through humour.*

**CLEESE:** Oh yes, but trying to get rid of it through art is nothing to do with solving the problem. People talk about art as being therapeutic. I think by and large that doesn't work, which is why so many playwrights write the same play many, many times! They're obsessing about themes, and I don't really think they work them out by writing about them. A lot of people think that art is a kind of therapy. Well, maybe it stops people from going *completely* mad, but I don't think it helps people very much.

*Does it help an audience?*

**CLEESE:** No, I don't think so! I think very few things have any kind of lasting emotional effect. It's like New Year's resolutions, or weekend psychology courses, EST, those kinds of things. Robin Skynner once said to me, 'Trying to change your life is like steering the *Queen Elizabeth*; you start turning the wheel, twenty minutes later the boat just *slightly* moves right.'

*Do you think it would be harder today than when Python started
for the kind of innovation associated with Python to succeed?*

**CLEESE:** If you do something that's genuinely original, it's very hard for people to grab it. I asked a publicist, 'What's the hardest kind of movie to publicize?' And he said, 'Anything original.' For it to find an audience, if it doesn't have a good first Friday, basically you're in trouble, whereas in the old days a movie could sit in a cinema for a time. I think one of the great things about *A Fish Called Wanda* was that we opened it in a very small number of cinemas – two in New York and one in LA, I think – for the first two weeks, so people were slowly able to get used to the fact that it was a bit odd.

So you've got this awful thing, that the first Friday is all-dependent on the publicity campaign – because by definition very few people have seen the movie – and if you have something that's *very* original, that's the thing that's hardest to publicize. And if you don't get a good first Friday, then it's no longer possible to keep it in the movie house long enough for it to find an audience. So I think this is operating to some extent against originality.

---

In 1984, Terry Gilliam directed *Brazil*, a neo-Orwellian look at a dystopian society, co-authored with Tom Stoppard and Charles McKeown. Sam Lowry (a petty bureaucrat played by Jonathan Pryce) upsets the system by trying to locate his dream girl, a woman suspected of having links to terrorists. Unknowingly helping Sam in his search is an old friend, Jack Lint, whose ambition has guided him far up the career ladder at the Ministry of Information, where he pulls in a paycheck by interrogating and torturing prisoners.

Gilliam asked Michael Palin to play the role of Jack, trading on the actor's affability in order to depict a likable but morally corrupt person. Their collaboration represented an exceptional example of humour being used to support and heighten dramatic ideas, in this case issues of loyalty and morality, leading to the film's most chilling moment: when Jack encounters Sam himself strapped in the chair awaiting 'information retrieval'.

---

**PALIN:** I don't think Terry did have me specifically in mind when he wrote Jack Lint. I think that probably Terry once he'd written it may have thought of me because we worked quite closely on *Jabberwocky* and *Time Bandits* and I think he felt sort of – not exactly morally obliged, just because we were good friends and had worked productively before – to offer me something on *Brazil*.

Producer Arnon Milchan dangled before Terry the prospect of major stars, including Robert De Niro. De Niro was shown the script and said, of all the parts he'd like to do, Jack Lint was the one. So Terry said – this is Terry's story anyway – 'I'm sorry, my friend Mike is going to do that; you have to choose something else!' So that must be a rare example of De Niro being turned down.

We talked about the nature of evil if you like, and the way it manifests itself. Terry and I both felt that it is a cliché and possibly an absurd generalization to think that all evil people *look* evil and have scars on their faces and go *heh-heh-heh* and all that. We felt that very often the most dangerous people are the ones who appear most plausible and most charming. So that was how we set about the idea of playing Jack Lint as someone who was everything that Jonathan Pryce's character *wasn't*: he was stable, he had a family, he was settled, comfortable, hardworking, charming, sociable – and utterly and totally unscrupulous. That was the way we felt we could bring out the evil in Jack Lint.

I had a great problem with playing Jack, as I'd not really played a character like this before. It was also scheduled for the first day of shooting and it was about the most complicated scene in the film, which was really in retrospect a ridiculous bit of scheduling – you don't schedule your hardest scene involving complicated character dialogue until your cast have had time to get to know who they're playing, what they're playing; you schedule some gentler stuff. But there we were, crack in. I'd just come from a week in the Belfast Festival doing a one-man show, so I was pretty exhausted, and we went in on day one and there was tremendous pressure to get the scene done, and get it done fast.

Now, all sorts of things militated against that. I'd not worked with Jonathan before. He's quite an intense actor, and I'm a – you know – Python actor; we're intense for short periods, but basically we rely on the love and the comfort and the ease and the bouncing off lines one from another. Jonathan was searching for exactly how he should play his character, which was going to have to go through the entire film – he had another three months to go. I felt the whole atmosphere was a bit tight and tense and I wasn't particularly happy with my performance by the end of the day (two days actually we spent).

We got it down and we'd done a couple of more scenes as well, and people were saying, 'Hey, we've got twelve pages of script under our belts. This is great, what a start!' I felt relieved that we'd done it, I thought we'd cracked it, but a little voice in the back of my mind said, 'You know, this could be better.' So I was actually quite relieved when after a month or so, Terry said, 'You know, there are some problems, it might be worth it trying this scene again.' And after I got over the hurt pride – couldn't get it right the first time – I realized yes, there were things wrong, and maybe we'd be able to improve on it.

We talked about it, and between us we came to the conclusion that the great thing about Jack is that he is a family man, that he is a personification of the good citizen. And there was no real indication of that in the first scene – it was just between the two of them. If we could have some elements of family life in it, sort of playing off Jack's family, then that would make it all the more dark. So Terry said, 'Well, let's go straight into it, let's give you a daughter.' My daughter at that time was only one year old, she wasn't eligible. And Terry said, 'Hey! I've got a daughter! I'll get Holly to do it.'

So several months after we'd shot the first scene we got back together again, and it just felt easier, it felt better. I enjoyed having Holly there, it gave me something to do, which enabled the jargon – Buttles and Tuttles and E-23 and B-24 and all that – and the sinister side of what Jack is saying to come out. You see there's blood on his coat, you assume he's orchestrated some awful torture. The next thing is he's playing with his daughter and at the same time says, 'Well, they have to be destroyed, you'd have to wipe him out,' and all that sort of thing.

Because that scene was eventually played with an element of humour, it actually concentrates the disturbing element much more. If it's just desk-to-desk, it is more like a stock scene out of any thriller, and you're not quite listening to the lines – you're just observing the tension be-

*Palin with Jonathan Pryce in an unused scene from* Brazil.

tween the two people. If you're *laughing*, then you're becoming much more involved in the scene. I think an audience is beginning to feel a sort of catharsis – you know, we've all been children, a lot of them have children, they've been through that before – and suddenly the chilling line will come through: 'There's nothing I can do for you, that's it.' I think it makes those lines much more memorable, makes Jack's attitude much more memorable.

It wasn't necessary to put it all on the line: here's a nasty man saying nasty things. Here is a *nice* man having a good time, but oh crikey! What he *said*! This is what it *means*, you know, when you're away from the family background, you see exactly what the implications are, and they're very unpleasant!

I think it was quite audacious of Terry to play it with Holly; it really worked extremely well. I can remember when we were doing reverses on Holly, and Terry had the studio cleared and operated the camera, and Maggie was there, so it was this little family group, and me in the background. And that's when she says the memorable line about 'I won't look at your willy'. So that felt very much better the second time around.

# THERE'S VIOLENCE TO BE DONE

Having exceeded their creative and financial expectations on *Brian*, there was pressure (not all from within the group) to follow up their success with another film. Because the group's members were going in different directions, however, they were limited in their ability to collaborate, pulled as they were by their own solo projects.

Shortly after *Life of Brian*, the Pythons began meeting to discuss a new film, but by mid-1980 they were getting nowhere – dissatisfied with the disjointed nature of their schedule, the quantity of prime material, and the lack of a clear focus on the script. It was during this time that they were approached to make a stage appearance in Los Angeles, which they taped and ultimately released as a theatrical film (*Monty Python Live at the Hollywood Bowl*). The show was a mixture of Python warhorses (the 'Dead Parrot' sketch), songs (many courtesy of Neil Innes), Gilliam animations, and film clips from *Fliegender Zirkus*. There was also other material both pre- and post-Python (such as an argument between the Pope and Michelangelo about why there are three Christs depicted in *The Last Supper*, and four wealthy Yorkshiremen engaged in a friendly rivalry about whose childhood was the most impoverished – a classic sketch from *At Last the 1948 Show*).

**GILLIAM:** There's a forgetfulness in Python. I'm like an elephant: I remember all the bad bits where somebody trod on my toe, where revenge is going to be meted out at some point. Mike doesn't; he remembers the fun and the good bits. It's like, 'He fucked us, Mike, you remember? He fucked us; why are you doing business with him, Mike?' And he's, 'Oh, really? Oh, I forgot all about that!'

Like with Denis O'Brien, Mike kept working with Denis for a long time. Well, Denis did a lot of *good* things, but the Hollywood Bowl thing was the moment when they were offering us X amount of money to go and do a Hollywood Bowl, guaranteed, go in there, five days, in/out. Denis was our manager then, he decided to interfere, [and] he completely fucked it up. We had taped the shows, and the money we were guaranteed we didn't get because Denis squandered it, wasted it, so we actually had to release the tape as a movie here in England to get the money that we'd *hoped* to get from the stage show; we didn't *want* it to go out as a movie. That's what he did. He used the money because he's managing it, but I said, 'Denis, you should have *asked* us if you were doing that.' He didn't see any need to do that; our money was his money, and *his* money was his money, and he blew it. How can anybody work with somebody like that again? It's crazy. Mike forgets!

I remember the bad things, he remembers the good things and forgets the bad things. I wish *I* could remember more good things! Life would be more pleasant.

## I DIDN'T KNOW AN ACCEPTABLE LEGAL PHRASE, M'LUD

As a curious footnote to the Pythons' estranged relationship with Denis O'Brien, *Life of Brian* eventually became the centrepiece of a legal action between the group and Paragon Entertainment, a Canadian company which had purchased Handmade Films in 1994. (Although noted as a quality producer of independent films, including *Mona Lisa, Withnail and I*, and *A Private Function*, Handmade suffered financial problems in the late eighties which led to a rift – and a lawsuit – between O'Brien and George Harrison. The company was dormant for a few years before Paragon bought the company's library, including *Brian*.) As in the ABC case, the Pythons objected to cuts made in television showings of *Brian* when Paragon licensed it to Channel 4 in the UK. The court action, resolved in early 1998, resulted in a victory for the Pythons, and they were awarded full ownership of the film.

*Cleese with Denis O'Brien at the Hollywood Bowl.*

**GOLDSTONE:** The ABC case enabled them to get the rights back to the entire series, which was a pretty unusual thing. But this was more about people who really felt very strongly about their work and objected to ABC cutting it and the BBC *allowing* it to be cut. Very few others would go to that sort of length. Even this *Life of Brian* case, it's been enormously expensive and I don't think anybody else would have gone to that length because you never know what the outcome would be – it wasn't ever a clear-cut case.

The great tragedy of the Paragon saga is that Handmade had kept all the out-takes and negatives of *Life of Brian* and then when Paragon bought it, they were very cheesy about a lot of things and weren't prepared to continue to pay for storage of all this material, and without consulting us they junked it all. So when it came to doing the laser disc version, there was very little to add on from scenes cut from the final release – like the Otto scene and the shepherds [who are oblivious to the angel's appearance in the beginning]. The negs weren't available; it was [only] the stuff that had been transferred onto video just by chance.

# THE MEANING OF LIFE

*The Grim Reaper on the set of* The Meaning of Life.

## IN FACT I WILL PERSONALLY MAKE SURE YOU HAVE A *DOUBLE* HELPING

Dissatisfied on a business level with the Hollywood Bowl experience (Denis O'Brien ended his tenure as the Pythons' manager shortly after), and remembering their success by holing up on a Caribbean island to work out the screenplay for *Life of Brian*, the Pythons tried again by departing for Jamaica, at which point the framework of *Meaning of Life* was realized.

The film is a broad meditation on the perilousness and absurdity of human existence that comes across visually as a mix of Federico Fellini, Ingmar Bergman, and Busby Berkeley. Rather than featuring a single narrative thread (as was the case with *Brian*), *The Meaning of Life* is a collection of sketches which provide many high points and some low ones, all reflecting a 'Seven Ages of Man'-type framework. The topics covered range from the expected ('Birth',

'Education', 'Fighting Each Other', 'Death') to the uncommon ('Live Organ Transplants'). Though the level of writing is quite high, there is an uneasy mix to the film as a whole (there is a certain repetition concerning dining, for example, as no fewer than eight scenes take place in restaurants, in nightclubs, at dinner parties, or at hastily erected dessert tables).

As an indication of how far the Pythons had come in mastering the humour of excess, the film's most memorable scene involves Mr Creosote, a restaurant patron weighing more than all the Pythons put together, who proceeds to spew vomit throughout the establishment, orders every item on the menu, and then – upon topping off his meal with a dainty after-dinner mint – explodes.

The most Pythonic element of the film is a linking device repeated throughout featuring the group as fish in a tank, whose laconic commentary on the film itself ('Not much happening at the moment, is there?') is a delight.

---

**GOLDSTONE:** *The Meaning of Life* definitely came about because *Life of Brian* had been very successful and there was pressure to come together again.

Denis O'Brien managed the group subsequently for a short while, but that created problems because what he was able to do was realize the film dreams of the individuals – *Time Bandits* was the first one to be made under the Python/Handmade relationship, and then *The Missionary*. Obviously, Eric had his own project that he wanted to do; I'm sure they all did. And ultimately Terry Gilliam and Michael Palin were the only people who benefited from that relationship.

Denis constantly tried to see whether he could encourage them to write something [as a group], but by the time they did, the relationship [with him] became a bit acrimonious and it was really up to me again to get it together.

# ALL MIXED UP IN A BUCKET

*Was it difficult for the group to work together again*
*after having concentrated on solo projects?*

**IDLE:** Not hard. John was the one who was reluctant; we simply started writing without him. But we found it hard to find a theme, even when he came aboard.

**JONES:** That was the trouble, really, it was getting increasingly hard to get together, and it showed, I think. We'd meet and we'd read out material, then we wouldn't meet again for another two months or something, and then we'd get together again, have another readout of material, and it seemed to be getting nowhere. I think we spent about a year doing that, meeting on and off and getting this pile of *stuff* together.

I always said, 'Let's do a sketch show, I'm sure we could do a sketch film and make it work,' just to show we can. Because there was this feeling that maybe a sketch film you couldn't sustain for more than an hour. And because we'd never done a sketch film – *And Now for Something Completely Different* I never really counted because I thought it was a bit half-assed, it wasn't conceived as a film, really.

And I'd been saying it ought to be somebody's life story. We were looking for a sort of archetypal idea to hang our material onto, really.

We had this pile of material we put into some shape, it was a bit like Buñuel's *The Discreet Charm of the Bourgeoisie,* where he kept turning into a dream. We went to Jamaica to write so we could have two weeks without being interrupted. We all read it on the plane over there, and I think all our hearts sank – we just thought, 'It isn't working, this repetitive thing just doesn't go.' I remember waking up in Jamaica [with] this sinking feeling in my stomach, the first time I'd had it since 1969 and the early days of editing, this feeling that something was wrong. We'd been talking, talking, going around in circles and not getting anywhere, and this was our third day by this time, and I thought, 'What have I got that

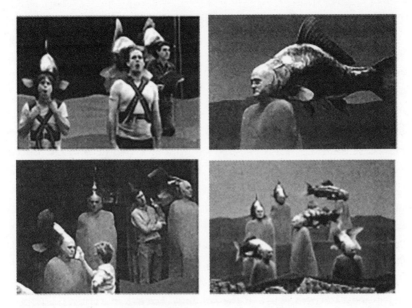

*Rehearsals and blue-screen filming of the fish.*

nobody else has got?' And I suddenly remembered I'd packed a script in which our continuity girl had done her timings, and her timings were different from ours – they were longer. The material that we all thought was 'A' material was seventy-four minutes or something by her timing; by ours it was like fifty minutes. And hers was probably more accurate.

So when we got down to breakfast, I said, 'I've got a proposal,' and Mike said *he'd* got a proposal. Mike's proposal was that we should all pack up and go home and turn it into a TV series. And my proposal was, 'What are we worried about? Because by these timings if we've got seventy-four minutes of ace material, we've only got to write another twenty minutes – surely we could do *that*. And *it's somebody's life story,* I'm sure!'

And they were all, 'Yeah, yeah, yeah . . .' And then somebody said it could be *anybody's* life story. And Eric said, 'Yeah, we could call it *The Meaning of Life.*' That's it! Just over that breakfast it suddenly came up.

I didn't come up with the idea, but I came up with the impetus, and then somebody else came up with the idea of 'Let's do it as the Seven Ages of Man,' and somebody came up with *The Meaning of Life* as the title, and then we knew where we were going. We then started putting the material into that kind of shape.

**IDLE:** We never found the theme till the end. I think it would have been perfect if we had given it one extra draft and it had become the Seven Ages of Man as well, with the story of *one* person, growing up at various ages through time. We nearly got there, but again John was reluctant to meet, so we just went ahead and shot it anyway. It still has great stuff in it and is still marvellously offensive!

**GILLIAM:** I actually think we didn't do the film we should have done. There was *Monty Python's World War III*, which I thought had some wonderful stuff in there, with all the soldiers wearing advertising, like race car drivers – ads are being taken out on all the soldiers, on the weapons, everything. It was the whole commercialization of war and atrocities, basically, and we played around with that for a long time; we incorporated some of the war stuff in *Meaning of Life*.

But then the one that I really liked was a whole Python film that was a court case. We were in the dock and the prosecution was trying to prove that what we were watching, this film we had made, is *not* a film, it's a tax dodge. 'Your Honour, a case in point: here's a scene, it's supposed to be *Scott of the Antarctic*, but it's taking place in Bermuda. Now *why* is this, Your Honour?' And so we'd be running all these wonderful sketches and ideas and then keep cutting back to the court case, which is trying to prove that this is a tax dodge. At the same time we were actually going to take advertising in the film, we would get sponsors and we'd do ads in the film, and so we'd literally get paid lots of money for doing these ads, and we thought we could finance this thing with all the presales of all the advertising we were going to do in it, *and* make an incredibly funny film, *and* [have] this weird connecting thing of this court case commenting on the very film that we're watching and what it is and what it isn't, and *why* it is or isn't a 'film'. In the end we were going to be found guilty, that in fact what people had been sitting watching was *not* a film, it *was* a tax dodge, and then we were all going to be punished! And that's where in *Meaning of Life*, where Graham's chased to death by half-naked girls, that was in fact going to be one of the deaths.

Anyway, we decided on *The Meaning of Life*, which basically ended up being the Seven Stages of Man or whatever. And it's fine, we at least take on a good title! I think the stages of man we got in there is very, very slight, to say the least. But the material in the film is some of the best stuff we've ever done. Also the performances are just fantastic. But to me, it's less of a film than the other ones.

I bumped into Henry Jaglom, who thinks it's a total masterpiece. I bumped into Mike Nichols; *he* says it's a true masterpiece. So I'm getting these people running around who are saying that and I don't know what to make of it; because when it's good, it's *really* good, but there're real shitty bits that just don't work!

**GOLDSTONE:** When I went out to raise the money for *Meaning of Life*, it was already a given that the Pythons would have to have final cut and artistic control – that precedent had been set. It already existed on *Holy Grail* (because there was nobody to question it) and *Life of Brian*. Also what they were very keen about by then was having proper fees up front, which we hadn't done substantially in the others – certainly not on *Holy Grail* – so that needed a major studio to do that level of fee.

The actual title *The Meaning of Life* didn't come in until a bit later; it was called *Monty Python's Fish Film* or something like that.

There was a little bidding war; I mean, every studio wanted the next Python film, and I just felt Universal was the most easygoing in a way. It was being run by Ned Tannen at the time. They were having these huge hits, doing all these teenage movies and doing very well with them. We were very confident about who they were and [they] didn't mind letting filmmakers get on with it.

It was kind of interesting how the thing happened as well; I didn't show them the screenplay, I just did one page, which was the lyrics of a song that Eric had written about what was going to be in this movie,[*] and they bought it on that.

Things had changed internally though in Python by then. This was now 1982, and they'd all been doing their own things for a while, so this new movie somehow wasn't done with quite the same blinding commitment as the earlier ones. There were distractions. There was no one inherent problem, but there was kind of a latitude that was not quite as pioneering. Although there's some great stuff, classic sequences, as a whole it still is a series of sketches [without] the narrative drive that *Brian* had.

**NANCY LEWIS:** On *The Meaning of Life*, they brought me over to be the director of Python Relations, because they wanted the fish thing and all of that to be kept fairly undercover, and not ruin the jokes. And then they moved the release date back and put it out earlier than expected, so all the sort of long-term publicity things we planned? Threw them out the window.

I think it was a difficult movie for some of them. John was getting bored, [but] they were all very involved. They would all go along to the dailies, as I recall, more so I think than actors might ordinarily on something on which they were just performing. They actually worked wonderfully together. There is a wonderful chemistry between them, I think they feed off each other – certainly they did performance-wise.

---

[*]    'There's everything in this movie,
Everything that fits,
From the meaning of life in the Universe,
To girls with great big tits . . .'

# AH! AND WHAT SORT OF THING IS THAT?

The first big set piece of the film involved hordes of Catholics –
men, women, children, nuns, stilt-walkers, cadavers! – singing and
dancing, *Annie*-like, in praise of the Church's prohibition against
contraception ('Every sperm is sacred . . .'). The outlandish design
of the sketch is itself a spoof of Hollywood musicals, but the vicari-
ous kick of the number is to see tiny children actually singing the
word 'sperm'. It reminds one of a Lenny Bruce monologue about
the desensitization of language – when words are robbed of their
power to shock, the speaker is thoroughly robbed of *his* power
over others.

*How was directing children in those sequences?*

**JONES:** It wasn't difficult at all. Once the parents had all read the script
and knew what the children would be doing and what they were singing,
then it was fine. It didn't worry the children. I mean, the kids either knew
what it was or they didn't know, and if they didn't know then it was no
problem. They weren't embarrassed. In fact, the little girl was terrific; she
was miming to one of the other girls who had a great voice who was about
twelve – she actually sang that bit – and the six-year-old was miming to
that, but we had about four takes of her doing it and she was absolutely
spot-on every time.

There was only one bit we changed in deference to the nannies who
were there. Mike had to do all this stuff about, 'If I wore a little rubber
thing on the end of my cock we wouldn't be in the trouble we are in now.'
And in fact he said to the children 'on the end of my sock'. And then we
put 'cock' in at the dubbing.

Arlene Phillips was the choreographer. We weren't deliberately parodying anything. It was in a very *Oliver!* style, although I'm not sure I've
even seen *Oliver!* But I know what it's like! Arlene came up with ideas

*Exterior shot of Mr Creosote, with auxilary transportation.*

and I sort of came up with ideas and then we designed each shot, really.

I'd not had any schooling in directing, really, but I just find story-boarding helps you know where you are. I'm not really good at thinking on my feet, so I want to sort out everything first. The way I work, I first draw pathetic little pictures, diagram sketches, really, of each scene. It helps me in things like realizing I needed kids up the top of the frame, and so a staircase needs to go around the room [instead of] the left-hand side to make the room look *full* of children.

I've gone through the script and I usually have my storyboard num-bers and shot numbers in the script as well, roughly, so I know what it's covering. And then when we're shooting, I write the slate number on my drawing, and then I even put the take numbers in, so I've got this wonderful ready reference. When we're editing, I can just look at the scene and say, 'Oh, we want shot so-and-so, there it is, and we want take number so-and-so of that.' It's much better than the normal way where they've got two books, one in slate order – one, two, three, four – and the other in script order. My method, you can see immediately what shots you're looking for.

In the Creosote scene our production designer came up with a revamp of one of the other sets, a restaurant set earlier on, and I said, 'Oh, it's not big enough.' So he did another, bigger one, and I said, 'No, no, it isn't big enough.' I said it's like one of London's clubs, [or] like La Coupole in Paris. Eventually he and I went around London to see what I meant. I think we got to the RAC

*Jones in mid-make-up as Mr Creosote.*

Club, and I said, 'It's *this* sort of size, this is the kind of thing.' And he immediately said, 'Oh, I know, we can do it in Porchester Street Baths and dress it up like a restaurant.' I couldn't really think why I wanted it to be such a big restaurant, but I think if it were a small restaurant it would be too claustrophobic. You wanted these events to be going on disturbing *some* of the people around Mr Creosote, but not everybody in the restaurant.

### Plus he has to fit in there!

**JONES:** That's right! Creosote was quite hard. I was a bit nervous about doing that, actually; originally I said Terry Gilliam ought to do it, and then Terry persuaded me that *I* ought to do it. I was a bit worried because it was a big make-up job, three and a half hours.

And of course the biggest thing was to get the vomit to look real. I didn't want it to squirt out, I wanted it to sort of bludge out – go *blurp!* We had a device, a tube that didn't go into my mouth, it was at the side of the mouth, and I had to be at [an] absolute right angle. It looked fine when we tested it and everything, we shot the first day, and then we went to see the rushes, it didn't work. What we hadn't realized was that when the liquid came out of the side, there was a shadow from my face on the liquid, so you *saw* it wasn't coming out of my mouth.

So we were a bit alarmed when we saw that, and thought, 'Fuck, it's not working.' But Richard Conway, our special effects guy, got a fail-safe device which actually went into my mouth. Although it came out as more of a spray, you had no fears [of detection].

Still, there's one shot where my mouth shut and the stuff's coming out! I think just after when John is hovering over me with the menu, and it's just come out and hit the menu and at some point I shut my mouth and there was still stuff coming out but nobody really noticed!

We had a big catapult; we had to throw it at the crowd. We knew the trajectory, we'd worked out where it would land. The catapult held like twenty or thirty gallons and hit everything spot-on. But for that we had to select the extras with the cheap costumes!

**LEWIS:** That was really quite glorious, Mr Creosote. They mixed up this sort of vegetable mixture and Russian salad dressing, and they were shooting for a couple of days at least in this hall, and the place was to be used for a wedding afterwards. It was very hot, it smelled so dreadful, by the end of the shoot you couldn't open that room because [with] the heat and this mixture sitting there, it was one of the most revolting things! That smell comes back to me now, it was terrible! I often wondered how the wedding went. They must have managed to get it out. I'm sure when they rented [the place], they just wrote these things down in their books: 'Ah, couple days' filming, fine . . . wedding the next day, fine . . .'

*The Crimson Permanent Assurance skirting the shoals of bankruptcy, barely.*

## PEOPLE ARE NOT WEARING ENOUGH HATS

**GILLIAM:** *The Crimson Permanent Assurance,* this idea of this building setting sail and all that, is a romantic idea that these little old guys can take on these modern monsters. It's a bit like Saddam Hussein taking on America; it's a foolish, romantic idea. And I sort of give them their moment, and they defeat them, but in the end it's a silly idea and they fall off the edge of the earth! Because it doesn't really work that way in the real world.

It was originally a cartoon, and I just felt, I don't want to do that. By then I was so terribly keen to escape from animation. I wanted to convince them that I could make my own little film – which was initially within the body of the main film. I had my own sound stage, my own everything. They were making their film over there and I was

*Gilliam on the galley slave set of* Crimson Permanent Assurance.

making mine. I still did bits of animation just to justify my supposed 'real' job, but *Crimson Permanent* was just right because I got to play with models, taking stuff that we'd done in *Time Bandits* and stuff which hopefully we'd be able to do in *Brazil* and play with them. And I really enjoyed doing that.

**JONES:** We originally thought he was doing a five-minute animation, it was only when we heard that Terry wanted *another* million dollars or whatever it was, we suddenly realized it was a whole different feature going on! We kept going to his studio next door, and he had these *huge* sets compared to what we had.

**GILLIAM:** But what was interesting afterwards when we started cutting it down, it just wouldn't stay in the film. And I cut it shorter and shorter, and the others kept saying, 'No, it's *still* too long.' The rhythms of it are just totally different rhythms than Python rhythms, it's not like that – it's very *long*!

THE MEANING OF LIFE    297

**JONES:** Of course, that originally came about three-quarters of a way through the film, and it never worked when it came there. We'd show the film, and everybody would say, 'Well, yeah, *hate* that pirate number.' And Terry said, 'I think it would work at the beginning of the film.'

**GILLIAM:** I made the quantum leap – just pull it *outside* the film – and then it became a better idea. Because not only is it a short subject before the film, but then it *attacks* the main film later on; you win both ways.

Still the great thing with Python was that we were able to do this, to have that kind of freedom to just pull things apart completely, change the shape of the form or whatever.

**CLEESE:** I was annoyed with him because he went over budget and instead of producing what we'd asked for (which I think was seven minutes), I think he produced twenty-three! I thought he was capable of being completely overtaken by his artistic ego and losing boundaries almost completely. And I felt annoyed with John Goldstone, the producer, that John would not restrain him.

**GOLDSTONE:** The one major problem on *Meaning of Life* was the Terry Gilliam sequence, which did run out of control. I think everyone was a bit pissed off at what he was doing, because he was clearly spending more money than we'd ever reckoned with. Actually, somehow we did manage to contain it within the money that Universal had given us, but it cost far too much for what it was.

The atmosphere was strained, I must say, because it was difficult to justify. And then to find that it didn't work within the context of the film was a bit of a disappointment as well. One of the problems was that it was so grand in itself it didn't fit within the scale of the rest of the film, and so this decision was made to make it the short that preceded it. It's probably the most expensive short ever made!

**JONES:** It was quite obvious that the pirate stuff had to come at the beginning, once we'd done it like that. The only trouble was that then the beginning of *Meaning of Life,* which was the hospital stuff, suffered. The hospital scenes were never as funny as they were when we kicked straight off with them; they always had a huge reaction, and they didn't get quite such a big reaction after *The Crimson Permanent Assurance.*

**GILLIAM:** When I saw it in Cannes, *Crimson Permanent* comes on a huge screen, great sound, it's like we're in a big film, we're in a *movie*! And then the film comes on and it's like television, like *big* television. Now what's interesting is when you see it on video, *Crimson Permanent* doesn't quite do it as far as I'm concerned, but the rest of the film is *perfect*. It seems to me it's the right scale; the television screen is the perfect scale to see it. It's like Marty Scorsese's *King of Comedy*. I saw it on the big screen, had mixed feelings; saw it on television, and said, 'Yeah, that's it.' I don't quite understand how it all works, [but] this sense of scale is really important.

## WELL, THAT'S CAST RATHER A GLOOM OVER THE EVENING, HASN'T IT?

**GILLIAM:** It was a funny experience, *Meaning of Life.* I really felt more separated because I was in my little world, hopping in occasionally to do something in the other. We were no longer working as this tight unit, like on *Brian*. I think by *Meaning of Life* the writing was much more separate, everyone was doing their own thing more, and then we just stitched it together.

**JULIAN DOYLE:** One of the things about sketch films is you must end well. Like my old jazz teacher used to say, 'Your applause on the end of a jazz song is how long you hold the last note.' So you must leave them with a good memory at the end of a sketch film because they haven't got an

*Idle as the waiter, who may actually know the meaning of life.*

overall experience of the thing; they just think it's been fun if they *feel* fun as they leave the cinema.

Now we get to Creosote, fine – the funniest scene in the film, everybody is rolling around laughing. We then [go into] the restaurant clearing up, and then we have a shaggy dog story: a waiter saying, 'Come, follow me.' Now the audience is [still] laughing because Creosote's funny, but in fact that [next sketch] is killing us: we are slowly dying as that scene is going on. And we get to the end [of that scene where] we tell the audience to 'fuck off!' That's what he says to them. 'You've just seen the best scene in the film, and now I'm going to tell you the answer to the meaning of life, follow me, follow me, follow me,' tells us his life story, then he says, 'Fuck off!'

Death. We have killed our audience.

After Creosote, we need to be out of that film as quickly as possible with our best stuff and *only* our best stuff. My feeling is that Creosote exploding should have been the precursor to Death: the guy chased by the women jumping off the cliff, quickly [moving] into the Grim Reaper coming around the dinner table. *Everything* should be about Death.

Also, the audience are expecting gags in your credits; that film had nothing, just a piece of music with a TV floating away. What we should have had was the credits would start, and then we reprise Creosote [with the] cleaning up going on in the restaurant. So they're cleaning up the restaurant, and the guy says, 'Listen, since we're right at the end of the film now, I'll tell you what the meaning of life is.' So the credits are rolling, rolling – we had loads of stuff of him walking and saying, 'Follow me, follow me,' all the way through the credits – the credits finish, he's *still* saying, 'Follow me!' Half the audience are standing in the aisle *waiting to hear* the meaning of life, and you run it for as long as you like! And then the guy tells you to 'fuck off!' That would have been the ending that would have made that film.

I don't think you can tell an audience to fuck off and *then* try to keep them after that point! The other thing is, by reprising the Creosote restaurant we would have *reminded* everybody about the funniest thing in the film.

### *Was that suggested structure seriously considered?*

**DOYLE:** Well, I talked to Terry Jones and he liked what the cleaning lady was saying – he played the cleaning lady – and he felt it would detract from it by putting it at the end of the film. The others weren't around and they never heard about it. So I just didn't get anywhere with the idea, and I couldn't convince Terry that that was the way to go.

I have these horrible thoughts of where films can be better; they sort of stick with me. I don't think you can get *Holy Grail* much better, I don't think you can get *Life of Brian* much better – Otto would have helped a little. [But] *Meaning of Life* could have been a better film.

**PALIN:** I tend to think that the only creative work thrives on economy, in a sense. More money doesn't mean better comedy, I don't think it ever has; I think it's quite irrelevant. The best comedy is some sort of complaint or conflict, anyway – that's what it's about – so it's probably better if the comedy writers are up against it than if they're being softened up with large amounts of money, because then you become formulaic. And I think that was important to me in the early *Python* shows, because we didn't have much money and we had lots and lots of ideas. [We tried to] find how we could put these ideas across, so people worked incredibly hard, Gilliam especially on his animation. There are some costumes and all that, being clearly inventive, and that spirit of invention was very, very important. I think possibly as we came to the third series, got a little bit more money and were more accepted, maybe the invention weakened a little, but it might be just that we'd done so much.

My assessment looking back on it was that it was the first couple of series that really all of us were flying on all cylinders. There was a tremendous amount of work put into each show, because we said, 'We've got this freedom, we don't have much money, but we're going to fill these shows brim-full, we're going to make them so rich.' And then as it got to the third series, things just became a little bit more indulgent, possibly slightly more repetitive. And I think again with the films, probably in its way *Holy Grail* was much more inventive than *The Meaning of Life*, which had more money – if we'd wanted a battlefield we could *have* one, with plenty of soldiers and all that sort of thing. And so, yes, I think that when Python was forced to be inventive for whatever reason – a lack of funds, usually – that's when we were at our best.

It's not a general rule, because I think there were things that we did in *The Meaning of Life* – for instance, the 'Sperm Song' – which we couldn't have done unless we had some money. And that was a really good use of money; whereas before it would have been just a neat idea, we made it into something with quite a towering impression, a sequence to stand in comparison with the best Hollywood musical sequences. And you could only do that with a bit of money.

**CLEESE:** Everything that was good about *Life of Brian* was bad about *Meaning of Life*. *Life of Brian*, we knew instinctively what we were writing about, everybody was writing well, the story (which we're not very

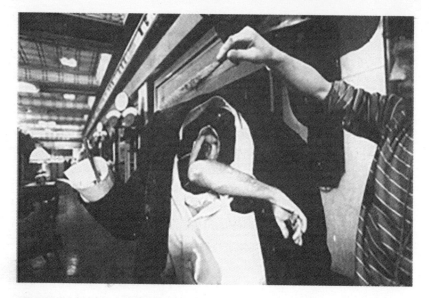

*Thankless acting assignment, from 'Find the Fish'.*

good at) developed remarkably easily and organically, we knew that we were onto something good and funny and meaningful, and the shooting process was a joy – except the last few days when I got a rotten chest infection – I remember saying to someone, 'Being crucified is bad enough, it's no fun when you have the flu as well.'

That was a great project, and then we made a terrible mistake: when *Life of Brian* came out and it was such a big hit (a *very* big hit by our standards), Denis O'Brien said to us – and it remains to this day the single most misleading bit of information I've ever been given – 'If you guys make another film almost straightaway, you'll never have to work again in your lives.' And that was very attractive to me, because work is not my strong suit. And so we started trying to create a film, even though we needed a break from each other – not because we weren't getting on, but we just needed to regenerate. We went straight into writing *Meaning of Life*, we broke up for a time and went off and did our own projects, we got back together, we wrote again, we broke again, we got back together and on and on and on. And all we did was accumulate material, a third of which was really good, a third of which was okay, a third of which I thought was not good enough.

I'm not entirely sure how pleased I am that we did it. I thought it was a very scrappy, rather unsatisfactory film, and for every good bit of material I thought there were several bits that weren't. I never thought it really came together, and I thought it was a perfect example of us starting on something before we were ready. And also at the end I disagreed with a number of the editorial decisions that the group had made, and I thought, well, at my age (by that time I was forty-three), I've reached the point where I ought to be making my own mistakes and not other people's.

I think there was a general sense that it had not been a very satisfactory experience, and while I don't remember a conscious decision being made not to make another film, I think it was like when you go to a restaurant that isn't very good: you don't actually *say*, 'I'm never going back there again,' you just suddenly discover three years later that you've never been drawn back. I think it was like that.

**GOLDSTONE:** It didn't do more [business] than *Life of Brian* because in a way it didn't satisfy the way *Life of Brian* did. Its individual moments were great, but the feeling people had coming out of the cinema wasn't the one that they came out of *Life of Brian* with. It's a film that they could sit through again and again and pick up on certain moments, but I think in terms of consumer satisfaction they were disappointed, and that's very important in terms of word of mouth and the success of a film. Also, it didn't have really the same kind of notoriety because the subject matter was very broad.

I reckon after *Meaning of Life* the chances of them doing another film are really slim. It may be the fact that *Meaning of Life* didn't work as well, but also there's the realization historically that it had taken two or three years to write and prepare each film, and to have to make that kind of commitment became virtually impossible for all of them to do.

**GILLIAM:** It was work habits that had changed. We weren't all at the same level trying to work just for the show. I mean, lifestyles were getting in the way: 'I'm a Hollywood Star, I need this . . .' It's not [that] one is right or wrong, it's just they're different ways of working. Work habits: that's the only way I can describe it.

*How do you think their work characterized the Pythons themselves?*

**GOLDSTONE:** They always had integrity and commitment to what they did. They wouldn't compromise, and were able to see that vision through. I'm sure that pays off because it's truth. It's not pandering to what's thought to be the commercial way of doing things. It's not just second-guessing what an audience will like. You do what you feel is right; sometimes it doesn't work, but it's that kind of commitment that clearly has worked for them.

I've never really thought about this before, but although *Meaning of Life* was uncompromising, probably because of what was happening to the group at the time, and the kind of tensions that existed, they somehow didn't quite see it through in the way they had the previous work. It's the sort of film that peaks too early, and it's downhill to the end – you can't do that. It may reflect something that was happening internally, a feeling that the interest was waning. That's the nature of screenwriting, where the third act often does not live up to the first two.

They wouldn't proceed with a movie until they all felt that the script was ready; that in itself was just so rare. In American movies an awful lot of work is invested in development of a project – or overdevelopment! In England it isn't the case; screenplays are generally *underwritten* except in a few rare examples.

It's such a miracle that films get made, and a lot of the influence has been television, which is never as diligent. Because they need to fill time slots, they will go with a second draft rather than a fourteenth, and it shows. But the films that have really broken through, interestingly, have been subject to very substantial writing and rewriting: *Four Weddings and a Funeral, A Fish Called Wanda. The Full Monty* was a long writing process, and I think that has something to say about the credibility of the project, as to what really has gone into it. When a film is put under scrutiny, every blemish will come through if it hasn't been properly thought [out].

Things are getting better here in terms of screenwriting, but it's never been a part of our history. We've had a culture that has always been theatre and (to a certain extent) television. Cinema is not the language that we think in, and it's only been since a new generation has been influenced by American cinema and has recognized something about film grammar that it is getting better and better.

So just that experience of the intensity of the writing and rewriting of Python scripts is a very good lesson.

**PALIN:** I think the fact that we'd struggled for a long time to get a script together, we were writing from almost as soon as we'd done *Brian*. And there were *tons* of stuff; far more material was thrown away during the writing of *Meaning of Life* than any other thing we'd done on *Python*. Tons of stuff just didn't quite work out. So yeah, in the end I suppose there was a feeling that we have to see it through because we'd invested so much time in the writing of it, [but] it never happened as neatly or organically as the other films. And although there are a number of things in *Meaning of Life* which are really exceptionally good – I mean, Mr Creosote and the 'Sperm Song', and there's a scene where Graham and Eric talk about contraception, which is just one of my favourite things – I didn't feel as a whole it was very satisfactory. It doesn't leave in your mind that wonderful world that *Brian* and *Grail* did, which was a pity. And Terry Gilliam's [work] wasn't assimilated in the way it should have been. I don't think to be honest it was the best use of Terry. I like *The Crimson Permanent Assurance,* but it was too long and too heavy and it should have been somehow integrated *into* the film.

---

At the 1983 Cannes Film Festival, *The Meaning of Life* received the
Jury Prize, a rarity for a comic film.

---

**GILLIAM:** I don't know what Cannes did. We made a splash there, but I
never got a feeling that [because of that] the writing about what we did
was any more serious or not. Cannes to me was just a funny time to be
inundated with all this madness, where the twenty-four hours of your
day, the big day (when you've got the press conference and the show),
everywhere you move there's a photographer, there's a microphone, you're
the centre of it, and the next day, *nothing*! You don't exist the next day.
That was the best thing to learn in Cannes: the fleetingness of fame.
Twenty-four hours is what you get in Cannes and then it's over!

The best memory I have of Cannes was at the Carlton Terrace. I see
Terry coming down through the interior part of it, there's a video crew
coming, he's grabbing people and saying, '¿Qué Monty Python? ¿Qué
Monty Python?' And people were responding or not responding, and he
was just *gone*, and he actually grabbed me without even recognizing who
I was and kept on talking to me: 'Who is Monty Python?' And I looked
at him and then he finally recognized it was me, and I started taking my
trousers down! And in the midst of all this, suddenly I feel this heat on
my back, it was like the sun was burning, it was really hot. And I turned
around and it was Jerry Lewis, beet-red, staring, just angry because we
were in his way. We were in France and the camera was interested in *us*,
and paying no attention to Jerry Lewis, and he *hated* us. It was just a great
moment.

I could actually feel the heat coming off of this man, this face was
ugly, so full of hatred, it was amazing. That's my memory of Cannes, and
also being there in the black ties and all that, and projectile-vomiting
on-screen. And the audience went with it, that's what was *really* funny,
because we didn't know, we thought they might just be so outraged. So
that was good.

And then the prize – I was off doing something else. Terry was the one that went back and got it. I've never really registered it, to be quite honest. It's like, 'Oh, we got a prize, good.' And that's about it. I think I've got a thing in its plastic folder still stuck up on the wall that [says] we'd won something. It was just really strange.

**IDLE:** It was the only studio picture we did, which means it will *never* go into profit!

✵   ✵   ✵

# LE MORTE D'ARTHUR

## FORGET ABOUT YOUR SIN – GIVE THE AUDIENCE A GRIN

In his naked account of his life and friendships, *A Liar's Autobiography* (published in 1980), Chapman wrote unapologetically about where the turns of fate had taken him, but seemed proud that he had in fact stood up to alcohol, which had grown to dominate him. His was a life marked by flirtations with disaster, whether it was engaging in obnoxious or rude behaviour in order to shock those in attendance, or indulging in hedonistic or death-defying thrills.

In the late 1980s, Chapman began touring (mainly at college campuses) with a one-man show that was a convivial mixture of reminiscences, jokes, and performance art. A typical start for the show would be his request to the audience for ten seconds' worth of shouted abuse ('It would certainly save a lot of time later on'). He made several guest appearances on American television, hosted a series on Cinemax, and worked on various projects, including a screenplay loosely based on the exploits of the Dangerous Sports Club, and an unsold pilot for an NBC series, *Jake's Journey*.

On October 4, 1989, almost twenty years to the day since the first broadcast of *Monty Python's Flying Circus*, Graham Chapman passed away at the age of forty-eight, following an extended battle against cancer. Having been weakened by his lengthy dance with alcoholism (he had started drinking at age fourteen), Chapman's late recovery from substance abuse perhaps had convinced him that his fight against cancer would prove equally successful. But his uncompromising lifestyle, which had earlier introduced a strain in his relationships with the other Pythons, seemed to forebode an early, tragic end. The death of Chapman also mirrored the dissolution of the group as a performing entity, for by that time Python existed pretty much only in reruns and in CD compilations of previously recorded albums.

---

*How did your relationship with Graham change when you were no longer writing with him regularly?*

**CLEESE:** Well, I think that there was a time when Graham felt, because we were a writing pair, that we were like a kind of professional marriage. And I remember in 1971 I lost some money on an unwise investment; I opened a health club and the guy who was running the health club dropped dead about three weeks after it opened, and it was all predicated on his participation. It was terrible, [but] I needed some money rapidly. And I spoke to Humphrey Barclay, who was doing *Doctor at Large,* and since Graham and I had done the pilot episode of that, I said to Humphrey, 'Can I write some episodes?' And when Graham found out I was writing on my own he was terribly upset, rather as though I wasn't allowed to, like I was *cheating* on him. As though it was simply not in the cards for me to be able to go off and do something on my own. And I remember thinking, 'Why would he feel that?' He felt very upset and complained to people about it, as though I was doing something morally wrong.

And then of course when I pulled out of the group and started writing with Connie, I was not only wanting to write with Connie but around about that time the last thing I wanted to do was go and write with a full-blown alcoholic. And I think he had all sorts of difficult feelings, whereas I was just glad to be out of there. I wanted to be with someone who would be on time and know what was going on. Now, after he cleaned his act up, it was good fun working with him again. But what happened was that we went from seeing a great deal of each other in 1972, '73, until I then started writing with Connie, so I wasn't seeing Graham during the day and I wasn't performing with him.

**GILLIAM:** There was a strange kind of self-destructiveness going on with Graham. In New York he used to come back, he was constantly getting hit by people, there was some transvestite who'd attacked him once – he came back all bloody.

In the end I used to get really pissed off at Graham, because it was becoming like Dorian Gray, and there was a portrait somewhere, but the portrait was a living person. John Tomiczek was his ward, this was a guy that turned up one day in the studio. John was like something out of *Death in Venice,* this totally androgynous creature, *beautiful* creature. It was hard to know whether John was a boy or a girl, he was just beautiful. And then it turned out later Graham had adopted him as his ward. I had no idea what if anything was going on between them, but he became his ward, because he'd come from this poor Liverpool family, lots of kids, and Graham took him on.

And as the years go by, Graham's drinking never affected him – he'd look the same – but John Tomiczek was putting on weight and bloating, and getting uglier. Graham was giving this kid everything, but he was somehow the living portrait of Graham Chapman. It got so bad there was a party at his place one night, we were all there, and somebody had been there [who] wasn't invited and Graham threw him out. Fifteen minutes later there was a knock at the door, and John went to the door and they were there and they slashed his face open with a razor. So not only was he bloated but now he was scarred. And this went on, and I was beginning to hate Graham: 'What do you think you're doing to this kid?' And Graham just sucked on his pipe, like there was no connection between his lifestyle and what was happening with John.

And in the end John died of a heart attack not long after Graham died, this *kid*. It was the most bizarre thing watching this happen. And Graham just floated through life sucking his pipe, it was a weird kind of total obliviousness to any responsibility. That was a time I began to get really worried, because it was one thing when Graham was really outrageous and funny, and then it sort of moved into something else and started first affecting him and then those around him, in a way that was affecting them worse than it was affecting him. He sort of passed this thing through himself and on to somebody else. It became really weird. I went through a long period when I was really angry with Graham, I thought, 'This is wrong, this is immoral,' and he felt one could be free in any way.

It's like – well, that's *Fear and Loathing in Las Vegas*: the bad side goes so far and then it comes out; you can't keep doing that, there's a *limit* to where you go.

**DAVID SHERLOCK:** It seems to me such a strange thing that Graham in life was not afraid of the physical act of death. He'd seen it, he dealt with it, he actually nursed very well a wonderful young cartoonist who was on *The Frost Show* who died of leukemia in St Bart's Hospital. Incidentally, Graham didn't quite finish his [medical] training, because in this country you had to do two years' internship and he never did that. He just couldn't be bothered, obviously, when he'd already started a career. I wouldn't say he practiced, but he occasionally would write prescriptions for people – he was very careful about for whom and what, and would often turn down requests.

Graham had fooled us in the last three weeks that he was going to survive; in fact, he even showed us an X-ray taken of his chest to show that there [was] no cancer left. I actually think they gave him any old X-ray; it's a known technique, particularly in the last weeks or so with someone who is obsessed with getting home, wants to be at home, cannot stand being in the hospital – he was a terrible patient, most doctors are! They knew they were sending him home to die, and probably he did because he kept up the illusion that he was getting better.

It was perfectly obvious; he had a relapse which was extremely traumatic, and from then on the next forty-eight hours were just whirlwind sensations, vague memories for me. It's like a nightmare, of course, because the very thing that we'd worked all year to try and prevent was happening and there was nothing I could do.

**CLEESE:** We had a dinner together about eighteen months before he died, and he was on about free radicals, and I was amazed at just how careful and disciplined he was about his eating, as though he was going to live forever. And then when we turned up at some meeting a year later, I hadn't seen him for a bit, he walked in and I suddenly heard this high-pitched voice. I thought he was clowning around, and I turned and was actually shocked; he looked *terrible*, some sort of red marking on his skin where he'd had some kind of radiation, and he was talking in a high voice. From that point on I saw quite a lot of him, and I was there when he died.

*What was your most surprising reaction to
the loss when Graham died?*

**CLEESE:** First of all, an enormous sense of sadness, and then the surprising bit (which kicked in after three or four days) was a sense of relief. Graham had an almost infinite capacity for fantasy. I discovered he really had a genuine problem about distinguishing reality from his own fantasy. And I was always worried (because he was chronically short of money) that he would one day go and sell his story or memoirs to one of the British Sunday tabloids. And I thought if he was out of sorts with the group at the time, there was always a danger – because he was very emotional – that a whole lot of his fantasy life would get put down on paper. You would then spend the rest of your life saying, 'No, it wasn't like *that*.' I remember thinking, 'Well, at least *that's* not going to happen.' Although he did in fact sell some sort of life story to the *Sun* not so long before he died and it was fine, I had that fear.

*He did come out with* A Liar's Autobiography.

**CLEESE:** Which was my idea, oddly enough. I was going to do a thing about winning the Cup Final, playing inside right with Stanley Matthews, and being on Everest with Hillary – a nice idea, and he kind of took it off me, which I was perfectly fine with. But once when I was really wanting to leave the group, he gave an interview to one of the tabloids in which he told a story that was so fantastic, something about the fact that I'd hidden his pipe and he chased me across the studio floor and rugby-tackled me and sat on my head! And it appeared, and I read it and thought, 'He's crazy!' He had no capacity a lot of the time of really knowing what had happened and what hadn't.

So there was a sense of relief, but also a great sense of loss, and I realized that the loss was not so much a loss in the present. In the previous years I hadn't seen him for ages so he wasn't a part of my life, so my sadness was thinking back to a time and thinking how positive and good most of it had been. It was positive and good from 1962 through *Python*, but when he became a drunk it was unpleasant.

**DOUGLAS ADAMS:** The last time I spoke to him would have been just a few days before he died. I hadn't spoken to him that regularly for quite a while, and I often wondered exactly what he knew at that point. He'd been discharged; effectively the doctors knew he wasn't going to make it, but there was no point in keeping him in hospital anymore. He must have known. But what Graham said absolutely to everybody, with complete conviction, was that he was now in remission and it was all going to be fine. And so when I talked to him he was very, very chatty and full of all the things he could now do: this project and that project and how great it was going to be, and all this kind of stuff. Four or five days later he was dead.

He must have known. I don't know whether he was just being very brave for everybody else or deluded.

*Would that have been like him, to pretend for the sake of others?*

**ADAMS:** But also self-delusion would have been like him. My guess is that there isn't actually one answer. I think probably intellectually he must have known, but probably the reality/distortion field we all maintain would have told him that *of course he can beat this,* just as his personal reality/distortion field would have told him all sorts of completely implausible things in the past.

It's funny, there was such an extraordinary warmth. I'm sort of sitting here, visualizing him puttering out of the room, just sort of *purring* with laughter.

**SHERLOCK:** The Pythons were wonderful to me after Gray died, particularly for the memorial in London. The funeral was in a very small crematorium in Kent, it only held eighty people, and although the Pythons wanted to come, his own family I think were too distressed. And as it was, it was far too public, because the world's press turned up (whether we liked it or not), and we were just not in any state to do that.

In fact, as we approached the crematorium there was this battery of cameras. I actually said to his nephews and nieces, who were in the same car with me, 'One thing you do *not* do is look right or left – you look straight ahead, or you keep your head down.' Because I had just seen Diana Dors'* funeral, where people were running over gravestones to talk, because they were in an emotional state; they couldn't know until they

---

* 'Britain's answer to Marilyn Monroe', who starred in such films as *Man Bait, Good Time Girl, The Unholy Wife,* and *Berserk!*

saw themselves on camera how it looked like they were *eagerly* running to talk to the cameramen about how much they loved Diana. I don't think that's the case at all, but that's how they *looked*, and I was not going to have that situation at Graham's funeral.

**ADAMS:** John Cleese said a number of things at Graham's memorial. He said he wanted to be the first person to say 'fuck' at a memorial service! But he also said, 'Graham was above all honest. He was frighteningly honest with himself and he was appallingly honest with other people. And he would hate it if I were [to] stand up at his memorial service and say anything less than the honest truth, which was that he was a freeloading bastard!' That caused a bit of a moment!

But you see the whole of that was true. I could see why John particularly and the rest of the Pythons would get pretty exasperated when in fact they felt he was maybe not pulling his weight and being drunk and troublesome. But nevertheless that kind of brutal honesty that he brought (even if it was a drunk's honesty, which is often completely self-deluded) was a very, very powerful force at work. It wouldn't be Python without any one of them, but one could see very strongly it wouldn't be Python without Graham.

**SHERLOCK:** I've had some of the most gracious letters from fans; the outpouring of emotion when he died was extraordinary. His brother and sister-in-law were in Canada when he died, and the university they were visiting was having a Graham celebration and dedicated a whole evening of student comedy to Graham and in particular one sketch where a group of students was singing 'Autumn Leaves', and as it happened thousands of leaves showered down until they were almost covered and they still kept on singing, and someone came with one of those leaf blowers that blew them away. His brother and sister-in-law were absolutely amazed that they should be so far from home and yet it was happening even there. And nobody knew they were there; it wasn't done for them, it was done for the students themselves, because they wanted to do something to at least mark his passing.

# THE 'IF YOU COULD SAVE ONLY ONE THING YOU'VE PRODUCED' CHAPTER

*An unfair question, but one which shall be asked anyway: a fire is raging in a warehouse which contains everything you have ever done. If you could run into the inferno and rescue but one item that would be preserved for future generations, what would it be?*

**IDLE:** My penis.

**GILLIAM:** I can't bring my three children out, that doesn't count? I produced those!

*Don't worry, the kids are safe.*

**GILLIAM:** I don't know if I agree with it, but I suppose I'd probably have to hold *Brazil* to be the one. I mean, it's still the one that's probably the truest, completest, most 'me' of anything. The most cathartic it was at the time I did it, and the most about things that were really driving me mad.

[But] the odd thing is, I'm not that person anymore, so it's actually saving somebody (or a *representation* of that person) who doesn't exist anymore. When I watch it I'm kind of astonished by it, that I made it; all I know is that *I* didn't; a guy named Terry Gilliam who looks a lot like me did it years ago, but it was *another* guy. Maybe that's the guy I'd like to save, the guy that made that.

Then I look at *Fisher King*, and I say, 'I like that, that's the sweetest one. Maybe I ought to keep the sweetest one.' Then *Time Bandits* is – I don't know, I'd probably be so busy trying to make up my mind they'd *all* burn – then I'd probably go down with them!

**PALIN:** In the category of Python material I would say in *Life of Brian*, the scene with the Centurion sending people off to be crucified ('Crucifixion? Good, out of the door, line on the left, one cross each. Next?'). I just love that character, because there's all these people surrounding this centurion, Nisus Wettus, who's trying to do his best, decent chap, out of a good school, been posted to Judea, surrounded by these complete lunatics.

And the other would be from 'Roger of the Raj' (an episode of *Ripping Yarns*): Lord Bartlesham, this terribly decent chap stuck in this little terrible reactionary world, and his wife. They're just fun, the two of them together:

### LORD BARTLESHAM:

Just suppose for a minute that when Wallenstein reached the gates of Magdeburg in 1631, instead of razing the city to the ground and putting its inhabitants to the sword, he'd said, *What a lovely place! How lucky you are to live here. I live in Sweden, you must come and see me some time.* Just think what a difference it would have made. He'd have gone down in history as a nice chap, instead of the Butcher of Magdeburg.

### LADY BARTLESHAM:

Eat up, dear, and stop talking piffle.

I'm a great fan of the 'Fish Slapping Dance'; if all the work I'd ever done was going to be destroyed, I could save one minute of it, I'd rather save the 'Fish Slapping Dance'. These sketches you can debate one against the other; the 'Fish Slapping Dance', there's something so elementally silly about it, it works so satisfactorily, that I would put that on the list.

**JONES:** Maybe my children's books, *Fairy Tales* and *Fantastic Stories*.

**CLEESE:** You're assuming my cats are safely out? My Modigliani and my cats?

*Only your work is at risk.*

**CLEESE:** Oh, I'd let it all burn! I actually don't feel any of it's very important. I mean, I wish I had an answer for you, but I don't have, not one. I think *Life of Brian* is the best of the Python movies, and there's two or three *Fawlty Towers* I'm very very fond of: the rat and the psychiatrist and the dead body. But I have to say none of them matter to me very much, do you know what I mean?

I'm not someone who looks back; that's my temperament. Somebody once said you only really start to age when you look back; well, that's not the reason that I don't look back. I don't look back because I'm the sort of person who doesn't look back, I've not much interest in it at all. There will come a time when I do look back, and then I think I'll get quite a lot of pleasure out of plying through old *Fawlty Towers*, looking through scrapbooks, but right at the moment I'm much more interested in the next lot of things I have to do. And that isn't a choice, that's not an attitude; that comes from the sort of person you are. I have no control over it.

# TWENTY-FIRST-CENTURY PYTHON

*Reunited in Aspen, 1998.*

## THANK GOD FOR THAT. FOR ONE GHASTLY MOMENT I THOUGHT I WAS . . . TOO LATE.

On March 7, 1998, HBO brought together the Pythons for an informal stage appearance during the US Comedy Arts Festival in Aspen, Colorado, taping the proceedings for broadcast. Apart from being the first public appearance of all five surviving Pythons in many years, the occasion became noteworthy for the almost sacrilegious handling of the supposed 'ashes' of Graham Chapman, which were brought onstage in his stead and which ended up being vacuumed by a Dustbuster.

The Aspen appearance merely fuelled speculation and rumours that – in anticipation of Python's thirtieth anniversary in 1999 – the group would reunite for a stage show, a tour, or even another movie.

---

**CLEESE:** What was really nice about Aspen and also the subsequent dinner that four of us had in London was just to see how well we all got on. As the main cause of dispute in the group (which was the material) has faded into the background, it enables us all to get on in the way that we basically always did get on – a personal level. The relationships have always been quite good; it's been the work that's thrown up the cause of the disagreements. And we got on well, and that's why we thought it would be fun to do something [for the thirtieth anniversary].

But then the very next day Terry Gilliam said to Michael Palin and Terry Jones that he didn't really want to do it, which is *not* what he said in

*Gilliam kicking over the 'ashes' of Chapman at the Aspen reunion.*

the room. And then some weeks, months later, Michael decided he didn't really want to do six or eight weeks, he really only wanted to do two. So trying to get everybody's needs together has proved very difficult.

You see, the show itself will be quite costly, so if we do two weeks, say in Las Vegas, all that ticket money may go just to pay for the production, so that the only money that comes to us would effectively be from the television sales, and by the time that's been split several ways – and there's been several weeks writing it, two weeks rehearsal, two weeks performing – it's not a particularly exciting offer compared to what we get for movies. But we may decide to do it anyway just out of affection for Python, and because it marks the thirtieth anniversary quite well.

**GILLIAM:** That Aspen thing, it was like *aspic*. We were up there, I thought we were almost mummified! There's a crowd down there, three or four rows back, the entire cast of *Cheers*, Ted Danson and Woody Harrelson, grinning with these beaming Moonie smiles: *'It's the Pythons!'* And we're just talking like, [*imitating an old fogey*] 'Well, in my day when we used to do comedy . . .' And the audience was so happy, they loved it so much. We didn't have to *do* anything; we were feeding them, they were *inhaling* us. I don't know if you can do that night after night, week after week, city after city, and have any self-respect left! Any soul left, anything.

It was really interesting, because the HBO people were coming with all these ideas, they were going to do the urn and everybody was going along with it – this was in the planning stage – and I just thought there's something awful about this *pretending* that Graham's there. I just thought, 'I'm going to knock the urn over.' And then suddenly it's all right, because this pretense led to something outrageous. But it was weird.

We once had an offer to do an HBO thing in Las Vegas, and I wanted to show it with showgirls, still doing the sketches in the middle but with girls on the sides – just something *awful*. But if you're going to do it in Las Vegas, then you've got to *deal* with Las Vegas in one form or another. It's *not* Drury Lane.

☞

I was talking to Mike – what we should be getting is the Pythonettes. You get six young beautiful girls who would do all the sketches. *'This parrot is de-ceased!'* And they have nice tits and everything, and we'd sit there on the side of the stage: 'Yes, these are the girls, they're doing great. *Well done,* girls!' Do the whole show like that, and we'd take the bows at the end of each scene! I don't think we'd make many cities before the word was out.

**IDLE:** Aspen was very beneficial for us. We got a chance to see each other again – apart from Terry Gilliam, who was still in his fascist 'I'm a Director' stage and wouldn't have dinner with us but went running off to hang out with Hunter S. Thompson. What a lapse of taste! Still, he's a Yank, you know.

Whether we will ever be able to agree on anything ever again is moot. I think groups use up all their agreements early and then all that is left is to disagree. But I'm not sure whether I agree with that . . .

*How do you think Graham's absence*
*affects the workings of the group now?*

**PALIN:** I think it's very significant. I think it makes it extremely difficult to write new material, and in an odd way I think Graham will be missed more as a writer than as a performer, although he was very important for *Grail* and *Life of Brian* because he took the leading roles. He had the ability to play the leading man, and we don't have anyone quite like that. But he and John really created some of the best stuff Python's done; without Graham there, I don't think it's as easy for John to produce the material on his own. I think you'd find the same if I was writing with Terry and Terry wasn't there. I think a very, very important part of the balance was Graham's input – take him away and it isn't the same. There's no denying it; whatever we do now as Python, Python without Graham, you've either got to say, 'Well, we can still do something which people will enjoy without Graham,' or we can take the view, 'Rest it there; he's not replaceable, therefore anything we do without him will be slightly weaker,' in the way when we did the six shows without John they were show for show probably weaker than the rest of the series. We did miss John; we still produced some great stuff, but you can't say, 'This is still Python.' One has to go onward.

*It's like having Paul, George, and Ringo*
*perform as the Beatles without John.*

**PALIN:** Yes, exactly. I've never gone along with that, either; I never really *wanted* to see the three remaining Beatles play. How could the Beatles be the same without Lennon? So you have to admit the same would happen with Python; we'd be different.

But I always feel you should never be led by the fans, much as one is grateful for them. Or television people [who] say, 'We can make some money out of it.'

I think there are quite interesting parallels between *Meaning of Life* and the idea of a Python tour next year, both led largely by outsiders thinking they could make money out of us, which means also *we* can make a bit of money. They're just not organic. We are told, 'There is that market there, yes; we love Python, you must get together.' Fine, I accept that and I'm very grateful for it, but I don't think we can get together at all costs.

But on the other hand, Python's a sort of strange, resilient force. Despite all the years that have gone by, it's still something which we shared and which we feel we created and *only* the group of us created. We may have our differences about things, [but] undoubtedly as a group we'll be there. It can be something which is still considered to be valuable and successful, and that's an animal which you can't ignore! It's like, the fire is not burning brightly but the embers are still there; you just blow on them and the flames will come up again. That is why the Python project's still around, still in the air; there is something there that could be used. And I think it's a very interesting debate as to whether we *should* use it or not.

**GILLIAM:** I think we've gone much further apart than we think we have, that's what worries me. We can get together and work for a day or two and we can feel it all, or we can get on stage (although with the HBO thing it was nothing but talking), and when we do get together, ideas start coming up, it gets really funny, it's really nice. But I don't know where that ballast is that Graham was. And Mike and Terry are not a writing team in the way they were; Eric is still fine, but he hasn't done anything really for a while.

I don't know how, I almost feel I would have to end up being in there writing with John and being *Splunge!* and I don't want to do that, because I *can't stand* writing with John! Writing with John is one of the most boring things in the world because he's *so* methodical. We did it on *Meaning of Life.* Because we were all out in Jamaica, we split into two groups, and I got stuck with John and Graham, and I couldn't stand the pace. One can throw in ideas fast and furious but then [it's] this nitpicking, and I couldn't deal with it. You need someone like Graham sitting there sucking on his pipe [while] John nitpicks.

Even Eric would find it difficult. Everybody would find it difficult writing with John because you just have to work at a different pace. And John's brilliant, there's nothing less than brilliance there, but it's again a work pace or habit.

My gut tells me the group doesn't work, and then I keep thinking when we start [talking about new projects], hopefully we can resurrect a lot of old stuff, but number one, who replaces Graham in the performances? You can spread it out a little bit, but it's still not quite the same, and I can't fill a gap that's as big – I can take a little bit, but it's not what I'm good at, I don't want to do that, really. And I mean Terry got excited about the stage show and started writing some stuff, but this doesn't excite me. Maybe it would have felt like a good idea twenty-five years ago, but now it doesn't. It feels like an *old* idea, and it seems to me if we were to work we would have to come up with new and fresh ideas to excite us all, and if we can't do that . . .

We started talking about doing a film a year ago, and it got very

TWENTY-FIRST-CENTURY PYTHON

funny. It was about another crusade, the Last Crusade, we try to gather these old knights together who are all married and settled down – *us!* – which is a smart thing. And then we had this great idea about Graham coming along as a holy relic, a box with these bones in it. And he could *talk* because we've got old material from Graham, from records and things, we've got his voice, and so Graham could be there doing stuff and he's in this terrible box we've got to drag around.

A stage show might be easier, because it's just a couple of sketches. We'd need some new sketches – John's probably got a few stuck away in a drawer! But I can't personally think of anything worse than getting up there and reciting that old stuff again. So I'm not being very positive these days!

I think the smartest thing we did was getting out when we got out. We sort of became Comedy James Deans – we killed ourselves. I'd rather the legend be kept alive with the few remaining artifacts rather than, 'James Dean is alive and onstage? Oh fuck, we don't want to see that, do we?' I mean it's good just to see, 'Oh, *that's* what he looks like now – he's *bald?*'

I just thought we did the smart thing: we killed ourselves and that was the end of it. We always said it was the six of us or nothing. And the only reason for doing the stage show it seems to me is greed, and *that's* not motivating me much nowadays.

*Having established a career for yourself, what responsibility do you still feel towards the group?*

**GILLIAM:** Hmm, I don't. I think the responsibility is to make sure we don't sell out what we've done, that's my feeling. I think we did rather well at controlling stuff and not compromising it.

The fact that we own the television shows is still one of the most extraordinary things because *nobody* owns their own shows. Except maybe us and Lucille Ball! She was shrewd, she was a real sharp lady.

It may be that's why on the tour there's a sense that I don't want to sully something we've done more than we already have. We could exploit

---

things more, but they have to be done well, and there's a lot of stuff, merchandising, we've let go out that's mediocre, which bothers me. It's kind of like the responsibility to say, 'That's not good enough.' But I don't feel strongly enough to go out there and do it myself, so that's a very *lax* responsibility!

I don't know. We sort of argue about, 'Should we let the stuff go out and let commercials be put in now that it's been seen enough times and it's on videotape?' It's like this greed that's creeping in: okay, we've controlled it long enough, now let's just let it go out and make as much money as possible. There's a tendency for that argument to rise, and it worries me.

### *What would Lucy have done?*

**GILLIAM:** I don't know, that's kind of it! To me, so much is in the past, and yet it's always here. I mean, we've got the organization, these companies and things, it's kind of our pension fund, and our children's and children's children's futures, so you're sort of torn between 'Make more money for the kids' and all that, or do we just keep Python what it always was and protect that little thing, that little gem, however flawed it might be?

Some of the things that I haven't paid much attention to I think are pretty shoddy. With the CD-ROMs,[*] that was one of the things [where] we were trying to keep the quality up, being involved in those. I think the CD-ROMs are the best kind of reinvention of Python because it's a new format – you can juggle it, and it becomes even *more* non-linear than it was, and that's kind of interesting. They stand up on their own.

It's funny, I think Terry's still much deeper in Python than I am. I think Mike and I and John have probably moved away more. Terry's much more nostalgic about it, I think.

---

[*] Computer games including *Monty Python's Complete Waste of Time* and *The Quest for the Holy Grail* used elements from the films and TV programmes in absurd ways, such as a *Tetris*-like block game in which dead bodies had to be piled correctly.

*Is that because you had established a solo career away
from Python earlier than perhaps Terry Jones has?*

**GILLIAM:** It may be that, but the solo careers may be the product of us try-ing to escape, get away from Python! Terry has lingered in it longer. And Eric in a strange way has as well. John I know wanted to escape from it first, and I sort of, and Mike's been escaping from everybody! If he were living in a flat world, he could go and that would be the end of it. Now he's home again: 'Oh, shit! Let's go *another* way!' The world is round, that's the problem! It's been quite interesting to watch Mike be the most determined to keep moving.

**IDLE:** Like everyone else, I prefer my solo work, because it is mine. You cannot take credit for Python because it is a group effort. I like my play, my books, my songs, the Rutles, so much stuff. Python was just a part of my life; it isn't my fault people won't let it go! I have learned you cannot run away from it, you cannot hide from it, and to be polite at all times, but it ain't me, mate. Perhaps having a Beatle for a pal helped me some-what come to terms with it all.

**JOHN GOLDSTONE:** There was nothing that would really naturally bring them together; Gilliam had unquestionably established his position as a serious filmmaker, and John had gone on to his own businesses and ulti-mately *A Fish Called Wanda*, which surpassed everybody's expectations.

And yet what was extraordinary was seeing the Aspen show: the chemistry that still remains is unquestionably still there, the way they play off each other is very funny.

**TERRY BEDFORD:** Python offended the Establishment in terms of the humour. Throughout that period of time there was a real tightening of the conservative background, which really brought about the Thatcher era – I think they were just closing ranks and making sure it didn't hap-pen again, basically!

I think one of the really scary things about the British film industry is that it should have embraced the Pythons wholeheartedly as being a really great asset. But they were shunned by the film industry; the Pythons offended them. Because truthfully, if they had carried on making those films we would have had a great tradition of film comedy here.

*'Offended' because the Pythons were outsiders and rather fiercely independent?*

**BEDFORD:** Yes. I think the British film industry at that time was really the Bonds and those kind of films. When I was doing *Jabberwocky*, you had George Lucas coming in and making *Star Wars*, and the stories that were coming back from the Lucas set down at Shepperton Studios were equally uncomplimentary as what the industry was making about *Jabberwocky*: 'These are amateur films that will never cut together, they'll never be successful.' And look at that!

**GILLIAM:** I don't think Python exists in the film world. You read the history of film, Monty Python's a footnote at best. And when you talk to film buffs in Europe, we were the films of the seventies to them. But we are not taken seriously in the world of filmmaking.

In a way it's probably a good thing, because if we were, we'd just be pretentious. But it does shock me how comedy is not allowed to be treated as serious filmmaking, and what we were doing, some of it I think is amazingly revolutionary, playing around with the medium: 'Pirandello takes over the cinema' in some cases. Nobody ever seems to write about it that way: 'It's just a bunch of funny sketches – some of them work, some don't.' We were playing with the medium and shifting it around, in the way we were playing with television, and we get no points for that.

I'm surprised because one can actually get one's academic intellectual teeth into this stuff. If there were a *Cahiers du Comedy* around, they could have a field day with it. But they don't. I'm actually glad that it doesn't get *too* carried away, but I also think it's crazy that they can't accept that we're serious filmmakers when we're doing stuff which just isn't following the rules.

**CLEESE:** Sometimes I switch on the BBC and find old *Python* shows on by accident. I watch them and some of the material, two or three things in every show, seem to be so utterly hopeless that I have no idea – and it's not just that they're not funny, but I don't know how we could have ever thought they *might* have been. All I know is that we were playing games with convention which no one had ever done before, and it was very startling the first time you do it. But once people get used to a convention being broken it's not startling at all, and then there's nothing left.

In fact, there were some Americans who when they saw *Monty Python* said, 'These guys are ripping off *Saturday Night Live*.' Whereas of course we were pre-*Saturday Night Live*. But if you'd seen *Saturday Night Live* and you hadn't seen *Python*, and *then* you see *Python*, those conventions had been broken already for the audience, even though *we* were doing that stuff first.

**NANCY LEWIS:** It was so exciting, because it was comparatively revolutionary what *Python* did. I know when *Saturday Night Live* was starting up, their premise was sort of based on a *Monty Python*-type approach. I don't know what happened to that, but it was never repeated, strangely. People tend to go back to blackouts at the end of sketches again.

Occasionally in advertising they'd try to do a Python-type thing. I've seen very Gilliamesque animation done in advertising; very little of general Python has been tried. It was unique; I think you need that web of disciplined writing, because you know the Pythons were very disciplined. The first time Michael or Eric, whoever did *Saturday Night Live* first – I remember getting the reaction from them to *Saturday Night Live* where it was, 'Hey, man, let's hang out all night, do whatever, and we'll turn out some funny stuff!' Which is so different, it wasn't a real disciplined approach. It takes a lot of work, I think, to be as consistently funny as Python.

**BARRY TOOK:** My big error, to be absolutely honest with you, was that I said, 'Python will not be a major success, but it will be very influential.' And I was utterly wrong, because it *wasn't* influential at all – nobody else apart from undergraduates copied it – and it was *enormously* successful! One of the most successful things ever made in this country. Talk about the Department of Cloudy Crystal Ball, my word!

☀    ☀    ☀

# SPAMALOT

## WE'RE OPERA-MAD IN CAMELOT, WE SING FROM THE DIAPHRAGM A LOT

As the Pythons all went their separate ways on non-Python projects – from films and documentaries to books, video games, and political columns – Idle was interested in returning musical comedy to the Broadway stage. He proclaimed that shows in the era of Andrew Lloyd Webber were no longer fun, featuring 'people with plates on their faces'.

He said he first pitched to Mel Brooks the idea of adapting his 1968 film *The Producers* (about two schemers who back a Broadway show that's destined to be a flop in order to scam the investors, only to watch in horror as their show becomes a verified hit), but the filmmaker decided against it. Brooks would later change his mind and take it on himself, and his 2001 musical *The Producers* proved a blockbuster. The show's box office receipts and twelve Tony Awards (a record) convinced Idle the time was right for even more fun on Broadway, and he believed that a musical adaptation of *Monty Python and the Holy Grail* would be the silly, vaudevillian entertainment that theatregoers craved. But turning a beloved film into a stage show is not for the faint of heart; for every *Producers* that is a hit, there are several (like 1988's *Carrie: The Musical*, which closed after five performances) that don't make it.

Before raising the idea with the other Pythons (who might have vetoed it), Idle worked for two years on the project, collaborating with composer John Du Prez (an arranger on *Life of Brian* and *Time Bandits*, and composer for *The Meaning of Life*, *A Private Function*, and *A Fish Called Wanda*). In Idle's rendition, King Arthur's quest for the Holy Grail becomes a quest for a magical land called Broadway, where a fabled Grail is said to be, and where (as Sir Robin sings) you can't succeed if you haven't any Jews. The Lady of the Lake, a mere mention in the film, becomes a musical diva who shares a power ballad with Sir Galahad ('The Song That Goes Like This'). And Lancelot, who protests an accusation of being gay in the movie, here comes all out, because, hey, it's Broadway!

After creating demo versions of the songs, Idle shipped off a CD to each Python. With positive responses in hand, he and Du Prez moved forward, under the reins of veteran director Mike Nichols (whose stage successes included *Barefoot in the Park*, *The Odd Couple*, *Luv*, *The Real Thing*, and *Annie*).

The stage show *Monty Python's Spamalot* condenses characters but re-creates many of the film's most memorable sequences, from taunting French knights to a killer rabbit that imparts a rather glorious beheading. All the Black Knight's limbs are even hacked off before our eyes. Dennis, the argumentative peasant in 'Constitutional Peasants', becomes Sir Galahad; the corpse collector and the depositor of someone 'not quite dead' become Sir Robin and Sir Lancelot, who join Arthur's crusade. But some of the film's sketches were cut in previews, including the 'burn the witch' sequence, along with a song written for the cow that gets catapulted over a castle wall.

With a cast featuring Tim Curry as Arthur, David Hyde Pierce,

Hank Azaria, Sara Ramirez, Christopher Sieber, Michael Mc-Grath, and Steve Rosen, the Knights of the Round Table opened in New York on March 17, 2005, and would continue to clap their coconuts on the Great White Way for four years, receiving fourteen Tony nominations and three awards – for Best Musical, Best Director, and Best Featured Actress in a Musical (Ramirez). The original cast album won a Grammy Award. The 2006 London production was also nominated for seven Olivier Awards. Regional and touring companies brought the show across the world, to Las Vegas, Australia, Canada, the Czech Republic, France, Germany, Hungary, Japan, Mexico, the Netherlands, Norway, Poland, South Korea, Spain, Switzerland, and Sweden... but not Malaysia (it was banned by authorities there).

---

*How did Eric win you all over to allow the film to be adapted, (a) because it sounded like an odd idea, and (b) because the track record of films turned into Broadway musicals is not that great?*

**PALIN:** My initial reaction [was] we've got to be careful about this. It's using something that already exists and possibly diluting it, or at least transforming it into something which may not be a good thing. For a long time we all sort of saw Python as the Holy Writ, in a way. We fought against ABC to keep it off of American television because they had diluted the show and edited it, in this case without our permission. So there were real echoes of that, I think, when Eric came up with *Spamalot*. And I suppose I was in that kind of protective, foggy, paranoid way where we felt, *What's going to happen here? Who's going to be in it? Are other people going to be saying our lines? Is this a good thing?* So there were doubts, definitely doubts.

But I don't think anybody ever felt like saying, 'Eric, you can't do this.' That was an option. But Eric was very good, [he] sent us songs, sent us examples of what it might sound like. I must say, the songs we liked very much. That was probably what sold us. Beyond that I'm not quite sure.

The other element was how we'd be paid for all this. We have one member of the Python team creating a show really on his own and yet with all our material – what do we charge, what our rights were, all that sort of thing. That became a slightly complicated area, and I think probably made others a little wary of signing on the dotted line. But in the end, I can't really remember why, we generally agreed because we liked the sound of it. And at that time Python was not playing much anywhere. It was definitely not playing on television in England – I suppose it was [in] various parts throughout the world, maybe in America. We had no new films out. I think it was a chance to keep Python bubbling over, and so yeah, I think there was general agreement that Eric should go ahead.

**CLEESE:** He didn't really have to win us over because he wasn't asking us to take part. He said that he would like to do this. We had the same reaction: we didn't believe in it!

Well, it's not a terribly good story, *Holy Grail*. *Life of Brian* is a good story. *Holy Grail* is just a succession of (some of them) extraordinarily funny sketches sort of stitched together with a rather thin plot. And none of us were interested in going back to it. I just thought, 'That's fine if Eric wants to go off and play with that,' but I did not consider it a very promising idea.

**GILLIAM:** We didn't think it was probably likely, but if he wanted to do it, Eric always wrote good songs – that was the one thing he was guaranteed to provide interesting stuff. It was fun. And he just wanted to do a musical. He'd always wanted to do that. We didn't care. In fact that's why we did a really bad deal, because we didn't think he'd ever pull it off.

*David Hyde Pierce, Hank Azaria, Christopher Sieber, Steve Rosen, and Tim Curry in Monty Python's Spamalot.*

***Did you think it was not possible to turn* Holy Grail *into a stage show, or did you not see the point of it?***

**GILLIAM:** No, I think we were all busy doing our own things, we couldn't care less! [*laughs*] By that point, the group had pretty much disassembled, and it was Eric's project. And it was only when we saw things like the programme – oh, wait, Python was barely mentioned! I don't think our names were even in it originally. And that was quite extraordinary. But Eric did the work, he got Mike Nichols involved, he made it work in that sense, and writing songs like 'You Gotta Have a Jew'. They were wonderful songs, right up to Mel Brooks' level of songwriting.

*Eric claims that he brought the idea of turning*
*The Producers into a stage show to Mel Brooks.*

**GILLIAM:** Oh, come on!

*He's said Brooks originally turned him down, and then years later*
*turned around and did it himself.*

**GILLIAM:** He couldn't have. Maybe, I don't know. Eric takes credit for a lot of things!

**CLEESE:** He sent us some songs. And there was one that we all absolutely adored, which is 'The Song That Goes Like This'. We thought that was absolutely brilliant. We thought there were other good songs, and some that weren't, so we said, 'Yes, sure, continue to go ahead. Nobody was going to stand in the way, but you don't need anyone's help.' Nobody's going to upset their schedule in order to join in.

And then after a time, I heard that he had got his good friend Mike Nichols involved and that was the moment when I thought, 'Oh, ho!' Because I think Mike Nichols is just about the greatest of the post-war generation as a director and as a writer and as a performer. I don't know if *writing's* quite the right word, but he was a wonderful improviser. And a lovely man. I was lucky enough to meet him, and unlucky enough not to be able to be in two films which he was closely associated with: *Remains of the Day* and *Birdcage*. I wasn't able to do either because of scheduling.

Once Eric had brought him in, I thought, 'Well, Eric is marvellous in lyrics, marvellous in jokes, but I don't think that Eric's strongest area is script,' and I thought, 'If he's got Mike Nichols looking after the structure, this is going to be a seriously promising event.'

*Christopher Sieber as Sir Galahad and Sara Ramirez as the Lady of the Lake.*

## BUT MANY TIMES WE'RE GIVEN RHYMES THAT ARE QUITE UN-SINGABLE

*You'd worked with Mike Nichols in* The Birdcage. *Was that how you came to be cast in* Spamalot? *And what did getting to play in the Python sandbox, as it were, mean to you?*

**HANK AZARIA:** Mike Nichols, we loved each other. And he champions people. Mike made us feel extremely special, would think of us for the right job and give it to us, and he took tremendous joy in that. And I was lucky enough to have that with Mike twice. Just knowing me, how he knew me as a guy who likes to do voices and imitate and also really throw myself into physical comedy, he just thought I'd be right for it, and he just reached out and asked me if I would do it. Can you imagine how quickly I said yes to that?

Talk about a dream come true, or a wish fulfilment that I didn't even know I had. I mean, I also would love to play shortstop for the New York Mets, and put an S on my chest and fly over the city. Those two things are not going to happen. I swear to you being able to jump in on some kind of Python production and be a Python was on that level for me.

I was a child who was raised by the television set. My grandmother gave me a TV when I was five, and my parents were foolish enough to put it in my room, so I was watching Johnny Carson by the time I was five. I just saw everything, and certainly anything comedically. And I was a fan of Python the very second I saw the very first airing of *Flying Circus* on PBS in New York. It completely blew my mind. The idea that grown men could be that silly, first of all, just absolutely destroyed me at age ten or eleven. I didn't get all the references until I was a few years older, but I could tell – similar to Woody Allen – that they were very, very smart and very learned and historically accurate, and that made a huge impression on me as well. 'Cause I was in the midst of my own kind of obsessive prep school education at the time and they felt like kindred spirits in that way. I asked Eric how much of that comedy came out of just rebelling against how oppressed you felt by your education, and he said, 'Oh my God, a ton of it.' I really related to it. It really meant a lot to me, not just it had made me laugh but just knowing there were adults like that running around the world was a bright spot of my childhood.

I'm one of those kids that memorized all of that, all of *Holy Grail,* all of *Life of Brian,* all of *Meaning of Life,* all of the television series. You give me a line, I can spit back to you the line that's coming; I was that ready to go.

**CLEESE:** I happened to be in the area when they started to rehearse. I went to the very first day of rehearsal – Eric was very pleased I did that – and [was] amazed because Nichols already had a couple of dances which looked to be terribly good and it was the second day of rehearsal, I don't understand how he'd done it – maybe the dancers had started early?

**AZARIA:** It was like a workshop. We kept presenting almost every day a different version of it. Eric would go home and write that night and then he'd come back the next day with a different version. We kept refining and refining and refining through Chicago, 'cause we were in previews. The show was very different in how it started at previews and how it ended, including what joke would work where. How to end the darn thing was really a problem, how to tie together all the story lines to give everybody a semi-satisfying little beginning/middle/end.

The other thing I think that's interesting that Eric pointed out, that they realized halfway through, is that in the movie what holds it all together is those guys. You know, it's Cleese as Tim the Enchanter and as Lancelot and as the guy bringing out the dead guy, and that's sort of a through line. That doesn't work onstage (a) because we're not as iconic as those guys, and (b) there's no close-ups! You don't know it's me! If I come out in a wig you don't know it's me. You don't know that I'm Tim the Enchanter. It doesn't create a through line. And so we had to abandon that idea halfway through rehearsal when you realize you need to have a through line, or you need to just not worry about having one at all.

Because Mike and Eric and choreographer Casey Nicholaw were so concerned about structure all the time and making the macro work, making the story lines work, making the musical numbers work, and more importantly the transitions from one scene or number to another, we were sort of left on our own to work out the comedy. I could have had a lot more freedom than I even took. Mostly it was about trying to hit the laughs, do as good a job imitating mostly John, a little bit of Eric as I could, and then justifying whatever stage moves I needed to make, like flying onto stage as Tim the Enchanter, or make an exit as the Knight of 'Ni', make it all work as smoothly as I could. Towards the end when we were in Chicago, I actually said to Mike, 'Look, I need you to at least one time look at what I'm doing onstage and tell me what's funny and what isn't.' He always just trusted us – 'Oh, you guys'll make this work.' And we mostly did, but he figured that making the structure and the staging right would best serve us, and it did. But, Mike, please, you gotta just pay attention to me for one afternoon! And he did.

*Did you feel he put too much trust in you, especially as*
*this was your first Broadway show?*

**AZARIA:** Mike had many amazing aphorisms; one was, 'Directing is 90 per cent casting.' Mike felt that if he cast it right – in everything he did, movie, play, anything – that you should be left to your own devices. And he would say this or that here and there, and they were usually really brilliant, genius things. But mostly he let you do your thing and trusted that you would self-correct. And he was right most of the time.

*How did you approach playing characters – Sir Lancelot,*
*Tim the Enchanter, the French Taunter, and the Knight*
*Who Says 'Ni!' – that were so vivid from the film?*

**AZARIA:** I probably treated the material with too much reverence. I kept trying to re-create the movie as literally as I could. It became obvious halfway through rehearsal that you have to transpose it into a stage production, and a musical, so those have special needs.

The one regret I have, I'm a mimic and I worship John Cleese and all those guys, and so I was trying so much to literally re-create their rhythm down to the sound, down to the letter, and a lot of that was great and fun. Looking back on it, I think it would have been probably more fun, even a better homage, to make it more my own and get into the spirit of what they were doing. Those guys were such good actors, and they threw themselves emotionally into all these sketches, and I think the best way to tribute them is to do one's own version of that. Which I did, but I wish I'd done even more of it. You get older, you get wiser!

**CLEESE:** I saw it on the first night [in New York] and I thought it was splendid. I thought Eric'd done a marvellous job. I think the only Python who didn't like it [was] Terry Jones, who is often difficult to please. He wasn't very keen on it at all. He seemed to think that something had been lost. I don't know what he felt. We tried to explain to him it's like a pantomime, and the audience is involved and it's silly. All the rest of

*The French guards (from top: Thomas Cannizzaro, Christian Borle, Hank Azaria, and Greg Reuter).*

us thought it was terrific. It was a great pleasure to go on at the end and stand with all the performers and sing something.

**PALIN:** I first saw the show in America, I thought this was a pretty good show. I wasn't happy with absolutely all of it. But on the whole I thought it was something bright and lively, very well performed, and with some new songs that were particularly good. I thought Eric and John Du Prez between them had written some marvellous new material. One looked around and the audience were going mad. You realize, however possessive we wanted to be about the Holy Writ of Python, this particular version was still considered by the audience to be Python, to be a celebration of a movie, the *Holy Grail,* they'd all liked. And I suppose that was for me the final moment when I said, 'This was a good thing, a very good thing.'

On the whole I was happy with seeing other people playing that material, which was not something I expected to be happy with. I don't know, one feels of Python sketches, you put the Python name to that character, you see people playing that character, and that's the way it was. We had never delegated our material to anybody else, certainly on that scale. I had certain reservations about that but generally speaking whenever I have seen it – I've seen two or three productions of it – I come away very happy! It's as simple as that. Eric and John had got together a very good team, I thought the designer was excellent, it moved along at a great pace and didn't take itself too seriously. So, these were all parts of the Python instruction booklet, as it were.

*The audience was bringing their love for the film to the show, which must have been a help to you and the rest of the cast.*

**AZARIA:** It was, but we had two kinds of audiences essentially seeing the show: Python fans and musical theatre fans, and there's some overlap there but not a ton. And you could sort of tell by the first five minutes in [from] how the audience was responding whether they were a musical theatre crowd or they were a Python crowd. The musical theatre crowd loved all the tropes and the meta references, very similar to *The Producers* in making fun of Broadway tropes. They loved all that. Whereas the Python fans almost didn't get those too much and just loved the re-creation of the movie and the Python bits. On the best nights it kind of would ignite and both factions would get delighted and hit a frenzy. We had a lot of nights like that, it was really gratifying. But I came to it [with] much more a movie-guy feeling – almost overly so, almost to a fault – that I wanted to carry the tradition of the movie and these guys as an homage to them and almost take a backseat to all that. So, I felt like I was always playing to the Python folks in the crowd.

*The actors seemed like fans who enjoyed
playing in the Python sandbox.*

**PALIN:** Exactly. I'm always kind of surprised by how warmly people feel towards Python. Simon Russell Beale, who is a brilliant theatre actor in England, he can take his pick of whatever parts he wants, decides to play a season as King Arthur in *Spamalot,* just because he loves the part, he loves the idea of it, and he loves Monty Python. That's quite something, and something which I consistently underestimated in people.

*Why 'underestimated'?*

**PALIN:** Because I don't go around thinking this is the best thing we've ever done, or best thing I've ever done, about anything I've done. [There's] always sort of a layer of me which says, 'Okay, this is looking good, this is fine, but I know X, Y, and Z don't like it.' I'm always aware of that negative shadow somewhere. I think that's better than being complacent and feeling everything you do works for everybody. The great thing about Python is it didn't work for everybody, which is part of its strength.

And I would have to be persuaded by people that they liked Python that much that they would give up several months of their acting career to go onstage. I learned from that. I learned that [Simon] loved it very much, thought it was a great show, and he made something of it. He could see that the part was something he could really enjoy. It's very nice for people to come along and say this really is good. [*laughs*] I need a little bit of that now and then!

*I imagine you might have different feelings if someone else
performed the 'Dead Parrot' sketch, because that is so much you.*

**PALIN:** Yes, yes, I accept that. But I'm much, much less possessive now than I used to be. The idea of other people doing Python material doesn't fill me with horror or depress me in any way. Have a go now! I feel just as the years have passed I've become a little bit less possessive, a little bit more open about Python material, largely I think because we established, if you like, the baseline of how a sketch should be done.

And nowadays people can always go back to the original, it's always there somewhere on YouTube. This was different from when we started on the BBC and *Python* went out one night and if you missed it that night, that was it – it wasn't even on video until much later. But now everything is available, people can have a look if they want. The 'Dead Parrot' sketch is a very good piece of writing, and I'm absolutely happy to see other people have a go at it, especially as we're not performing it much at the moment. That was what made the O2 show in London so special, that we got the chance forty years on to play our own sketches so people could see us doing it, and the reaction to that was so strong and so warm, I couldn't see that same reaction happening for another group of people playing Python. There's a degree to which us playing our own sketches – people know it, people look for that and they enjoy it in that way, but I don't feel in any way now about *preventing* people from doing Python sketches should they want to. And they do, all over, all the time.

I mean, if I were at school I would love to do something like Python. A Python sketch to me would have that sort of light, bright, full of fun that comes with youth, you know? And it's a bit rude! It's not like doing a bit out of Shakespeare, I suppose!

**CLEESE:** No, I have no problem at all with other people [playing Python], and sometimes I learn something.

For example, a couple of years ago we did a stage version of *Fawlty Towers* in Australia, played the big cities there. It was extremely good. It wasn't as well received in a couple of the cities (in Adelaide and in Perth) as it should have been. But it was very, very well received in Sydney, very good press in the newspapers in Melbourne and Brisbane. And people said, 'How do you think about this other guy [Stephen Hall] playing Basil Fawlty?' I said, 'I think he's terrific!' [*laughs*]

It's not a problem, I don't feel possessive about it. And if somebody else turns up and does a Python sketch, I say, 'How very interesting, I wonder what Eddie Izzard will make of that?' There's no sense of territory as far as I'm concerned. But that may be because I'm much more a writer temperamentally than I am an actor. Maybe an actor would feel differently.

**AZARIA:** Simon Russell Beale really made it his own. If I were playing Arthur, I would have tried to do the best Graham Chapman I could have, which would have been a mistake. But Simon kind of played it with a wide-eyed wonder; he was on a childlike journey of discovery. Whereas Tim played it much more cynical, aware he was in a musical. He played it much more from a meta standpoint, but that's really who Tim was, the guy who had done a million musicals and was very aware of the traditions he was parodying from panto and musical theatre. And it works beautifully with Tim doing that, and it worked amazingly well with Simon playing it pretty straight. So, there was a lot of room for interpretation. Mostly they were playing straight men, and they did their own versions of it.

## HE HASN'T GOT SHIT ALL OVER HIM

**GILLIAM:** The fact that *Spamalot* works is terrific. But I remember both Terry Jones and I were very critical of it when we first saw it. 'Ah, he's messing with what was great about the film,' was all we could see. That was coming from our point of view. But it plays and it's very good.

*Because it didn't look like a gritty, messy, medieval period film?*

**GILLIAM:** Yeah. The humour in *Grail* came out of a real place. Everything that we were doing was creating a reality – mud, dirt, filth, all of those things – and the jokes came out of that. And onstage none of that texture was there. And yet, it obviously triggered great memories for all the people who loved the film, and he wrote some wonderful songs and did some terrific stuff. But it wasn't what Terry and I were trying to do.

The others weren't interested in the mud and the filth and the discomfort we were feeling that was essential to make the jokes work. And so Eric's is the comfortable version of it that Cleese wouldn't have been moaning about if he were in it, because he would have been comfortable.

**AZARIA:** I would venture to say that doing a musical is a more physically comfortable experience than making that movie! Yeah, they pride themselves on the realism, which does make things a lot funnier. And one of the things I responded to even as a child was, my God, this thing's real, and yet it's absurdly funny.

The stage show was a musical, that's what it felt like. There was no dirt, no adverse weather conditions or trudging up hills. But musicals are rigorous and this was [high] on the rigorous scale. All of us were playing five, six, seven different roles. We'd have to sprint backstage to make our costume changes. I couldn't keep weight on performing this show, which was a wonderful problem to have for a middle-aged Jewish guy like myself. But it was strenuous. A lot of people's knees blew out and elbows blew out. And I remember there were times running up those steps, 'Wow, I don't know whether I'm going to make it up these steps today! It's really fifty-fifty.'

I remember they cut a number in Chicago – they cut three or four numbers, as you do on a musical, you need to pare it back – and I remember being so relieved, not because I didn't like the number, but I swear to you I didn't think I could physically make it through the show. I cannot dance again right now! It was such a relief to not have to run around the extra nine minutes we would have had to run around if that number had stayed in.

**GILLIAM:** I thought the show basically worked better than I expected. I think what I enjoyed the most of all was when it came to London and Simon Russell Beale played Arthur, and he found a way of doing it that was totally original, he really just blew me away how good he was. In the Broadway version I think people were trying too hard to imitate the original performances.

### What did Simon do differently? Was he more Shakespearean?

**GILLIAM:** It was just his whole bearing: *I am a great king*, and yet there's a little touch, *I don't really do this kind of work normally.* And he did a moment that I just treasured. One of his dismounts from the non-horses, as he came off he slipped on an imaginary pebble as he put his foot to the ground, and he did this wonderful slip. And it was such a brilliant moment because nobody had ever done anything like that, making a dismount more believable by stepping on a stone that slips in front of his foot. And it's little details like that, because he's such a great actor, he would just find the moments to play it. It was incredibly solemn the way he was doing it, but it was incredibly funny!

### What characters did you most enjoy playing?

**AZARIA:** I really like doing the Knight of 'Ni!' and the Taunter, just to be that unbridled level of silly, and to discover that you kind of can't push it too far. Steve Martin used to joke you can't be sad playing the banjo, it's just not possible – if you're making those sounds, you just can't feel depression. That's the way I felt doing the French Taunter and the 'Ni!' Knight. You can't be bummed when you're being that silly. And the sounds of those characters are like happy childhood memories associated with them.

**CLEESE:** People thought of course that we all made a lot of money out of it. And we didn't. We made surprisingly little out of it!

❄   ❄   ❄

# DÉJÀ REVUE

## REMEMBER, IT'S YOUR LAST CHANCE ANYHOW

The success of *Spamalot* may have renewed curiosity in the Pythons' archive of work, but at that time, the group's members were all pursuing their own interests, with little evidence of passion to collaborate under the Python umbrella. Palin continued doing travel series' and began publishing his diaries; Jones presented TV documentaries on history and wrote children's books and a medieval true-crime book, *Who Murdered Chaucer?*; Gilliam, after the collapse of his film *The Man Who Killed Don Quixote*, alternated between attempts to revive the production and shooting *Tideland* and *The Imaginarium of Doctor Parnassus* (which itself was almost shuttered owing to the death of Heath Ledger); and Cleese acted in Bond films (as Q opposite Pierce Brosnan) and animated features (including *Charlotte's Web* and the *Shrek* series). Idle,

*Audience member Talia Lindner, age ten, is put through the paces of the 'Spanish Inquisition' sketch.*

meanwhile, after performing in *The Greedy Bastard Tour*, created an oratorio based on *Life of Brian*, called *Not the Messiah (He's a Very Naughty Boy)*.

In 2009, upon the occasion of the group's fortieth anniversary, the British Academy of Film and Television Arts presented a lifetime achievement award to the Pythons at the Ziegfeld Theatre in New York City.[*] It was their first public appearance together since Aspen, eleven years earlier. A feature-length version of a new retrospective documentary series, *Monty Python: Almost the Truth: The Lawyer's Cut*, was also screened.

During a Q & A session, a ten-year-old girl, Talia Lindner, was

---

[*]   When asked why BAFTA gave them an award in New York City instead of London, Gilliam replied, 'I have no idea! Maybe we were in the wrong place, and they had an award that had to be given out that week!'

invited from the audience to perform her rendition of the 'Spanish Inquisition' sketch ('I didn't expect a sort of Spanish Inquisition.' 'Nobody expects the Spanish Inquisition!'). Palin seemed to express his joy about avoiding a possible Python reunion show when he exclaimed, 'What we just need are four more like her and we can piss off! Beautiful!'

Despite the warm reception that the five Pythons – and a life-sized cardboard stand-up of Chapman – received from the audience, even from a Groucho Marx fan ('I think you're at the wrong reunion!' castigated Idle), rumours of a possible stage show or film went nowhere, as each was busy with his own career.

But then, as so frequently happens, lawyers got involved.

In 2012, Mark Forstater, who was producer of *Monty Python and the Holy Grail*, initiated legal action against the Pythons, claiming a share of royalties and merchandising profits from *Spamalot*. The Pythons argued that Forstater had already been overpaid for royalties owing to an accounting error that extended back to the time of *Holy Grail*.

The High Court judge noted that Palin had made a 1975 diary entry which read: '... as we are a soft lot and not at all businesslike, I think it would be in the finest traditions of Python irrationality if we gave Mark an extra £1,000 and a silver tray with some cut-glass sherry glasses and told him to stop writing to us for more money. Beyond that even I am not prepared to go. Oh, all right, some cheese straws to go with the sherry glasses.'

In July 2013 Mr Justice Norris ruled in favour of Forstater. Cleese called the judge's ruling 'a very silly decision', but it was one that cost the Pythons dearly, with royalties and lawyers' fees amounting to £800,000.

With the Python bank account perilously void of rain-washed florins, glittering guineas, romantic rubles, and sunburnt Australian dollars, a reunion suddenly seemed lucratively attractive.

**GILLIAM:** How we lost that case was quite amazing. I remember the first meeting with the lawyers I just started asking certain questions that were the very things the case failed on, and they just seemed to be obvious things. But they were, 'No, no, no, it's all fine.' Suddenly the Python pension fund was drained.

**CLEESE:** We had a meeting in the St James Hotel with a lovely guy called Jim Beach. Jim had been my lawyer at one time. He was at Cambridge with me; he was a year younger than me, and when I left Cambridge I gave him my notebooks that I'd taken in law lectures. Subsequently he became a solicitor, and he became my solicitor, so I always thought it rather funny that my solicitor had passed his exams on my notes!

He was also a major figure in the Footlights. He was in Eric's number two year [when] Eric was president, he played the piano extremely well, he just had a great sense of show business. He stopped being a lawyer as such and went off and was the manager of Queen. And so he understands big deals; he understands when people do extreme things.

And we told him [our] situation. And I remember he came in, we were all sitting around a rectangular table and he was in the middle, and he said, 'Well, I've been looking at this – you're fucked!' Which we laughed a great deal over.

And then we said, 'Well, what do we do?' He said, 'Well, the only thing you can do is do a big show.'

We looked at him – 'Well, what do you mean?'

'You've got to play an arena. Do an arena show and you'll make enough money to pay off these lawyers' fees.'

Eric fortunately had a few days off – he didn't have anything on his plate at the moment, and he'd made so much money with *Spamalot*, the rest of us were racing around – and he put a show together based on what we'd done when we were on tour in '73, and Drury Lane in '74. We'd done the Hollywood Bowl, [so] we knew what an arena show was, [though] it was a lot less than sixteen thousand!

*Reunited in the rehearsal hall for the 2014 O2 stage show.*

**GILLIAM:** At the same time we were discussing with the *South Park* guys about teaming up with a company they had just formed, to get some money back in the collection plate. And once again it's Eric, who's always wanted to do theatre, do stage shows, that's the stuff he really loves. The show [came up], *boom!* – that's it. It focused everybody's mind, having this big hole in the finances.

*So, was the impetus to play the O2 Arena*
*primarily to refill the coffers?*

**CLEESE:** I think the truth is that was largely the idea on day one. But one of the things I notice as you get older is things changing the whole time, and they never stay the same. People's motivations are changing. I think that trying to freeze things in a moment in time is okay, providing you realize it's always changing.

The real incentive – because you can't control what you get excited about – was when we had that reading when Eric put the script together.

He'd done a wonderful job. I mean, the first half was almost exactly what we [ended up doing] in the O2. This was three days after we'd decided to do it! And we started roaring with laughter hearing these sketches that we'd written years before. And it was as simple as that. The moment we found it really funny, we thought, 'Oh well, this is going to be fun.'

**JONES:** Of course, I'm excited about getting back together again – it's not every day you have a reunion after thirty or more years – but there's a little worry at the back of my mind. Will it go off okay? Can I remember the words? Of course we are all going to make a lot of money out of it, but is the O2 too big for our little TV show? . . .
 The O2 intimidates me. No! It terrifies me.

*In retrospect, given the success of the O2 reunion, which was*
*precipitated by the court case, do you think you all should send*
*Mark Forstater Christmas cards thanking him?*

**PALIN:** Well, I think we'd have to send Christmas cards to John Cleese's third wife as well!* And possibly to the people who Terry J. got the mortgage of his house from. They were also elements in the need to get some money. I don't think the Forstater case was the primary thing, although we did spend a lot of money on it.
 Certainly John, and I think Terry, were quite desperate for some funds at the time, and I don't think any of the rest of us felt bitter about that, and probably somewhere in the back of our minds felt, 'How can we help?' Certainly in Terry's case. So, when we got together, the discussion turned to how could we make some money, 'cause Python income generally was decreasing. The money was not coming in the way it had done

---

\* Owing to the specificities of California divorce laws, the dissolution of Cleese's marriage, in 2008, to Alyce Faye Eichelberger meant he was to pay $20 million, which he helped finance by embarking on a worldwide 'Alimony Tour'. Cleese has since finished paying off the debt, and married his fourth (and final) wife, Jennifer Wade.

ten to fifteen years before. So when we get together and have a meeting, and we had changed managers (which I think was quite an important thing to have done), Jim Beach, who was a friend of all of us really but particularly a friend of John and Eric from Cambridge, had the confidence and the vision of a man who has been guiding the career of Queen, which, even since Freddie Mercury died, had done better and better. He's able to use and market that material brilliantly.

And so when he says, 'A couple of nights at a big venue like the O2 would clear all of your bills,' no one's ever proposed anything like that.

*Palin and Cleese, and a Norwegian Blue pining for the fjords, at the O2 in London, 2014.*

And within seconds we all agreed, something which had taken many, many years to get to that point.

## WELL, I'LL ASK HIM BUT I DON'T THINK HE'LL BE VERY KEEN

*One of the things you told me back in 1998 when you were suggesting a Python reunion was not all that attractive to you (certainly not for purely mercenary reasons) was, 'Python's a sort of strange, resilient force . . . It's like, the fire is not burning brightly but the embers are still there; you just blow on them and the flames will come up again.' And that seems to have been prescient.*

**PALIN:** It's a metaphor that sort of pinpoints the truth. I think I'd stand by that. A lot of what I said twenty years ago I probably wouldn't stand by, but that, yeah!

I think in the back of our minds there was a desire to help all the Pythons, to make sure that everybody made some money out of it. People who'd put a lot of time and work into it in the past deserved the money back, and also – as I said in what you quoted back to me – the embers were still burning, and nobody felt strongly enough to say, 'I don't ever want to do Python again.' So it all just came together like a flash, we all said, 'Yes, let's do it!' and that was that.

*How easy was it to clear schedules, because everyone is off doing their own thing, and you're off all over the world!*

**PALIN:** We managed it, because we knew we had to. A lot of it depended on when the O2 would be free. You had to think several months ahead. But I think in agreeing to do it, we all accepted this was a major thing, and there had to be something very, very important to stop us participating at that particular time. We were all very constructive about the dates and when we could possibly do it, and when Jim Beach found the dates in July, we said, 'Yeah, that's fine.' I can't remember what I was doing at that time but I certainly was able to drop everything during that period, and there wasn't anybody I think who said, 'No, I can't do that date.' In fact, quite the opposite!

# YOU TRY TELLING THE YOUNG PEOPLE OF TODAY THAT, AND THEY WON'T BELIEVE YOU

On November 21, 2013, the five Pythons appeared in a press conference to announce they would return to the stage, at the O2 Arena in London, promising comedy, music, 'and a tiny bit of ancient sex'. Cleese did beg off performing a silly walk, following hip and knee replacement surgery (Idle helpfully suggested the assistance of a 'silly walker').

But would people pay to see a group of septuagenarians who hadn't performed live together in more than thirty years? Palin was practical in his optimism: 'It's easier to be silly after seventy,' he said. But the proof came once tickets went on sale online: the first show's sixteen thousand tickets sold out in a gobsmacking 43.5 seconds.

**CLEESE:** It was a huge surprise. [The series] hasn't been on screens as much as it has in America [where] it's always going out. In America the younger generation does know about Python and loves it; in England the younger generation doesn't. When we saw the first sixteen thousand seats sold in forty-four seconds or whatever it was, we looked at each other in astonishment.

**PALIN:** It was originally two shows and they sold out. The next thing I knew we were being asked to do five shows. And at that time I did feel,

*Celebrity mystery guest Mike Myers, star of* Austin Powers.

'Wow, this is pushing it out a bit. They sold out two, but five?' And it's a physical commitment for these gigantic shows – are we all really up for it? In the end, Jim thought we could sell the tickets, everyone was up for it, okay, let's do five. I can then remember I was up in Scotland doing something up there, came back to London to find an email that we'd actually now extended to ten! By that time no one had even asked!

But there was kind of a thrill to the process by then. We were only doing these extra shows because the demand was so strong. How we'd sell the tickets and what the show would actually consist of was a little worrying for me, but it was never a worry strong enough to make me feel we shouldn't be doing this. There was a momentum, which was great.

# THAT INCREDIBLE FEELING THAT WE'VE EXPERIENCED SOMETHING BEFORE

*Were each of you jockeying for your own material that should be in the show?*

**PALIN:** No. As I remember, Eric, as he's done *Spamalot*, took charge of the project and he said, 'I'll send this list of materials; send a list of sketches you think should be in.' You have to have somebody really at the centre gathering all this together, and Eric volunteered. We all sent him what we thought were the sketches that should be in there. One or two were unusual. Obviously 'Dead Parrot', 'Argument', 'Lumberjack', 'Penguin on the Television', 'I Like Chinese', they were all bankers. But there were others, like the scene out of *The Meaning of Life* where Terry and I (or in the film Graham and Eric) are looking at the Catholics and deciding what a great thing it was to be a Protestant because they could go down to the drugstore and order a condom ('Because I am a Protestant!'), which I always liked. That was suggested. We wanted to get a few fresh things in; we didn't want it to be just the big hits.

*Was there any pressure to write new material, so the show could be sold as premiering new Python sketches?*

**PALIN:** That's a good question; I don't think so. Without being absolutely certain, my feeling was pretty soon we decided people would want to see the 'best of'. All of us had seen groups on stage who decide not to play their old material and just do their new album and been perhaps a bit disappointed. I think we felt with Python this is a once-and-for-all farewell show; we've got to go out with some of the sketches that people expect to see. In the linking material, yeah, there was a feeling that we should put in stuff that was new and fresh.

The 'Blackmail' sketch, which grew into something where you would introduce a different guest star each night – to be honest I didn't think

'Blackmail' was good enough to be in the show. But Eric by that time had got to work with Arlene Phillips and got dancers and music, and again it had a sort of life of its own, that song, and in the end it turned out to be very successful. People liked it. I still feel the 'Blackmail' sketch perhaps wasn't the perfect thing to do, but Eric had managed to create a presentation of it which was full-on and very lively and very good to watch. This was the new area – linking material and songs and dances and the staging, all of which had really come down to Eric primarily, and Terry Gilliam in some of the designs. But it was Eric's show, really.

*Is part of your reticence about something like 'Blackmail' because you'd written it so long ago, and you have certain associations with when you originally performed it?*

**PALIN:** Well, when we did it for the BBC it was pretty rough and ready. This was not material that had been honed over many weeks and brought to fruition after hours and hours of hard labour. A lot of the material we did for the television show was very spontaneous, written very quickly. We worked very rapidly and we got through it with a lot of cheek and audacity and speed and all that sort of thing. I never felt with 'Blackmail' in particular there was a definitive version.

What I suppose I was worried about was, does an audience see a version as definitive? Forget what I might have felt when I wrote it and how it might be improved, there are certain things the audience loves to see and they don't want to see things changed. They want the familiar words and lines and all that. That was a factor in selecting the sketches that we were going to do. But 'Blackmail' was always one of those 'means to an end' rather than an end itself. I was quite up for it to be changed, because I still didn't think it was the strongest material. But the presentation gave it a strength, and gave it a purpose in the show, which was to bring in some poor star or celebrity with a bag over their heads, which worked very well.

*An author may feel possessive towards a sketch or a character*
*he's created. But an audience can, too, and not want it to be*
*changed. They wouldn't want Mick Jagger to change the lyrics of*
*'Satisfaction'; they'd just want him to sing it as he always has.*

**PALIN:** Yeah, well, if you talk about something like the 'Dead Parrot' sketch, that's in the canon now, there is an authorized version of that, and I think if you got just one word wrong – if you got 'pining' in the wrong place – people who spot that, it would spoil the recitation. There are certain items like that; 'Argument' as well, possibly. But beyond that we could be a little more flexible with some of the material.

What the audience was going to make of our show before we actually went on stage was something I don't think any of the Pythons could have foreseen. Although we felt we got the materials, they're Python fans coming to see it, there was a lingering doubt and lingering nervousness probably in all of us as to how this was all going to come together. Was there a possibility that people would see men forty years older doing sketches which they did as young men and feel, 'No, this is all too much, they can't hack it anymore'? Once we started it was okay, and I realized we could hack it, but you couldn't address that lingering concern until you actually did the shows. We did some rehearsal but we just really didn't know until you're there in front of a big audience how things were going to go. I think in the end we made a pretty good selection.

*Lingering doubts never stopped Mick Jagger.*

**PALIN:** No, no. But that's Mick Jagger for you! I don't think he has lingering doubts. I'm going back to not just Jagger but, say, 'Satisfaction', and I would compare that in their canon to something like 'Dead Parrot'. People know that so well, unless you completely fuck it up, it's going to be great. It was the ones slightly lower down the order that we weren't absolutely sure about. And also Mick Jagger remains pretty fit, he leaps around. I think some of us were a little bit worried about athleticism on stage. But again that didn't seem to matter. We were like men possessed once we got going.

*Cardinal Fang goes airborne in the 'Spanish Inquisition' sketch.*

There's an amazing photo taken when Terry Gilliam and myself leap into the room as the Spanish Inquisition. I did what I thought was a fairly formidable jump, and behind me Terry Gilliam was doing this extraordinary leap which makes it look like he was on a magic carpet. There was no carpet there! There he is, suspended four feet off the ground. It's quite an extraordinary thing that I thought an old bloke like him shouldn't be doing! It was a bit like somebody possessed, and he perhaps was. Perhaps we all were!

It's the only way to do that show. There was no point just strolling on and saying, 'We've got a few sketches for you tonight.' You have to respond to this approbation and love and warmth from the audience. You have to do your best!

**CLEESE:** I don't know that we were feeling that anxious about it because the atmosphere was so extraordinary. Anyone who went to that show needed to realize this is not an ordinary theatrical event. One of my older friends went with that frame of mind; it wasn't that at all. It was an event in which the audience was playing a huge part. How many times do you go to the theatre where the audience knows a lot of the dialogue? It's not a very common experience!

# HE USED TO MAKE THEM HAPPY IN LITTLE WAYS

*Monty Python Live (Mostly): One Down, Five to Go* opened at the O2 Arena in London on July 1, 2014. Directed by Idle and Aubrey Powell, and choreographed by Arlene Phillips, the show played ten dates to sold-out crowds finishing on July 20. The final night's performance was carried live via satellite in the UK and other countries, and to approximately two thousand cinemas around the world.

In addition to the hooded 'Blackmail' mystery guests unveiled at each performance, theoretical physicist Stephen Hawking (in a speeding wheelchair) made a cameo in a filmed sketch, demonstrating his own form of physics by knocking over fellow professor Brian Cox, prior to performing his cover version of 'The Galaxy Song'.

Because Idle's expanded 'Penis Song' was scheduled during the show's first act – before 9 p.m., British broadcasting's 'watershed' cutoff for family-appropriate viewing – the UKTV Gold channel broadcast cut away briefly to Palin (in drag!) apologizing for the 'particularly rude song'.

**GILLIAM:** I remember being in the Tardis at the start of the show, we're all in there squeezed into this box about to go on in front of sixteen thousand people, and it was a very nice feeling in a sense. Like, our little family was back together for a brief moment, all in this tiny little box!

**CLEESE:** It was a pretty complicated show – my show consists of a chair, a table, and a glass of water!

One of the great pleasures of actually being in the O2 was to look at the audience and then to meet some of them afterwards and find they were from Mexico and Poland and India and South Africa, America, Brazil. I mean, places where people didn't know us at all, there were these die-hard fans dressed in silly costumes. There was something very, what is the word? Ecumenical! [*Laughs*] It was great to see so many people from so many cultures who love the show.

*In some respects the reunion was an introduction to a whole new generation of fans, not just a nostalgia trip for baby boomers.*

**PALIN:** We didn't really know who was making up the audience. After we'd done the first or second shows, gradually the word would come back that people who were our age came with their grandchildren and things like that. There were fifteen-year-olds flocking to us backstage to say hello. That's something I suppose we didn't realize until the shows themselves started. There's been very, very little in terms of Python activity over quite a long period, since probably *The Meaning of Life*. I knew that there were people who were the same age as my children who were enjoying Python, who weren't born when we did it. I knew that from meeting people and getting letters, but in terms of how big a proportion of the audience that was and how many different generations would really enjoy it, there'd been no real way of judging it until we got together at the O2. We could only see a short way out into the audience of course, [but] there were lots of people a good bit younger than ourselves and they were screaming and yelling! That was wonderful, part of this great liberation of getting out there and hearing that reaction, and gradually realizing this reaction was not just from different generations but lots of different countries. We'd heard that people came from Spain and Serbia and Argentina dressed as cardinals, with parrots on their shoulders, so it was an international thing as well.

But when you're on a stage, you don't quite know what's going on out there. It wasn't really until we put together the documentary that I saw

*The O₂ Arena, filled to the rafters with Python fans.*

for the first time people who'd bought tickets, who'd come thousands of miles to see the show, and they were a very generally silly bunch who really enjoyed themselves and let their hair down.

**CLEESE:** We knew that the first night would be a bit rough, because hiring the O2 is so expensive you can't have a proper dress rehearsal. It was a point that critics completely missed. You'd think a critic might have noticed that. The reviews were strangely grudging. We hadn't several shows out of town to practice, and the critics by and large didn't like the show. I didn't think it would matter. They don't like to be reminded that they don't have the power that they used to. Ten shows, 160,000 seats!

*A theory on the brontosaurus by (Miss) Anne Elk.*

## WELL, WHY ARE ANY OF US HERE? WHEN YOU COME DOWN TO IT, IT'S ALL SO MEANINGLESS

*Back in 1998, talking about the prospective reunions for which people kept trying to entice the Pythons, you told me, 'I can't personally think of anything worse than getting up there and reciting that old stuff again.'*

**GILLIAM**: [*laughs*] Did I really say that? What an idiot!

*How did you take on performing more, which is something you generally don't do?*

**GILLIAM:** I was terrified! Because I'm not as good as they are; they are really good. I can pull some faces and play a few grotesques. I just thought, 'What am I doing here?'

I was rehearsing the second opera.[*] I was in a completely different frame of mind doing another kind of job. And all of it was happening at the same time, and I thought, 'This is all a joke, I don't want to be doing it.' Without Graham I had to do more things. I thought, 'I gotta do stuff I wouldn't have normally done.'

But in high school I was a cheerleader, in college I was a cheerleader, so I've always enjoyed being in front of crowds. Once you get out in front of a crowd, it was actually fun playing around, jumping around, costume changes, all of that stuff. What was going on backstage is more fun than what's going on out front. It was a nice way of spending a few weeks. It was strangely enjoyable, even though at the time I thought it was a bad idea.

What intrigued me the most is how well received the cartoons were. At the time I was reading the reviews of it, it's like, the sketches had become so well-known and the cartoons had been forgotten in many ways other than just a vague, 'Oh, those cutout cartoons are amazing.' But suddenly seeing the stuff up on the screen again, people's reactions were amazing. Some of the reviews were saying this was the freshest part of the show because the other stuff had become so familiar having been done a lot, or had been repeated by people not us, and had become part of the culture: 'This parrot is dead', things like that.

### Did it inspire you to get back into animation?

**GILLIAM:** No, not really. I did a couple of little bits and pieces [for the reunion], but that's history. I can't do that again. It just takes too much out of me. My mind doesn't work like that anymore. Even doing a couple of little bits, at that moment I'm thinking about how do you do an opera onstage, then suddenly I had to do this animation? I didn't even have the tools anymore.

---

[*] *Benvenuto Cellini* by Berlioz, staged by the English National Opera in June 2014.

I just think the fact that it worked as well as it did was the big surprise. I think we all were surprised. We spend our time not really thinking about the impact we've had on the world, and so when we actually did go out in the front and realize, 'Whoa! Apparently we had quite an impact!' That's a nice surprise.

I always felt I was a very fringe side of the whole thing. But it was the audience; that's what I think made it. It was so easy, so in love with Python, that almost anything you did got a laugh. I really enjoyed feeling sixteen thousand people out there from all over the world just loving to see Python, a bunch of old guys dancing round onstage doing old material!

We talked about maybe only doing one or two shows, we weren't sure if we could fill the place. I think that's what's interesting, how either naive we were or just maybe not really aware of how powerful or important and beloved we were around the world. We just thought maybe we could pull off a couple of shows. We could probably have done more even. I think that was a surprise to everybody, because we had all gone our separate ways and were making our way through life in whatever success we had in different realms, and *bingo!* That happened. And it was great.

**CLEESE:** Python fans are rather nice people! They have a sense of humour, they're not showing off, they're having a good time and laughing a lot. So the opening night was much more relaxed than you'd think because of the wonderful atmosphere.

Then, two things happened for me that were very significant: On the second night, I came out to do the 'Spanish Loonies', and they were in the orchestra pit and when they finished playing a little tune in the beginning, the orchestra all shouted '*Olé!*' and sat down. And I was standing there in front of sixteen thousand people, and it broke me up. I'd not said a word. It was right at the top of the show, and I stood there shaking with laughter. That's how relaxed I was.

And that night something strange happened backstage: When Terry Jones took his guitar off in rapid change he hit himself above the

*The boys are back.*

eye with the guitar. When you're changing in a hurry you don't notice it. Came on to do the 'Four Yorkshiremen' in the white tuxedos, and we did a few lines of dialogue, and when he spoke for the first time I looked at him and he had blood running down the side of his face. And I was very thrown by it. I thought, 'Christ, is he all right?' And I fluffed my line.

I saw Eddie Izzard backstage immediately afterwards because he was just wandering around sort of being supportive, and I said, 'Sorry, I screwed that sketch up,' because I've always been a perfectionist. He said, 'You don't understand. These people know these sketches perfectly well. They'd rather see something completely new happen than to see the same one again.'

And I was released from the anxiety I'd always had of trying to make it perfect. And I went down there each night not knowing what was going to happen, and quite likely to do something silly, like trying to break Eric Idle up in the 'Anne Elk' sketch by coughing more, just playing around. It's what they wanted! They don't want perfect reproductions of sketches that they knew anyway. It was much more exciting if something happened and they saw it but no one else ever would.

It was a glorious event, and at the end of it we all got on very, very well.

## MY NIPPLES EXPLODE WITH DELIGHT!

*Once the show's success proved the continued popularity of Python, was there an impetus on your part, or from others, to exploit that with a new Python record, Python book, Python movie, because there was an obvious, eager market for it?*

**PALIN:** No, oddly enough we didn't go through all that. It was generally felt that what we were doing was our last outing for Python. And my worries had always been that we weren't the same group, [as] Graham Chapman was missing, and Graham was a vital part of Python. No one could act the parts the way Graham acted them, no one could write the sort of strange, bizarre stuff that Graham was able to come up with.

Once we did agree to do the O2, I thought we could just manage that, but I'm afraid it was clear even during that performance that Terry Jones wasn't totally happy with live performing. He was brilliant in the show but learning lines was beginning to worry him. So there was a feeling that this was probably going to be our last outing. Everything should be concentrated on getting the show right. Beyond that, we felt, most of the material had been seen anyway, it's there in some shape or form. Undoubtedly there would be a live video of the show, but that was about all. I don't know if we did a book, probably it was suggested, but I don't think it actually happened.

There was a feeling that this was the conclusion. And I don't think that everybody shared that feeling at quite the same time and in quite the same way, and there were some in the group who really felt, 'This is a money-spinner, let's go do it in New York, and beyond!' I just was never up to that. I felt that there perhaps had to be a point when we said this was it. And I thought London, the home city of Python, was the place to make our last stand, as it were. If we then went to New York – and there were plenty of offers from all over the world – would we have got as good a show together? Would we have been as excited by it somewhere else as we were in London? I wasn't sure. You'd be very, very hard-put to say to Chicago or Los Angeles or Frankfurt or Adelaide or Sydney or wherever, 'No, sorry, we're only doing one place abroad.' It looked to me as though it would be down a slippery slope and we would end up doing something for money and not the joy, thrill, and excitement of it.

So that was the feeling: let's just get these ten shows done and done well, and the last night was the last night. There weren't any tears or anything like that. It was just great. All the shows had been good. I personally felt there were signs towards the end of the run that people were beginning to feel, 'Oh God, do we have to do this again?' I can tell, I know those signs, and I know that's not good for Python. We have to feel the spontaneity. We have to feel the excitement. We have to feel this is something wonderfully different to be doing. And we did that for those ten shows. I don't think we'd manage to re-create that for the shows beyond that. That's my personal opinion.

**CLEESE:** We had lunch the next day after the last performance, and Eric said it was a sweet good-bye. And the extraordinary thing was there was no sense of regret. There was no sense of, 'Oh, it's finally come to an end.' We had a great time, and what a lovely way for the audience coming to thank us for making them laugh. It was all completely satisfactory.

And since then we were offered $10 million to do the show in Australia. Michael just said he didn't want to do it. Oh well, fair enough, we don't want to force someone to do something, because it won't work. And after that, we then realized that Terry's memory was definitely deteriorating and that there definitely wouldn't be any more.

*The last hurrah.*

**JONES:** I wanted to go on to perform other things, but Mike Palin didn't want to do it. And I think it was a fine idea to move on. I think it's done the trick.

**GILLIAM:** It was great that we did the show because it is the last thing we'll be doing. It's a nice way to call it a day, I would say – be that much loved by so many people, and then get out while we're ahead, is my feeling.

☞

# I THOUGHT IT WAS BECAUSE YOU WERE INTERESTED IN ME AS A HUMAN BEING

The following year, in 2015, the Tribeca Film Festival in New York City honoured the group with a retrospective of their films, including a fortieth-anniversary screening of *Monty Python and the Holy Grail*, at which all five Pythons appeared and engaged in a freewheeling post-screening Q & A session with moderator John Oliver.

**CLEESE:** He was interviewing us at the Beacon Theatre. And we started, the sound was terrible – so bad that three of us on the end couldn't hear what was going on. So I thought, 'I gotta do something about this,' 'cause you can't sit there for an hour if you can't hear what's going on. So I went off and got a chair. And then we went into a complete routine of moving chairs around. One point we all moved our chairs up around John Oliver, and then they all went away again, and then I sat very close to John Oliver. And he was about to ask a question and I said to him, 'I love you.' He was [stomping his feet] laughing so much! It's wonderful when you laugh like that.

And that's exactly what Chapman and I used to do. That's what I've always tried to do, is to make people really laugh. That's what I'm trying to do most of the time, laugh as much as possible, which is much harder than making 'em go, 'Hmmmmm.' I realized very early on it's much easier to be clever than to be funny, much easier. It's much harder to make them laugh to the point they're almost physically out of control.

There were moments when we were writing together when we thought of a funny idea. And we used to get absolutely hysterical – the joy, the energy from suddenly seeing the comic possibilities of a situation. And the fact that we were now going to explore that and write it was absolutely wonderful. It was like watching the winning goal in a game, you know what I mean? It was just extraordinary. And I managed to induce it in John Oliver!

---

The Tribeca reunion was all five Pythons' last public appearance together.

---

# EXITING THE STAGE

## LIFE'S A GAME, YOU SOMETIMES WIN OR LOSE . . .

In 2015 Terry Jones directed two films – the sci-fi comedy *Absolutely Anything*, starring Simon Pegg and featuring Cleese, Gilliam, Idle, and Palin as the voices of aliens toying with humankind, and *Boom Bust Boom*, a documentary about capitalism and the euphoria that drives economic bubbles and depressions, presented by puppets.

But Jones had begun complaining about memory issues during the O2 shows. It was a problem that would appear even more severe at the Tribeca Film Festival appearance, when his answers were short or clipped and he seemed less engaged than usual. And in September 2015, Jones was diagnosed with frontotemporal dementia (FTD), a condition that affects parts of the brain controlling language and social behaviour.

His dementia was made public the following year, and in

October 2016, when he appeared at the BAFTA Awards to accept a lifetime honour, he managed two words – 'Quiet down!' – as his son, Bill, spoke for him. Yet while Jones retreated from public view for the most part, he still continued to pursue activities, such as participating in the Alzheimer's Society's Memory Walk.

**GILLIAM:** I'm not sure at that point [at Tribeca] we actually did know he had dementia. When we were doing the stage show, yes, he was having trouble remembering his lines, but that was the only thing; he could still deliver the stuff with all the energy that was needed.

I was more aware with Terry when we were doing the shows [that] the drivers were getting very irritated with his behaviour, because in the cab with him there was only one way home, and if you didn't turn left, went straight, he would actually berate the driver, he would rap on the back of the seat. That was very weird. In the cab I couldn't maintain a conversation with Terry, he wasn't responding really in many ways.

**CLEESE:** Terry said he was having memory problems. But we're all getting older so we didn't think it was significant. In fact I made a joke about it, which I wouldn't do now, knowing what the reality was.

But then after the show he had it diagnosed, and we suddenly realized this is not going to get any better, which we didn't know at the time.

There's not much you can do. He's physically healthy, he goes on walks, but he can't follow conversations anymore, and that's terribly sad.

**PALIN:** I could see something happening to Terry. I could see his memory going and all that. And then I learned a lot about that particular condition. It's just the way it is. Terry has a particularly unfortunate form of dementia which deprives him of speech. Terry was a very expressive person; Terry loved words, he loved debating, he loved provoking, he loved joking, he loved giving opinions and having arguments. His wit was so good, [as was] his ability to talk to anybody about anything. His feelings, his passions were all tied up in words and speech, so it was a very, very cruel form of dementia to be diagnosed with.

Once you're diagnosed with it, there's not really much you could do. It's not like you're in hospital for a disease that can be alleviated and perhaps turned around. It is a withdrawal. There's no sort of route back from it, which is the hardest thing about it. It's cruel.

But on the other hand, it's happened, and there was no one moment where we all sat down and said, 'Oh, this is dreadful.' It just leaked out what was going on.

I suppose I see Terry slightly more than most of the others so I knew what was going on in there. I go and see Terry and I talk to him and he occasionally says something back. But generally I just babble on about things, because I have no way of knowing – I don't think anybody has – exactly what he's taking in and feeling. I'm encouraged by the fact that he looks well, he's got a good colour, he's got the energy to go on long walks still. It's not like someone physically falling apart. But it is just sort of the curtain closing, and that's very sad to see. It makes one want to hug him even harder!

### *Will he still engage, even if he can't speak?*

**PALIN:** Terry will appear to recognize people and then he'll sort of switch off. We had a Python meeting recently – we have to get together to discuss various things – and Terry was there throughout the meeting. I don't know quite how much he took in, but he did intervene at one point. He seemed quite agitated, and I kind of knew what he wanted, the others weren't quite sure, and I said, 'No, he's saying it's lunchtime!' I thought, 'That's great, good old Terry! Wants something to eat and drink, not sitting around listening to all these old gits discussing fine legal problems and all that sort of thing.' Those little moments, I just want to say, 'Terry, you're there, aren't you? You're laughing at us!'

*Is his sense of humour still present or accessible?*

**PALIN:** No. It's very hard to get any real signal from him as to what he's feeling. He'll smile every now and then, there'll be a little chuckle, but you're not quite sure what it's connected to, but it's still something to be treasured. Because it's a progressive illness, it's not something which is going to get better. It's irreversible.

I'm just glad that I can see him. Actually I don't see him enough, but I do go round to his house, sit there for a bit, have a chat with whoever's there and with Terry, and just being with him I feel purely selfish. It's rather beneficial to me. I feel our connection is still there. And I suppose the time may come when he just doesn't know who I am and doesn't want to see me, but that's not happened yet, so I enjoy seeing him, to be honest.

**GILLIAM:** It got stranger and stranger, and now, he looks like Terry, he's better groomed, better dressed, physically looks better than ever, and yet when I look at his eyes now, I don't know who this person is. It's really disturbing, and it really gets me depressed. I just don't know how to deal with him because I just don't know who's inside anymore – if anybody's inside.

*Does he recognize you?*

**GILLIAM:** I can't tell! The last time I went up to him, I couldn't tell if he knew who I was, and because we were always sort of combative there's always a nice, interesting friction between us, and now there's this benign character who looks lost, who doesn't seem to connect with the world. I literally do not know who he is, because Terry was this other person, and here's this guy who looks like Terry – and isn't. I was talking to Mike the other day about it. He looks after Terry, he sees him a lot, and he's convinced that Terry does respond, but it's not happening with me, is all I know. He seems to be quite blank: *who is this person who's talking to me?*

I've got a theory he's the White Rabbit from *Alice in Wonderland*.

Because Mike has said when he was over last, he's always gone somewhere else and he's always late for something else, but there isn't anything else, except just going home and being in a secure place that he understands and feels at ease in. It's this weird, 'I'm late, I'm late, for a very important date,' I keep hearing. He doesn't say that, but that's kind of what it's like.

For me it's very, very disturbing and depressing, maybe because we were so close. And maybe it's because I think I may be going down the same road. I keep looking for the symptoms! Are Terry and I going to be together again soon, wherever Dementia Land takes you?

Terry always had an opinion. We could always get immediately into an argument about something. Cantankerous, opinionated, angry. It used to get irritating because he was always right about everything, always thinking political, going on about the state of the nation. All of that stuff was there – and now, this sort of benign, placid, lost look in his eyes, this person standing there pretending to be Terry. It's not fully anybody as far as I can see.

*It's like taking away Beethoven's hearing, ripping away a defining feature of his personality.*

**GILLIAM:** I know! And I just don't know what he is feeling, how he's dealing with this, whether he's aware of it, or if he's just confused. Mike says that Terry just sits and watches a lot of films, old musicals in particular because he always loved old musicals, so he can be in a world that's familiar and that constantly repeats itself again and again. It doesn't change, and that must be maybe very comforting.

Terry Jones is no longer inhabiting the body that was Terry Jones.

# FINAL THOUGHTS

## OF COURSE IN THOSE DAYS I WAS ONLY A TEA BOY

*Twenty years ago, you said you were not someone who looks back at things you've done in the past, that that was not your temperament. And yet in the intervening time you've written a wonderfully entertaining memoir* * *that was very reflective.*

**CLEESE:** Oh yes. You have to get the balance right. If you're driven forward and never look back you'll probably never learn anything, so you have to look back by the right amount, whatever that might be, you see what I mean?

The reason I wrote the autobiography was, I had lunch many years before with Michael Caine. I like Michael enormously. And he was in a

---

* *So, Anyway . . .*, published in 2014, and a *New York Times* bestseller.

wonderful mood and I said, 'Why are you in such a great mood?' And he said, 'I just finished my autobiography.' And I was fascinated. 'Well, did you enjoy it?' thinking that for example Sean Connery had actually abandoned his because it brought up so many unpleasant things. And he said, 'I loved it; it was like recovering bits of my life that I'd lost.' And that was what I found. As I started to think back I would suddenly remember Andrew Sanger-Davies, or the way that Sanger-Davies walked and we used to call him 'Andrew Sanger-Wagtail' – his head bobbed forward – all this kind of thing came back.

The nice thing was, when the sadder moments came back I didn't feel sad anymore. I was able to remember, 'Oh yes, I was sad at that time, I was very in love with that girl and she treated me like shit,' but you don't feel it anymore because you know it doesn't matter. So, you recall what happened but you're not recalling all the negative feelings, because if you had been through therapy you've been through them anyway.

So, I think there was only one time, and it was in fact to do with feeling ineffectual. I felt very ineffectual in a relationship with one girl and I think that that affected me for a couple of days as I thought about it; otherwise there were no ill effects of going back to parts of my life. It's like everybody's life – there are good bits and difficult bits.

I shall write a second volume, there's no question about that. It's just a question of what I'm doing right at the moment. I'm seventy-eight, which is quite old. It's not seventy-eight like when my parents were seventy-eight, but you know it's still quite old. There are certain things I want to do that involve physical activity, like acting, and there are certain things I want to do, like writing, which I can pretty much do if I'm sitting in an armchair. So it seems sensible to do the more active things now, and postpone the writing until such time that I can't do any of the performing or running around.

*That sounds like great planning!*

**CLEESE:** Well, I think you just look at it quite calmly. I think that one of the things I learned from therapy is common sense. And I think very few of us live commonsensical lives. You see people rushing around determined to make another million dollars when they've got more than they can spend anyway. My attitude to them is, 'Poor things, I wish they'd get into therapy,' 'cause it does liberate. I'm happier now than I've ever been. It's partly because I have a really nice wife who makes me laugh immoderately, and it's partly because I have very few goals. If somebody said to me, 'For God's sake, you could win an Oscar if you work really hard on this movie for two years,' I would say to him genuinely, 'That's very nice, but I have more interesting ways of spending two years, and I don't really need the Oscar.' Because what I do enjoy doing is sitting around where there's some sunshine and a swimming pool with my wife and the cats and doing a bit of writing. That makes me very happy. I need very little more than that, except good wine!

> *It sounds like you might not have managed writing an autobiography if you hadn't already experienced therapy.*

**CLEESE:** I think if you have therapy that's good (if it wasn't any good it's like going to a bad doctor, it doesn't help), then basically you'd have a liberating feeling, because you explore areas that have been repressed because they are uncomfortable, and as you explore them they become more and more comfortable, so it means you could now go into those areas quite easily instead of shying way from them. That's liberating in that sense.

It seems it's good for artists. I think there is a confusion that you often hear, and I've had this when I was talking to Terry Gilliam a couple of years ago shortly before he went completely mad. I said to Terry, who had always pooh-poohed any kind of therapy – as so often people do who badly need it – I said to him what I think happens is you become less hampered. As you get to understand yourself more, your unconscious doesn't have quite so much power over you because you become more conscious of what it's up to. Therefore, if you're more conscious of what you're doing in life you're more liable to make better decisions.

A lot of artists are very, very driven and that may be good, it's a choice. There's a very good side to being driven in terms of what you produce, [but] it doesn't necessarily mean that your life is so good. So, what I think therapy does is that it makes you less driven but more creative. It gives more options into your life.

*I wanted to ask about the value you place on humour to improve one's life, particularly today to counteract the current political climate. In 1998 you said to me you did not think that art in itself could serve as a means of therapy for artists: 'A lot of people think that art is a kind of therapy. Well, maybe it stops people from going* **completely** *mad, but I don't think it helps people very much.' And when I asked if you thought it helped an audience – the recipients of that art – you said you thought not. Do you still believe that?*

**CLEESE:** It's helpful to the artist to be freer. But in all probability the artist, the writer, or whatever will be already freer than the audience, which means that he can lead the audience into areas that the audience may well find uncomfortable.

What I've found is if you start dealing with taboos – dead bodies, that kind of thing, both in Python and *Fawlty Towers* – there's a little bit of anxiety in the audience because it's a taboo subject. It might be violence like the Black Knight, it might be sex. Anxiety actually makes the laugh bigger than it would be if it was not a taboo subject. That's why there are so many not-very-funny sex jokes. It's to do with anxiety about sex – people laugh partly out of relief. It's not real laughter, it's a cover-up. It's a smoke screen.

There's no question that the effect of laughter physiologically is to relax people. There's an aspect to humour which is that it does help people to get through things. I was in Sarajevo last year and I was hearing about the four-year siege of Sarajevo, and they were very clear that they had a rather dark sense of humour, the Bosnians, and that they laughed very specifically at Monty Python. They used to show Monty Python shows in a secret cinema that wasn't getting shelled, and they said being able to laugh together at their situation somehow made it better. In other words, it made it better psychologically to them. It didn't do anything materially, but it made them feel better.

[Eric and I] had this strange experience of going on stage the night after the election, when Trump was elected.[*] Eric said, 'You need us this evening.' And the audience realized we were going to be able to help people's psychological condition and make them laugh a bit.

So, I think that laughing in itself is good. It has an effect on your physiology, it has a slightly relaxing effect, so even if the laughter doesn't do anything about the situation, it helps you a little bit to deal with it.

## YOU ALWAYS TALK, YOU AMERICANS, YOU TALK AND YOU TALK AND SAY 'LET ME TELL YOU SOMETHING' AND 'I JUST WANT TO SAY THIS'

**GILLIAM:** It's so funny, there's Python – it's already carved in our gravestone, we know that. And it seems so long ago. Even the 2014 show seems like a million years ago. And yet, every time anything comes up, we're still Pythons. It's very weird, that's all I can say!

*It is a part of you no matter what you do solo-wise.*

**GILLIAM:** Yeah, I know. But at the same time, I've forgotten so much of it. Usually [when] somebody's doing something from one of the sketches, it takes me quite a bit to get what they're on about. And yet, at the same time people keep talking to me as if I still do animation. I haven't done animation in a million years. We're sort of locked in amber that was

---

[*] Following the 2015 Tribeca Film Festival, Cleese and Idle – the only two up for more live appearances – went on tour. Their show, *Together Again at Last . . . for the Very First Time* – featuring sketches, Cleese's storytelling, and Idle's songs – played in Australia, Canada, and the US.

around in those days, and that's who we are. To so many people we're still judged by Python; if there's something about a film I've done, they always stick Python on it. That seems to have made a greater effect than all the work subsequently. It's a great thing in a sense, because yeah, we did do something that has stuck. It just happened, and there's all these fans out there – you bump into people and they get all excited! It's almost like it's another person, a person I no longer am. I wonder if the Marx Brothers felt this? How few things they did, and yet they all went to their graves as the Marx Brothers; that's who they were. The difference is, they didn't do all as varied a collection of things as we've done over the years. We've all gone in quite different ways.

*While Harpo was always Harpo.*

**GILLIAM:** Yep! Groucho at least got his own quiz show!

*But Python started in 1969, and if you think back to what was on TV in the 1960s that has any sort of cultural currency nowadays, there's* Star Trek *and* Python, *maybe* Doctor Who, *and that's it!*

**GILLIAM:** Yeah. And they're not very representative of the times! *Star Trek,* what is it? Why Python? I suppose they both appeal to nerds in different ways; there's a nerdishness in Python that seems to work. It was also the smart kids that got it first and then it trickled down. What's funny, that still happens. I bump into people who are telling me they're introducing their kids to Python. The kids are like eleven years old, and they're – *bingo!* – into it.

I was talking to a guy from one of the big production companies, we were talking about a project, and he was telling me about how his mother, when he was five years old, dressed him as a Gumby and took him to the Hollywood Bowl show. That was one of his biggest memories of childhood!

The other thing that's shocking is, I still keep thinking I'm only a certain age. The guys who made *Lost in La Mancha*[*] have done a documentary now on *Quixote,* but it's really more about me than the film. But it goes back – there I am in the Python years, looking like that, and then suddenly I see my face as it is now. And I can't believe it; I can't even see the connection with the guy back then, except that if I don't have to look at myself in a mirror or a plate-glass window I still think I probably look more like *that* than I actually do. Which is probably the result of we being photographed a lot; we were hot! And so those images when I see them, 'Oh, that's who I am!'

I wish I could get rid of the Python stuff in a weird way. Because it just keeps surprising me when I least expect it.

### What do you mean?

**GILLIAM:** I'm not sure what I mean by that, but it feels like there's a part of me locked in that time. I want to be free of that so I can just move on with my death or any other things that are waiting for me.

### And instead there's this Jurassic Python trapped in amber.

**GILLIAM:** Yep! That's it. I actually think hard about what we did, because people remember it better than I think we do. That's what's odd. It takes people jogging my memory to bring back what we were doing and how we did it, because it actually happened over a very short period of time really, the main stuff. And that's what defined us.

But when we get together, we're just old! Eric is the one that still thrives on Python, or needs it more than the rest of us, I think. He holds on to it. That's why he directed the stage show and [wrote] *Spamalot*. He needs Python more than the rest of us do.

---

[*]    Keith Fulton and Louis Pepe's 2003 documentary recounting the disasters that plagued Gilliam's early attempt to film *The Man Who Killed Don Quixote* with Jean Rochefort and Johnny Depp. They recently produced a documentary on Gilliam's completion of the film, in 2018, with Jonathan Pryce and Adam Driver.

I've gone on and done all these other things, having some considerable effect in one way or another, and I think for me it's just trying to keep surprising myself and hopefully at least fool myself that I'm young even though I'm not. It might keep me alive a few more years. Everybody else has sort of settled into a living-legend status.

*Their dotage?*

**GILLIAM:** Come on, guys! I guess because I'm an American* the spring has been wound up tighter than English people who were privileged and went to Oxford and Cambridge! Whatever it is, it's interesting. I just would like to get another thing or two done before I kick the bucket, that's all, before I'm eighty, which is approaching fairly quickly!

## 'YOU MUST TRY AND MAKE EVERYONE HAPPY AND BRING PEACE AND CONTENTMENT EVERYWHERE YOU GO.' SO, I BECAME A WAITER.

*When you did your first travel series, it was promoted as 'Monty Python's Michael Palin goes around the world in eighty days.' And now your travel shows are promoted as 'Michael Palin . . .' So, is it satisfying for you that audiences see you as the guy who went to Everest rather than the guy who dressed up as the Spanish Inquisition?*

**PALIN:** It's quite a different audience for the travel shows, but I deliberately avoided using my Python persona or Python references in the travel shows. Not entirely – I have sung 'Lumberjack Song' to a yak herder in Bhutan, but that's because he asked me to sing and I couldn't think of

---

* Not anymore! In 2006 Gilliam renounced his American citizenship, for estate tax reasons.

anything else! But generally speaking I've been careful to not play on the Python label at all. People are always calling you an ex-Python, certainly. That's another part of me, that's fine, that's great.

By the time it came to *Full Circle* and *Himalaya* and *Sahara* and all those, people weren't asking me, 'Why weren't you making it more Pythonic? Why didn't you make this funny?' They were very much enjoying it for what it was. I appreciated that. And I always wanted to make sure that I enjoyed the full benefits of being freed of, not tied to, any particular group, producer, script, company. I could really go where the wind blew, and I've been able to do that. I've made some documentaries about the last day of the First World War, interviews with people like Jan Morris and artists like Andrew Wyeth. People come to me and say, 'Hey, we like what you do, this is something different, how about doing it?' That's very much in the spirit of Python, I think. I've been able to distinguish those sorts of programmes from my Python persona.

An interesting thing with Terry's illness: When Terry went public, I just put something on my website about my feelings about Terry, and it got an enormous reaction. One realized then the warmth and love for Python is quite strong. It sounds rather sentimental but there was no other word for it: People felt that what happened to Terry Jones happened to someone they knew in their family, as it were – the family of Python.

I'm really very, very pleased that in the last twenty years I've been free to go off and try lots of different things, I've never been hampered by Python at all, and yet Python when revived is still a pleasure to talk about and think about and to be respected for. (If that's not too pompous a word!)

*No, you can respect something and laugh at it!*

**PALIN:** Yeah, I think it's a sense of respect to be able to laugh at it, actually!

*Especially after all these years. I just have to think of 'Fish Slapping Dance' and I have to laugh – it always utterly gets me.*

**PALIN:** I was probably about twenty-seven when I did that, it was so long ago. And normally you think of things in your childhood, you think, 'Oh forget that!' Celebrating Python is celebrating childhood, I think. We were assumed to be very sophisticated because we talked about Proust and all that, but the treatment we gave it was always very childlike – not childish, but childlike. We mess around and we seek out pomposity so that we could then puncture it, and we could be very silly.

Forty years on, Terry Gilliam dressed as a cardinal comes leaping four feet into the air on the stage of the O2. It's just wonderful! An assertion that the life force goes on, and can still be funny and still make people laugh. That's what's so good. We do laugh a lot still whenever we get together and we're all fairly mischievous; we do still have that spirit which we had when I was getting knocked into the Thames by a large fish!

*Python fans everywhere are thankful that you took that fall!*

**PALIN:** Well, I was pleased about that. People ask me the best thing you've ever done and I say well, it was my fall into that lock on 'Fish Slapping Dance'. It wasn't meant to be; when we rehearsed it the water in the lock was full. Came to the time, it had suddenly emptied, fifteen foot drop. The fact that I carried on – I didn't say, 'Let's wait until it's filled up,' I carried on, and I'm very, very proud about the actual angle of the fall, where I kept my legs fairly straight and my pith helmet hit the water first. That's something I'm very proud of!

*And in one take?*

**PALIN:** Oh yes!

Python is something which has such a strong identity in this country. Everybody knows Python in some shape or form. And instead of it over the years waning, newspapers will use lines like 'What have the French ever done for us?' or something like that. 'No one ever expected Trump!' It's very much in the currency still. Python is not going to disappear; it's not going to be forgotten. And there are now eight-, nine-, ten-year-olds who are discovering Python films and the television series. So it's going to go on.

It is very British, even though it had a vital American contribution. Its preoccupations and sense of mischief is a very British thing. And Python has always interested people because there were so many elements to it. Some people think it's very clever and intelligent, and some people say it's extremely silly and inconsequential, but not many people ignore it. Everyone has an opinion on it, and that will keep us in business for quite a few years.

# THE PYTHON OEUVRE

Episode 8 (Dec. 7, 1969)   Army Protection Racket; Buy a Bed; Hermits;
                           The Dead Parrot; Hell's Grannies
Episode 9 (Dec. 14, 1969)   A Man with a Tape Recorder Up His Nose;
                           The Lumberjack Song; The Visitors
Episode 10 (Dec. 21, 1969)   Vocational Guidance Counsellor; Pet
                           Conversions
Episode 11 (Dec. 28, 1969)   Interesting People; The Batley Townswomen's
                           Guild Presents the Battle of Pearl Harbor
Episode 12 (Jan. 4, 1970)   Falling from a Building; Mr Hilter and the
                           North Minehead By-Election; Ken Shabby
Episode 13 (Jan. 11, 1970)   Cinema Advertisements; Albatross;
                           Psychiatry (Hearing Folk Singers)

## MONTY PYTHON'S FLYING CIRCUS – SERIES II

Episode 14 (Sept. 15, 1970)   Face the Press; New Cooker Sketch; The
                           Ministry of Silly Walks; The Piranha Brothers
Episode 15 (Sept. 22, 1970)   Man-Powered Flight; The Spanish Inquisition;
                           The Semaphore Version of *Wuthering Heights;*
                           Court Charades
Episode 16 (Sept. 29, 1970)   Exploding Stuffed Animals; Flying Lessons;
                           Hijacked Plane; Poet Ewan McTeagle; Psychiatrist
                           Milkman; Déjà Vu
Episode 17 (Oct. 20, 1970)   Gumbys; Architect Sketch; How to Give Up
                           Being a Mason; The Bishop; Poet Reader; Chemist
                           Sketch; Police Constable Pan-Am
Episode 18 (Oct. 27, 1970)   Live from the Grill-o-Mat Snack Bar, Paignton;
                           Blackmail; Society for Putting Things on Top
                           of Other Things; A Man Alternately Rude and
                           Polite; Ken Clean-Air Systems
Episode 19 (Nov. 3, 1970)   Eric Dibley's *If;* Dung; Timmy William's Coffee
                           Time; Raymond Luxury Yacht; Election Night
                           Special
Episode 20 (Nov. 10, 1970)   The Attila the Hun Show; Secretary of State
                           Striptease; Killer Sheep; Village Idiots; Quiz Show
Episode 21 (Nov. 17, 1970)   Archaeology Today; Silly Vicar; Mr and Mrs Git;
                           Mosquito Hunters; Judges' Cloakroom;
                           Beethoven's Mynah Bird
Episode 22 (Nov. 24, 1970)   How to Recognize Different Parts of the Body;
                           The Man Who Contradicts People; The Death of
                           Mary Queen of Scots; Penguin on the Television
Episode 23 (Dec. 1, 1970)   French Film; Scott of the Antarctic; Conrad

| | |
|---|---|
| | Poohs and His Dancing Teeth; Fish Licence |
| Episode 24 (Dec. 8, 1970) | Conquistador Instant Coffee; It All Happened on the 11.20 from Hainault &c.; Toothy Film Director; Crackpot Religions; How Not to Be Seen |
| Episode 25 (Dec. 15, 1970) | The Black Eagle; Dirty Hungarian Phrasebook; World Forum; Art Gallery Strike; World War I Sketch; Hospital for Over-Acting; Flower Arrangement; Spam |
| Episode 26 (Dec. 22, 1970) | Royal Episode 13; Coal Mine; The Man Who Says Things in a Very Roundabout Way; Lifeboat; Undertaker Sketch |

### MONTY PYTHON'S FLYING CIRCUS – SERIES III

| | |
|---|---|
| Episode 27 (Oct. 19, 1972) | Njorl's Saga; Court Scene; Police Pursuit Inside Body; Mrs Premise and Mrs Conclusion Visit Jean-Paul Sartre |
| Episode 28 (Oct. 26, 1972) | Mr and Mrs Brian Norris's Ford Popular; How to Do It; Mrs Niggerbaiter; Farming Club; Fish Slapping Dance |
| Episode 29 (Nov. 2, 1972) | The Money Programme; Erizabeth L; Argument Clinic |
| Episode 30 (Nov. 9, 1972) | The Man Who Speaks in Anagrams; Merchant Banker; The House Hunters; The Man Who Makes People Laugh Uncontrollably; News Reader Gestures; BBC Announcers |
| Episode 31 (Nov. 16, 1972) | The All-England Summarize Proust Competition; Everest Climbed by Hairdressers; Fire Brigade; Travel Agent; (Miss) Anne Elk |
| Episode 32 (Nov. 23, 1972) | Gumby Brain Surgeon; Molluscs |
| Episode 33 (Nov. 30, 1972) | Biggles Dictates a Letter; Climbing Uxbridge Road; Lifeboat; Why Television Is Bad for Your Eyes; The Show So Far; Cheese Shop; Sam Peckinpah's *Salad Days* |
| Episode 34 (Dec. 7, 1972) | The Cycling Tour |
| Episode 35 (Dec. 14, 1972) | English Literature Housing Project; Mortuary Hour; The Cheap-Laughs |
| Episode 36 (Dec. 21, 1972) | Tudor Pornography; The Rev. Arthur Belling; The Free Repetition of Doubtful Words Thing; Is There?; Thripshaw's Disease |

| Episode 37 (Jan. 4, 1973) | Boxing Tonight; Dennis Moore; Astrology Sketch; Ideal Loon Exposition; Poetry at the Off-Licence; Prejudice |
| Episode 38 (Jan. 11, 1973) | A Book at Bedtime; *2001: A Space Odyssey* Bone; Penguins; Spot the Loony; Rival Documentaries |
| Episode 39 (Jan. 18, 1973) | Light Entertainment Awards; Oscar Wilde Sketch; Pasolini's *The Third Test Match;* Curry's Brains; International Wife-Swapping; The Dirty Vicar Sketch |

## MONTY PYTHON'S FLYING CIRCUS – SERIES IV

| Episode 40 (Oct. 31, 1974) | The Golden Age of Ballooning; The Norwegian Party |
| Episode 41 (Nov. 7, 1974) | Michael Ellis; Ant Poetry Reading |
| Episode 42 (Nov. 14, 1974) | Light Entertainment War; Courtmartial; Programme Planners; Woody and Tinny Words; Show Jumping |
| Episode 43 (Nov. 21, 1974) | Bogus Psychiatrists; Queen Victoria Handicap |
| Episode 44 (Nov. 28, 1974) | Postal Box Dedication; Mr Neutron; Conjuring Today |
| Episode 45 (Dec. 5, 1974) | Most Awful Family in Britain; Waiting Room Stabbing; The Man Who Finishes Other People's Sentences |

## MONTY PYTHON'S FLIEGENDER ZIRKUS

| Episode 1 (prod. 1971) | Little Red Riding Hood; Stake Your Claim; Silly Olympics; Colin 'Bomber' Harris Wrestles Himself; Bavarian Restaurant |
| Episode 2 (prod. 1972) | German vs. Greek Philosophers Football Match; Happy Valley |

### FILMS
*And Now for Something Completely Different* (1971)
*Monty Python and the Holy Grail* (1975)
*Life of Brian* (1979)
*Monty Python Live at the Hollywood Bowl* (1982)
*Monty Python's the Meaning of Life* (1983)
*Monty Python Live (Mostly) – One Down, Five to Go* (2014)

## RECORDINGS
(except reissues, promotional samplers, and singles)

*Monty Python's Flying Circus* (1970)

*Another Monty Python Record* (1971)

*Monty Python's Previous Record* (1972)

*The Monty Python Matching Tie and Handkerchief* (1973)

*Monty Python Live at the Theatre Royal, Drury Lane* (1974)

*The Album of the Soundtrack of the Trailer of the Film 'Monty Python and the Holy Grail'* (1975)

*Monty Python Live! At City Center* (1976)

*The Monty Python Instant Record Collection* (1977) (a.k.a. *The Instant Monty Python CD Collection*)

*Monty Python's Life of Brian* (1979)

*Monty Python's Contractual Obligation Album* (1980)

*Monty Python's the Meaning of Life* (1983)

*Monty Python's the Final Rip Off* (1988)

*Monty Python Sings* (1989)

*The Ultimate Monty Python Rip Off* (1994)

*Monty Python Sings (Again)* (2014)

*Monty Python's Total Rubbish: The Complete Collection* (2014)

## BOOKS
(except repackagings and abridgements)

*Monty Python's Big Red Book* (1972)

*The Brand New Monty Python Bok* (1973) (reissued as *The Brand New Monty Python Papperbok*)

*Monty Python and the Holy Grail (Book) «Mønti Pythøn ik den Hølie Gräilen (Bøk)»* (1977)

*Monty Python's the Life of Brian (of Nazareth)/MontyPythonScrapbook* (1979)

*Monty Python's the Meaning of Life* (1983)

*The Complete Monty Python's Flying Circus: All the Words* (1989) (a.k.a. *Monty Python's Flying Circus: Just the Words*)

*The Fairly Incomplete & Rather Badly Illustrated Monty Python Song Book* (1994)

*A Pocketful of Python Picked by Terry Jones* (1999)

*A Pocketful of Python Picked by John Cleese* (1999)

*A Pocketful of Python Picked by Terry Gilliam* (2000)

*A Pocketful of Python Picked by Michael Palin* (2000)

*A Pocketful of Python Picked by Eric Idle* (2002)

*The Pythons' Autobiography by the Pythons* (2005)

*The Very Best of Monty Python . . .* (A compendium of the five *Pocketful of Python* books) (2006)

*Monty Python Live!* (2009)

*Monty Python's Flying Circus: Hidden Treasures* (2017)

# SOURCES

*Interviews with the five surviving Pythons and their co-conspirators were conducted by the author in the summer and fall of 1998. Other interviews include:*

John Cleese: author interview in March 2018.

Terry Gilliam: author interviews in September 1986, September and December 1987, June 1990, March 1991, March 1996, and March 2018.

Michael Palin: author interviews on May 9, 1996 (originally conducted for the special-edition laser disc of Terry Gilliam's *Brazil*; excerpts used by permission of the Criterion Collection), and in November 2017.

Hank Azaria: author interview in May 2018.

### QUOTED SOURCES

| | |
|---|---|
| p. 21 | 'Once I had my little Bolex . . .' Gilliam at an American Museum of the Moving Image seminar, January 9, 1996. |
| p. 27 | 'The worst problem we had . . .' Cleese on *The Dick Cavett Show*, October 11–12, 1979. |
| p. 74 | 'I had a friend . . .' Ibid. |
| p. 78 | 'You know when you do something . . .' Ibid. |
| p. 119 | 'As soon as you start to try and analyse . . .' Jones in *Radio Times*, October 24, 1974. |

p. 187    'I remember when it was subtitled . . .' Gilliam, from the Criterion Collection laser disc commentary track of *Monty Python and the Holy Grail*, 1993.

p. 261    'The offence is what a friend of mine . . .' Cleese on *Dick Cavett*.

p. 318    Script excerpt, Palin and Jones, *More Ripping Yarns* (New York: Pantheon, 1980).

p. 331:   'people with plates on their faces,' Idle, 'Curtain Call,' *Los Angeles,* July 30, 2015.

p. 353:   'Of course, I'm excited about getting back together again . . .' Jones, 'Monty Python reunion: And now for something not completely different,' *The Guardian*, November 22, 2013.

p. 371:   'I wanted to go on to perform . . .' Jones, 'Terry Jones on four decades of Monty Python and Robin Williams' final film,' Deadline.com, December 14, 2014.

p. 372:   'He was interviewing us at the Beacon Theatre . . .' Cleese, 'Extended transcript: John Cleese,' CBSNews.com, October 25, 2015.

## PICTURE CREDITS

All photographs are copyright © Python (Monty) Pictures, Ltd., used by permission, except for the following:

Courtesy of John Cleese: page 13

Courtesy of Terry Gilliam: page 280

Courtesy of Terry Jones: pages 11, 19, 56, 100, 110, 125, 126, 206

Courtesy of Nancy Lewis: pages 186, 191, 197, 202

Courtesy of Ian MacNaughton: pages 36, 134, 141, 142

Courtesy of Paul Shammasian: page 352

Courtesy of Ludwig Shammasian: pages 354, 357, 364, 365

Copyright © BBC Photo Archives: pages 80, 137

Copyright © Neil Preston/HBO: pages 319, 320

Copyright © Joan Marcus: pages 335, 337, 341

Copyright © Jennifer Graylock: page 349

Copyright © Dave J. Hogan via Getty Images: pages 361, 368

Copyright © Andy Kropa/Invision/Associated Press: page 371

# BIBLIOGRAPHY

In addition to the original Python shows, books, and films, the following sources provided reference and background information:

## BOOKS
Chapman, Graham. *A Liar's Autobiography, Vol. II [sic]*. New York: Methuen, 1980.
Gilliam, Terry. *Animations of Mortality*. London: Methuen, 1978.
Hewison, Robert. *Monty Python: The Case Against*. New York: Grove Press, 1981.
Johnson, Kim 'Howard'. *The First 200 Years of Monty Python*. New York: St. Martin's Press, 1989.
Perry, George. *The Life of Python*. Boston: Little, Brown and Company, 1983.
Stephens, Frances. *Theatre World Annual 1965*. London: Iliffe Books, Ltd., 1964.
Wilmut, Roger. *The Goon Show Companion*. New York: St. Martin's Press, 1976.

## PERIODICALS AND ONLINE PUBLICATIONS
Berry, Charles. 'Dead Parrots & Creosote: Monty Python Leads a Silly Invasion.' *Rolling Stone*, September 27, 1973.
Brown, Mark. 'Monty Python comeback show tickets sell out in 43.5 seconds.' *The Guardian*, November 25, 2013.
Farmer, Brian. '"Seventh Python" has the last laugh with victory in battle over *Spamalot* royalties.' *The Independent* (UK), July 5, 2013.
Hertzberg, Hendrik. 'Naughty Bits.' *The New Yorker*, March 29, 1976.
Jones, Jonathan. 'And They Did Mention the War.' *The Guardian*, October 1, 1998.

Kreier, Beth Ann. 'Curling Up with Monty Python.' *Los Angeles Times*, July 31, 1975.

McCarthy, James. 'My Music: Eric Idle.' *Gramophone Magazine*, March 28, 2018.

McKie, Robin. 'Terry Jones: "I've got dementia. My frontal lobe has absconded."' *The Guardian*, April 16, 2017.

Meehan, Thomas. 'And Now for Something Completely Different.' *The New York Times Magazine*, April 18, 1975.

Morgan, David. 'Monty Python at 40: Not dead yet.' CBSNews.com, October 16, 2009.

———. '"Not dead yet!"': Monty Python to reunite for London stadium show.' CBSNews.com, November 21, 2013.

Rawls, Wendell, Jr. '"*Life of Brian*" Stirs Carolina Controversy.' *New York Times*, October 24, 1979.

Reynolds, Stanley. 'Python.' *The Times* (London), December 14, 1970.

Zehme, Bill. 'King Mike and the Quest for the Broadway Grail.' *New York*, March 14, 2005.

# INDEX

NOTE: Page references in *italics* refer to photos and illustrations.

# ABOUT THE AUTHOR

David Morgan is a senior producer for CBSNews.com, and for CBS's Emmy Award–winning newsmagazine *Sunday Morning*. He has written about film production and media issues for such publications as the *Los Angeles Times*, *Newsday*, *Sight & Sound*, *The Hollywood Reporter*, *Empire*, *The Independent*, *American Cinematographer*, *Millimeter*, *Cinefex*, *Ciak si Gira*, and *Flix*. He previously worked for ABCNews.com and the Environmental Defense Fund.

He is author of the film music book *Knowing the Score*, and editor of John Anderson's oral history of the Sundance Film Festival, *Sundancing*. He also co-produced, wrote, and animated supplementary materials for the Criterion Collection's special editions of Terry Gilliam's *Brazil* and *The Adventures of Baron Munchausen*, documenting and analysing the production of those films, and recorded audio commentary. His website is Wide Angle/Closeup: Conversations with Filmmakers.

He lives in New York City.